"[A] meticulously researched page turner that marries adventure stories with crime cliffhangers. Travelers will especially enjoy the colorful descriptions of Tahiti's culture and customs. Presser's eloquent writing and masterful storytelling will capture you from the very first sentence until the last."
—*Travel + Leisure*

"Sometimes, the greatest adventure doesn't require packing a suitcase....I gasped with Presser as he unveiled truths about settling of the island, and I wandered along with him as he discovered both the beauty and the complexity of that island today." —*Boston Herald*

"*The Far Land* uncovers the almost unbelievable true story of Pitcairn Island, while taking readers on an exciting journey to one of the most remote communities in the world....Presser excels at depicting the strangeness, but his novelistic account of what happened to the original colonists is stranger and bloodier—and unforgettable in its shocking details....*Lord of the Flies* pales in comparison."
—*Shelf Awareness*

"Through his modern retelling and examination of the *Bounty*'s history, Presser creates a temporal bridge that spans hundreds of years and masterfully connects the island's violent past to its tumultuous present." —*Afar*

"A highly accomplished travel writer, Brandon Presser's *The Far Land* hits a lot of my pleasure centers: remote islands, then-and-now non-fiction, historical mysteries and forthright travelogues. The first night I started reading, I dreamed about Pitcairn Island."
—Maggie Shipstead, *New York Times* bestselling author of *Great Circle*

"Brandon Presser moves far beyond the Mutiny on the *Bounty* to the devastating tale of the Pitcairn Island settlement, a real-life *Lord of the Flies* tragedy. As Brandon finds when he makes a protracted visit to the island, it's a story still unwinding and a definite reminder that island and paradise are two words which often don't go together. It's a tale which seamlessly blends his new take on the mutiny and its aftermath with his own experiences on Pitcairn today."
—Tony Wheeler, cofounder, Lonely Planet

THE FAR LAND

THE FAR
LAND

200 YEARS OF MURDER,
MANIA, AND MUTINY IN
THE SOUTH PACIFIC

BRANDON PRESSER

PUBLICAFFAIRS
NEW YORK

PublicAffairs
Hachette Book Group
1290 Avenue of the Americas, New York, NY 10104
www.publicaffairsbooks.com
@Public_Affairs

Printed in the United States of America

First Trade Paperback Edition: March 2024

Published by PublicAffairs, an imprint of Hachette Book Group, Inc. The PublicAffairs name and logo is a registered trademark of the Hachette Book Group.

The Hachette Speakers Bureau provides a wide range of authors for speaking events. To find out more, go to hachettespeakersbureau.com or email HachetteSpeakers@hbgusa.com.

PublicAffairs books may be purchased in bulk for business, educational, or promotional use. For more information, please contact your local bookseller or the Hachette Book Group Special Markets Department at special.markets@hbgusa.com.

The publisher is not responsible for websites (or their content) that are not owned by the publisher.

Print book interior design by Trish Wilkinson.

The Library of Congress has cataloged the hardcover edition as follows:

Names: Presser, Brandon, author.
Title: The far land : 200 years of murder, mania, and mutiny in the South Pacific / Brandon Presser.
Description: First edition. | New York, NY : PublicAffairs, 2022. | Includes bibliographical references and index.
Identifiers: LCCN 2021034506 | ISBN 9781541758575 (hardcover) | ISBN 9781541758599 (ebook)
Subjects: LCSH: Presser, Brandon—Travel—Pitcairn Islands. | Bounty Mutiny, 1789. | Pitcairn Islands—History. | Pitcairn Islands—Description and travel.
Classification: LCC DU800 .P74 2022 | DDC 996.18—dc23/eng/20211027
LC record available at https://lccn.loc.gov/2021034506

ISBNs: 9781541758575 (hardcover), 9781541758599 (ebook),
        9781541758582 (paperback)

CW

10 9 8 7 6 5 4 3 2 1

For my grandpa
and his untold stories of the South Pacific

CONTENTS

Author's Note   *ix*

Cast of Characters   *xi*

Maps   *xvi*

1   Turn On the Quiet   1

2   The Strangest Hello   5

3   Artocarpus Incisa   18

4   Discovery in the Age of the Superstore   32

5   A Score of Worlds   36

6   The Three Legs of Man   50

7   The Last Grande Dame of Tahiti   72

8   Mutiny on the *Bounty*   84

9   The Backwater Emissary   92

10   The Geometry of Solitude   105

11   The Fallout Zone   114

12   The Quiet   121

13   The Museum People   138

14   The Devil's Workshop   153

15	Pandora's Box	163
16	Dreadfruit	175
17	Portrait of a Family	184
18	Hunting Pigs	191
19	An Eye for an Eye	199
20	A Spider's Progress	207
21	The Book of Fear	215
22	Down Rope	223
23	Time, Chance, and Death	231
24	Far from Help	239
25	Bury the Hatchet	248
26	Children of Castaways	254
27	The Strangest Bonjour	259
28	Austerity	263

Epilogue: Turn Off the Quiet — 271

Acknowledgments — 279
Notes on References — 281
Select Bibliography — 301
Index — 309

AUTHOR'S NOTE

When I traveled to Pitcairn in 2018, it was not my intention to write a book about the infamous HMAV *Bounty*'s mutineers and their descendants. But the longer I spent there, the more questions I had: How did forty-eight people come to live on an island impossible to access by commercial conveyance? And what really happened to their forebearers who settled on the lonely rock some two hundred years prior? Every time I peeled back the proverbial onion, I found another layer that seemed more unbelievable than the last. This operatic saga of treason and obsession—paired with the abject strangeness of a modern society of castaways—was, quite simply, the most fantastical story I had ever come across in my fifteen-plus years as a journalist.

It's so incredible, in fact, that the history of the mutineers' violent undoing reads more like an epic novel. But I can assure you that this is indeed a work of nonfiction—every sentence on every page was weighed and considered after three long years of rigorous research, combing through hundreds of resources from old captains' logs and newspaper clippings to the other tomes penned by writers who have similarly descended down into the darkness of Pitcairn. Fact-finding continued beyond the library too; in-depth interviews and seminars with historians, psychologists, religious scholars, and experts on Polynesian culture helped paint a more fully formed perspective on both the causes and effects of tribalism, trauma, psychopathy, paranoia, and survival in the bleakest of conditions.

In the past, the Pitcairn chronicle has largely been illuminated through the mutineers' point of view (Fletcher Christian in particular). Here, great care has been taken to dismantle the misogyny and racism inherent in the white, colonial male gaze, offering broader insight into how this diverse cast of characters grappled with the overwhelming adversity of their very real fates. Relative to the British sailors, little is known about their Tahitian consorts, who—in previous accounts of the *Bounty*'s journey—have been othered and infantilized through the use of broken English. In this version, the dialogue attributed to the women (and some of the secondary seamen) has been tweaked to more accurately reflect the reality that they were just as rational, cunning, and self-actualizing as the men long considered the heroes of this tale. This is the only rejiggering in an otherwise authentic recounting of what took place following history's favorite mutiny: eighteen years of solitude on the most remotely inhabited island in the entire world.

Enthusiasts and academics will find a comprehensive reference and bibliographical section at the end of this book detailing each piece used to put this puzzle together; it is my hope and intention, however, that you simply enjoy the narrative herein as a story whose details happen to be wickedly true.

CAST OF CHARACTERS

THE *BOUNTY* CREWMEN

WILLIAM BLIGH: *commander*

JOHN FRYER: *master*

FLETCHER CHRISTIAN: *master's mate*

THOMAS HUGGAN (DOC): *surgeon*

JOHN HALLETT: *midshipman; Bligh's protégé*

THOMAS HAYWARD: *midshipman; Bligh's protégé*

PETER HEYWOOD: *midshipman; Christian's protégé*

EDWARD YOUNG: *midshipman*

WILLIAM BROWN: *assistant gardener*

THOMAS BURKITT: *able seaman*

CHARLES CHURCHILL: *master-at-arms*

ISAAC MARTIN: *able seaman*

WILLIAM MCCOY: *able seaman*

JOHN MILLS: *gunner's mate*

JOHN MILLWARD: *able seaman*

MATTHEW QUINTAL: *able seaman*

ALEXANDER SMITH: *able seaman*

MATTHEW THOMPSON: *able seaman*

JOHN WILLIAMS: *able seaman*

THE TAHITIAN WOMEN

MAUATUA: *leader of the Tahitian women; Christian's companion*

SUSANNAH: *an aristocratic Tahitian; Young's companion*

JENNY: *Mauatua's friend; a low-caste Tahitian*

FAAHOTU: *Mauatua's maid; a healer*

TEVARUA: *Susannah's maid; Quintal's companion*

OBUAREI: *Susannah's maid; Smith's companion*

NANCY: *Tararo's companion*

TEATUAHITEA: *Brown's companion*

TEIO: *McCoy's companion; Baby Sully's mother*

ON TAHITI

TEINA: *chieftain of a prominent Tahitian clan*

ITIA: *Teina's wife*

ON TUBUAI

TAMATOA: *chieftain of western Tubuai*

TINARAU: *chieftain of southern Tubuai; Christian's enemy*

TAAROA: *chieftain of northern Tubuai; Christian's ally*

THE POLYNESIAN MEN ON PITCAIRN

TETAHITI: *Tubuaian warrior; Christian's blood brother*

OHA: *Tubuaian teenager; Tetahiti's cousin*

MINARII: *Tahitian boy*

TEIMUA: *Tahitian nobleman*

NIAU: *Tahitian teenager*

TARARO: *nobleman from the island of Raiatea*

THE DESCENDANTS
(MODERN-DAY PITCAIRNERS)

STEVE CHRISTIAN: *patriarch of the Christians*
OLIVE CHRISTIAN: *Steve's wife*
CAROL WARREN: *matriarch of the Warrens*
JAY WARREN: *Carol's husband*
ISABEL CHRISTIAN: *Steve and Olive's granddaughter*
SHAWN CHRISTIAN: *Steve and Olive's son; mayor*
MERALDA WARREN: *Jay's sister*
SIMON YOUNG: *a recluse*

JAMES NORMAN HALL'S
DESCENDANTS ON TAHITI

KATE HALL: *granddaughter*
NANCY HALL RUTGERS: *daughter; Kate's aunt*

THE FAR LAND

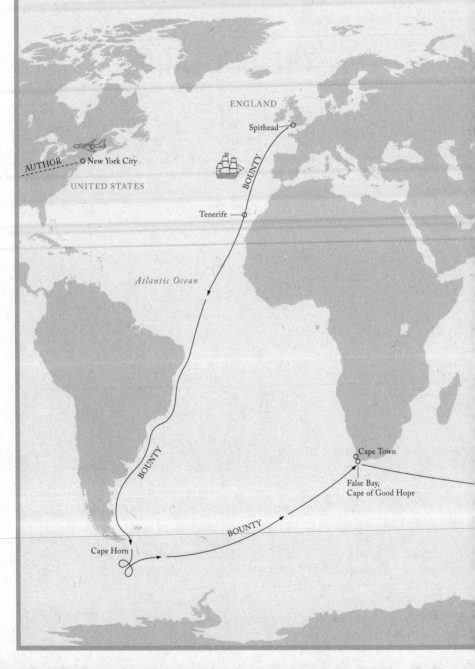

VOYAGE OF THE *BOUNTY*
& THE AUTHOR'S JOURNEY

ENGLAND

Spithead

AUTHOR - - - - O New York City

UNITED STATES

BOUNTY

Tenerife

Atlantic Ocean

BOUNTY

Cape Town

False Bay,
Cape of Good Hope

Cape Horn

BOUNTY

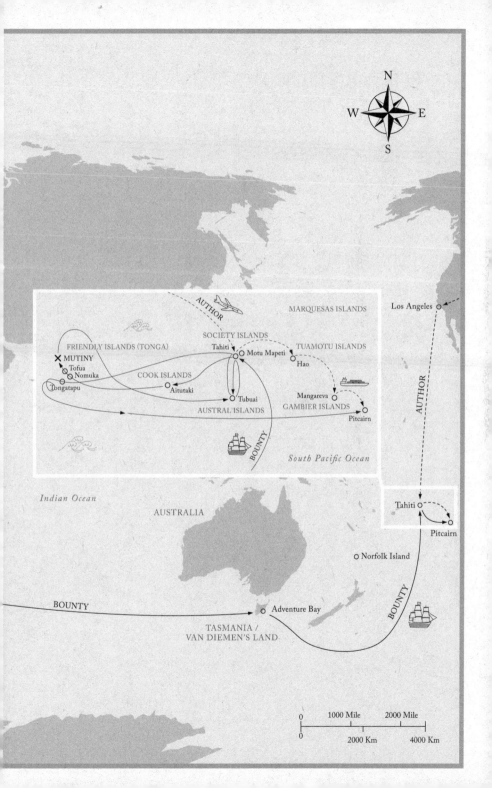

N
W   E
S

MARQUESAS ISLANDS

Los Angeles

AUTHOR

SOCIETY ISLANDS

FRIENDLY ISLANDS (TONGA)

Tahiti   Motu Mapeti   TUAMOTU ISLANDS

× MUTINY
Tofua
Nomuka   COOK ISLANDS
Tongatapu   Aitutaki

Hao

Tubuai
AUSTRAL ISLANDS

Mangareva
GAMBIER ISLANDS
Pitcairn

BOUNTY

South Pacific Ocean

Indian Ocean

AUSTRALIA

Tahiti
Pitcairn

Norfolk Island

BOUNTY   Adventure Bay

BOUNTY

TASMANIA /
VAN DIEMEN'S LAND

0   1000 Mile   2000 Mile
0   2000 Km   4000 Km

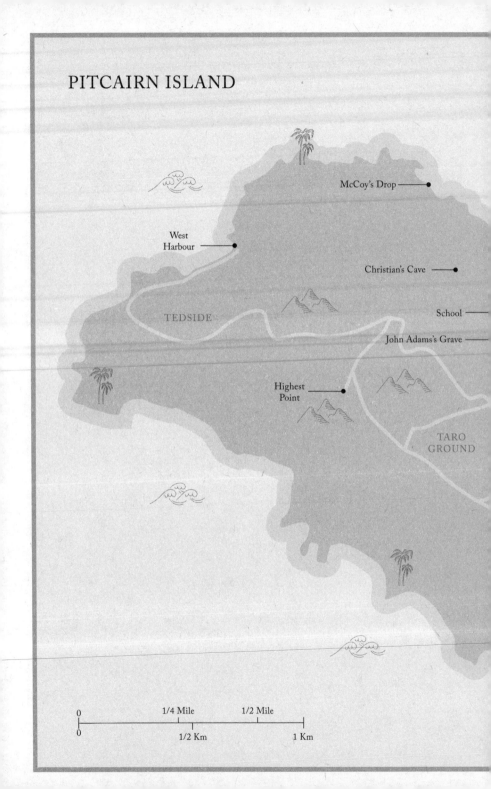

PITCAIRN ISLAND

McCoy's Drop ———— ●

West
Harbour ———— ●

Christian's Cave ———— ●

TEDSIDE

School ————

John Adams's Grave ————

Highest
Point ———— ●

TARO
GROUND

| 0 | 1/4 Mile | 1/2 Mile |
| 0 | 1/2 Km | 1 Km |

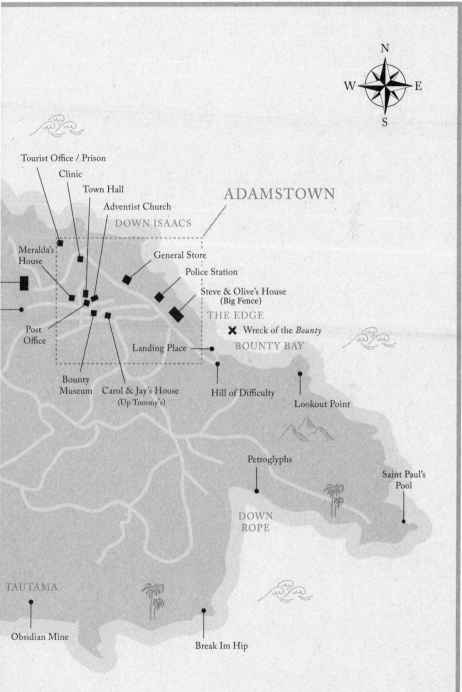

CHAPTER I

TURN ON THE QUIET

FEBRUARY 2018

The bed was twice as long as it was wide. A plank, really, with a yellowed mattress well worn by the various sleeping shapes of a family that had inhabited the house for generations. I lay flat on my back—it was too humid to tuck my legs under the sheets just yet, and the pedestal fan on the floor craned its neck high enough to let the little swivels of air tickle the bottoms of my feet.

Why were they late? I had already switched off the light—a futile attempt to slow the parade of roaches and moths that descended upon the dwelling every evening. I hid my iPhone deep beneath my pillow to check the time—the glow from the screen mustn't escape the room and alert the lurking creatures. It was 10:03 p.m. Yes, they were definitely late. Minutes felt like hours as I waited, gulping the fan's last breezy blasts, the mugginess still unabated.

I could hear them coming. The faint putter of their quad bikes grew louder as they trundled down the dirt track. They parked so close to the house that I could listen to their furtive footsteps as they searched for the dial in the overgrowth. And then it happened: everything shut off. My fan, the only noise, sputtered to a gentle halt, yielding to the oppressive, flat heat, which mummified me as I lay motionless in the dark. I was now keenly aware of my breathing as I began to descend—deeper and deeper—into this newfound sea of quietude, swimming through the leagues of soundlessness. There was no dull hum from the refrigerator in the kitchen, no distant ambulance rushing to save a life. Nighttime was different here. The silence was complete.

Every evening at 10 p.m. the island's power shut off. When I first arrived, the electric cuts would catch me off guard. Sometimes I'd be brushing my teeth, other times I'd be scribbling notes over a cup of tea. But now I was prepared: a cool shower first, a glass of water by the bed, and several crucial minutes of ventilated air before the stillness.

The island's lifeline was a single generator, but diesel fuel was costly and scarce, so a weekly schedule—like a chore wheel—was devised among the islanders denoting who, each night, would be responsible for staying up past their bedtime to turn on the quiet. Locals dreamed of a more sustainable energy source like solar panels, but progress is painfully slow in a place where everything arrives by a boat that takes three months to deliver its supplies. No airplane has ever landed here—the volcanic crags are too steep to support a runway, and the distances too vast for a small craft, like a helicopter, to make the trip. Only a hulking cargo freighter dares to brave the journey but four times a year, the same vessel that brought me here and the same one that will—God willing—get me off this rock on its next passage.

Until then, I would perform my nightly ritual—a study of silence.

It was still too hot to slip my feet under the covers. I wriggled my toes and made strange little shadows in the starlight that shone through the window. But there was no glass in the frame. No, there hadn't been a pane in the window for years—decades, maybe. The whole house had become overwhelmed by nature. Long vines reached through the shutters like the spindly tentacles of a kraken ready to drag the entire structure out to sea.

My thoughts turned to Fletcher Christian and how he had contemplated the quietness here. Did he fear he would perish from the unrelenting humidity? Did the shadows of the night play tricks on his stony gray eyes? Upon arriving on the island, Christian scoured his ship's timbers to build himself a cabin—now a whisper of a ruin beneath the floorboards of this rickety, shitty house. He then torched the rest of his vessel in the bay, forever condemning himself to life as a castaway.

CHRISTIAN WAS THE ringleader of a band of nine infamous mutineers who, in April 1789, commandeered His Majesty's Armed Vessel *Bounty* and, along with their Tahitian brides, launched a quest to find an idyllic island that had been incorrectly plotted in the British Navy's nautical logs. Dubbed Pitcairn, after the fifteen-year-old deckhand who had first spotted it, the green dot was scribbled on a big blue chart of the Pacific some two hundred miles west of its actual location due to an error in longitudinal reading. After many months at sea, Christian and his men finally found their promised paradise—by the end of their third year, almost all of the mutineers would be dead.

It wasn't fever or thirst that had racked the castaways, but the inextricable qualities of humanity that led to their most violent demises. You can call it love, jealousy, or greed, but really it was the need for power disguised as the pursuit of happiness.

Now, I don't want to spoil everything just yet, but in a way you already know this story. It's the oldest one the book: the ineffable quest to return to paradise. So foolish were the nine mutineers who pinned their Edenic dreams on a place fiercely governed by the laws of the wilderness. So foolish were the thousands of people who followed over the centuries, hoping to change their fate on this two-mile bump in the sea. They would all come to realize that we can travel to the farthest recesses of the planet, but we are never truly able to escape ourselves.

Perhaps I was a fool too, even though I knew full well that it would not be an island idyll. But Pitcairn called out to me nonetheless, much like it had to the liars, thieves, and despots of years gone by. And now, lying in my pooling sweat, it was hard to remember why.

Pitcairn has captured the imagination of many. Mark Twain wrote about it. Charles Nordhoff and James Norman Hall novelized the origin story of the island's settlement in a triad of spellbinding books. Oscar-nominated movies have been made, a Broadway musical too. But I was the only obsessive who had turned his infatuation into an actual trip—a journey famously described by a *National Geographic* explorer as taking longer than getting to the moon.

A journalist by trade, I couldn't shut off the electricity in my brain that had sparked years of travel across the world—from the glacial shelves of Svalbard to the tribal lands of Papua New Guinea—in search of my next story. I needed to know what happened when you fell off the map.

So from New York City I had set out in search of an outcrop not much larger than Central Park. Commercial liners dwindled to puddle jumpers—with each leg of the voyage the aircraft got smaller and smaller, like Russian dolls, until there were no more planes. Days and nights were then spent in the windowless hold of the rusting freighter as it cruised through seas so ruthless and vast that the British Navy, despite its best efforts, was never able to locate the mutineers' hideaway. The giant blue swells heaved the shipping vessel through one final swath of the Pacific—long thought to be lifeless—until it finally reached the last place on Earth.

Maybe Pitcairn was never meant to be found.

I should wait until the morning to ponder these questions further. Besides, the critters were coming now—spiders and vermin. I gently slid my legs under the covers and pulled the sheets up to my chin. Yes, tomorrow I'll boil a cup of water from the cistern and swirl in a heaping spoonful of Nescafé crystals. With the clarity of caffeine, I'll stare into the stony gray eyes of the descendants of Fletcher Christian from across the breakfast table and try to understand why, seven generations later, there are still forty-eight souls who have chosen to remain exiled in this wilderness.

Until then I must unbusy my mind and sleep—it's the only way to pass the time until dawn, when a spin of the chore wheel tasks the next castaway to flick on the diesel generator and rescue me from this silent, wretched heat.

CHAPTER 2

THE STRANGEST HELLO
FEBRUARY 1808

The hunt was over, but the deck of the *Topaz* remained varnished in burgundy like a banquet table after a bacchanal. There were no more seal pelts to be found as the small vessel drifted up from the bottom of the world toward the equator in its desperate search for supplies—the situation had become dire.

Captain Mayhew Folger slowly ran his tongue along the crowns of his teeth, examining every crooked ridge and valley—some porcelain, some bone. Saliva began to pool in his mouth as he desperately swallowed every drop of the sweaty, salty spittle. The sloshing of the half-empty casks was mocking him—but no, he must save the rum for trading when they finally reached civilization.

Although his crewmen loathed skimming the Antarctic waters for furs, Folger preferred the polar conditions to the vastness of the South Seas that now surrounded him. The chilly nip of the wind kept him alert, and the purple glow of the infinite sunshine had a captivating quality. He enjoyed sailing from iceberg to iceberg, stringing them together like pearls on a necklace. But now, the canvas jackets and woolen socks were buried deep within the ship's hold next to a final supply of sea biscuits pocked by burrowing maggots. Even in his linen tunic, his skin was irritated by the muggy midday heat.

The days were palpably shorter now, and there was something about the darkness of a tropical night that unnerved Folger; a stormy sky was indistinguishable from the rollicking waves. The light, refracted by the beads of humidity in the air, haunted him too, casting shadows on the distant clouds and creating peculiar shapes that piqued his imagination: a serpent, a tiger, his mother, a scythe.

Folger stared off the stern of the ship, bored. Today, his idle mind saw a sprawling city along the horizon—towering smokestacks and church spires looming over rows of town houses and factories. Perhaps it was Boston; it had been almost a year since he had left home.

"LAND!"

The excited cry from the crow's nest startled Folger; he clamped down on his tongue until it bled. "It's land, sir," repeated the young crewman as he negotiated his way through the tangle of cordage. He pointed in a westerly direction and handed Folger the spyglass. Through the rusting oculus appeared a snaggletooth of stone protruding from the rolling waves.

The *Topaz*'s two masts creaked and yawed as they altered course to race toward the islet against the quickening afternoon. Folger unfurled his nautical charts and studied them like an incantation. He moved his gaze from point to point, naming each dot on the map under his breath as he touched them with his quill: Nuka Hiva, Marutea, Mangareva, Tubuai. There was nothing, however, plotted in the seas that lay ahead.

Although not an explorer, Folger clenched his jaw in excited anticipation. It was the early nineteenth century—surely the entire world had been already discovered. So how then had this little island evaded the marauding English, French, Dutch, and Iberian navigators who greedily claimed each landfall in the name of their respective empires? It must be empty or of little worth.

A second call from up high interrupted Folger's quiet speculation. "FIRE! Captain, I see a fire!" By now the ship was close enough to appreciate the island's verticality: an impregnable battlement of granite and red rock with a carpet of lush green undergrowth. The castle governed a sprawling kingdom below—sharks and whales its loyal subjects. Without an obvious harbor, Folger dropped anchor only a few hundred yards offshore and was stunned to watch his entire rode unravel before the iron clunked against the ocean floor. High on the ridge, the glow of several campfires was easily noticeable in the waning twilight, and as evening set in the glittering embers became indistinguishable from the banner of stars.

Who were these isolated souls that had never been touched by the industrializing world?

Old tales of vicious savages quickly circulated among the crew. Feral tribesmen once ruled this faraway realm of the planet, and perhaps this was their final bastion. Some sailors begged to raise the anchor and steer the vessel away, others clamored to go ashore. Folger saw only one option: he would deploy two rowboats at first light to garner new provisions. Forfeiting the potential opportunity to restock their supplies would have mortal repercussions.

———————

WEARY FROM A restless night's sleep, Folger ordered all twenty of his crewmen to the main deck in the gravelly light before dawn to tug levers, source oars, and ready two dinghies to be lowered into the unrelenting swell. While monitoring their progress, he marveled at a time, years prior, when he had weighed the occupational hazards of captaining a merchant's vessel. Freezing to death on the ice sheets of Antarctica or being looted by pirates were the two main scenarios that worried his wife back home, but dying by the hand of a warrior from an undiscovered nation had never crossed his mind. It was, however, his decision to launch the exploratory foray, so he would be a man of intention and lead the party ashore. Folger paused to glimpse the horizon just as the rising sun splashed across the sea. He wondered if he'd live to see the end of this very short day.

A half whisper—"Captain"—broke Folger's introspection. His second mate was hastily pointing back toward the island, where a small outrigger canoe had been deployed from the shore. Uneasy, the crewman began to reach for a sealing pistol. Folger squeezed the sailor's forearm tightly, urging him to drop the firearm. "Let's not get ahead of ourselves."

From the mysterious island came three young oarsmen who fiercely paddled against the crashing waves. Each stroke, performed in unison, moved them closer to the *Topaz* with astonishing speed. Their clothing was rudimentary—small swatches of tapa cloth strung around their waists for modesty—save a straw hat with a wide brim and large black feather worn by the eldest of the three rowers, who steered the vessel from the back.

Folger locked eyes with the man in the hat: like two slate pebbles in shallow pools. He then raised both of his arms high in the air to show that he wasn't harboring a weapon. Through the biggest smile he could muster, Folger let out a booming "HELLO!" And the strangest, most unexpected sound was returned: a perfect echo— "Hello"—in crisp and proper English.

"Who are you?" the man in the straw hat continued.

Stunned, the sealers exchanged silent glances during an extended pause. They were over nine thousand miles from Great Britain.

"This is the ship *Topaz* of the United States of America. I am its master, Captain Mayhew Folger."

"We do not know of America . . . Is it in Ireland?"

By now the relentless swell was knocking the outrigger against the hull of Folger's ship. He flung a rope over to the islanders, and as they fastened the two vessels together he studied them more closely. Their tall, bare bodies showed not a trace of indulgence—each muscle and sinew rippled across their hairless chests. And although they spoke the king's English, they bore few European traits—their lean anatomies lacquered in the same auburn tint as the wood of their tiny craft. All three were teenagers but possessed a certain wide-eyed innocence often lost in adolescence.

"Who are *you*?" Folger continued the volley.

"We are good Englishmen."

"Where were you born?"

"In this place which you see."

"How then are you Englishmen if you were born on this island?"

"Because our father is an Englishman."

"Who is your father?"

"John."

"John, who?"

"Don't you know him? Our Father John?"

Folger paused. It was clear that the young men knew that a wide world existed beyond the confines of their tiny island, but they hadn't grasped the concept that humans are not all acquainted with one another.

The man in the hat broke the silence. "Then perhaps you know Captain Bligh?" Folger did. And the mood immediately shifted among his crew. Everyone in the seafaring world knew William Bligh, commander of the HMAV *Bounty*, who was famously betrayed by his lieutenant Fletcher Christian and several other sailors, then cast out into the abyss when they seized control of the ship. If Bligh had once surveyed this island then surely it would have been dutifully logged. Could Father John be one of the mutineers? They were never heard from again after commandeering Bligh's vessel. Was this their island hideaway?

"What is your name?" Folger asked.

"Thursday October Christian." He puffed his chest. "For the day and month on which I was born."

Christian. Yes, this couldn't be a coincidence. There must be a relation to Fletcher Christian. "I would like to invite you and your Father John aboard to be my personal guests," continued Folger, eager to learn more.

The three oarsmen unraveled the tethers and returned to their island with the invitation. For the next two hours, Folger paced back and forth with anticipation until he saw the raft reemerge from the island, but without an additional passenger. "Father John would like you to be our guest instead," Thursday October said, gliding up against the ship ready to welcome Folger on board.

Pangs of curiosity overpowered Folger's sensibilities. He dashed to his quarters and searched for his finery—a ruffled cravat and a navy blue tailcoat. There was no time to make a contingency plan should he be held prisoner on the island; he slid a furring knife deep in the pocket of his trousers as a precautionary measure.

Progress was slow as the fierce undertow dragged the canoe further out to sea before hurling it earthward on the crest of each tidal
crush. A final wave ambushed the oarsmen as they made landfall,
tossing Folger onto his hands and knees in the shallows of a small
beach. Sopping wet, he reached for Thursday October's helping
hand. The young men in their loincloths seemed unfazed, already
dried by the midday sun. Folger cursed the impracticality of his
overly formal vestments, which weighed him down like chain mail.

"Come. We invite you for a meal." Thursday October led the way
up a treacherous path snaking toward the settlement high above.
Folger gasped for breath as they climbed. "Had I known . . ." Step.
"I would have brought along a barrel of rum from my ship as a thank
you." Step. "Or even to trade for more supplies . . ." Step. "I would
be so grateful to benefit from your island's fecundity." Another step.

Thursday October stopped and looked back at Folger trying to
keep his balance. "We are a society free of vice and sin," he said,
then turned around to continue the lead. "We are in need of nothing
here." He paused once more at a felled coconut, smashing it open
with the single strike of a nearby rock, and handed it down to Folger. "But I can see that you are in need." Folger slurped the contents
of the coconut dry, letting the juice splash across his face. The sweet
fizz washed away the fetid aftertaste of cured meat and seawater that
had settled on his palate, and lent him enough vitality to finish the
slog up toward even ground.

On the plateau, the relentless foliage had been twisted and tamed
into what approximated an English common—a gated clearing patrolled by waddling chickens. On the far end of the pen sat a man
and woman under the sprawling canopy of a single banyan tree.
Rising when he noticed Folger's arrival, the man took several steps
forward until he reached the perimeter of the tree's shade, where he
waited. The woman stood close behind—his consort.

Folger hoisted his posture as he approached them and sucked
the air through his teeth, now blanched with coconut milk. "I'm
Captain Mayhew Folger of the American merchant vessel *Topaz*."

"I'm John Adams," the man said, his voice too gentle to escape
the shadows in which he remained. As they shook hands, Folger

studied him more closely. He had a dark complexion—so tan from the unyielding sun that it was hardly different from the tawny skin of the Polynesian woman at his side. Long, wiry shanks of hair—tendrils perpetually damp and encrusted with sand—tumbled down from a large straw hat that hid his balding crown. He was definitely an Englishman, and wore a sailor's costume stitched for a younger man—his belly now pressed against the white linen fabric, testing the threshold of its buttons. If he were truly a mutineer from the *Bounty*, then he couldn't be any older than forty or forty-five; the tropics had ravaged him. His eyes were sunken in—chasms, really—too deep to discern any meaning from his glances, but then Folger noticed a certain look of pity mirrored back in his direction.

Still wet, Folger attempted diplomatic airs in vain, combing his strands of straight brown hair with his fingers to distract from the gauntness of his face. He was surely five or ten years younger than Adams, and much more handsome, but navigating the depths of the Pacific had uglied his mien as well.

"You must be tired from your journey. We have prepared a banquet for you," Adams continued. "But first I'll need your knife."

Folger, surprised, feigned confusion. "My knife?"

"Yes, your knife. The one in your pocket. I need it." Adams's tone seemed suddenly stern as he extended an empty palm. Folger reluctantly ran his hands through the folds of his trousers, excavating the rusty blade.

"There is no violence here." Adams raised his other hand, lifting the bound pages of a tattered Bible into the sunlight.

"You are a society free of vice and sin," rehearsed Folger.

"Indeed."

Adams's wife took the weapon and vanished into the two-story house behind the great banyan. Folger slowly followed, passing a crackling fire that warmed an iron cauldron. He ran his fingers along the intricacies of the exterior walls—the remnants of a ship's keel, too elegant to have been crafted by the island's rudimentary tools—and glimpsed a room full of European furniture through the open entryway.

"I was told you've heard of the *Bounty*," interrupted Adams.

"Yes, I know of the *Bounty*. Everyone knows of the notorious Fletcher Christian and the *Bounty*." Folger had memorized the ship's manifest like a nursery rhyme, but John Adams was not one of the names of the nine mutineers. "It is you, however, that I do not know."

"I was there, I assure you. But that was a long time ago—another lifetime really . . ."

Folger wanted to prod further but was interrupted by a procession of islanders coming to examine their very first visitor. Under the generous awning of the banyan tree, they laid down the trappings of a feast: pale yams and plantains boiled in coconut milk, roasted chicken, grilled fish, and a whole hog speared from snout to tail. Over thirty people gathered in the square, mostly teenagers and children dressed in simple bark cloth like Thursday October. They were too bashful to make eye contact with Folger, save one young girl brandishing an undaunted smile of brilliant, bright teeth. She handed him a delicate hibiscus flower more radiant than the autumn maple leaves back home in New England and led him by the hand toward the outdoor hearth. Folger slinked off his coat, still sopping wet, and sat with the others on the ground as they passed around dishware—an indiscriminate assortment of naval china and hollowed-out gourds. Adams joined the circle and said grace:

> *Suffer me not, oh Lord to waste this*
> *Day in Sin or Folly but let me*
> *Worship Thee with much Delight.*
> *Teach me to know more of Thee and to*
> *Serve Thee better than I have ever done before.*
> *That I may be fitter to dwell in Heaven*
> *Where Thy Worship and Service are Everlasting.*

"Amen." Folger could barely temper his starvation as he inhaled the meat and vegetables, pausing only to field Adams's questions.

"Tell me, Captain, what have I missed after all this time?" Adams asked, half muffled as he mashed a boiled yam with his teeth. By Folger's calculations, it had been almost two decades since the *Bounty*'s mutineers sought refuge at the end of the world—a world that had changed so dramatically since the dawning of the new century. The Industrial Revolution was in full swing, inspiring thousands of new immigrants to cross the Atlantic. And the French had cut the heads off their monarchs, wanting *liberté* for all, only to embrace Napoleon's tyranny, which had plunged the republic into a series of bitter wars. Adams, delighted to learn of England's prosperity by comparison, sucked the morsels of stewed vegetables off the tips of his fingers in order to properly clap his hands. He then offered details about the *Bounty* in return: "In 1767 Captain Carteret, aboard the HMS *Swallow*, spotted land which he deemed 'so high it could be seen from fifteen leagues away.'"

"Pitcairn," Folger interrupted. He had a copy of Carteret's logs back on his ship. The island had been written off as a mirage as it was never spotted again.

"Yes. After we reclaimed our fates from Captain Bligh we spent months searching for a suitable home until we chanced upon Carteret's Pitcairn. And without a good anchorage, as you've seen—and a crew and a ship too weary for more seafaring—we ran the *Bounty* against the rocks and dismantled the vessel timber by timber to build our new island home, then destroyed the remains so as to not excite the curiosity of passersby."

"Where are the other mutineers now?" Folger wondered.

"Swept away by desperate contentions." Adams's voice got quieter.

The older women—of whom there were four or five—exchanged piercing glances with Adams. He began to measure his words. Folger remained silent, rapt.

"On our journey to Pitcairn we rescued six Polynesian sailors from a watery grave; they joined our colony, and, all told, we numbered around two dozen. The first few months were peaceful—we settled the land and constructed our farmsteads—but the tribesmen soon rose up, jealous of the harmonious relationships with our Tahitian brides. They stole our guns, killing all of my compatriots in a single night; there was a bullet meant for me, but by the grace of God I was spared. Our brave and vengeful wives righted the wrong, and we've been alone ever since, unbothered by the vicissitudes of civilization."

"I hope my presence hasn't disturbed your hidden community," Folger said, worried that Adams would resent his unintentional discovery.

"Secrets are like water. They seep into the crevices and cracks— every cleft and fissure. They fill holes, and sink even the mightiest of galleons."

"Like the *Bounty*?"

"The truth always leaks out. I know this to be an inevitability." Adams spoke more forcefully—his words weren't just for Folger, but a sermon for his shipwrecked congregation.

After the meal, Adams invited Folger to explore the rest of the island. They passed several more homes, each one a different configuration of *Bounty* timbers and indigenous thatch. A few of the children followed closely behind, tugging at Folger's trousers to point out strange insects and hand him an assortment of ripe fruit plucked from the trees. Pitcairn was small, but the turrets of earth and punishing incline created the illusion of vastness—a lost continent. From a lookout sheltered by a rocky overhang, Folger could see the *Topaz* far below, its two little masts bobbing in an otherwise empty sea—not a single speck of land could be spotted.

Folger noticed his shadow getting longer. "I should start making preparations to return to my ship." Adams quietly bowed his head, acknowledging Folger's request, and started down the trail leading back to the village. Deep in thought, they walked for many minutes until Adams spoke. "What will you tell your men about this day?"

"That a new country thrives here, and its citizens hold the answer to one of the world's greatest questions: the fate of the *Bounty*'s missing mutineers."

"And I should expect that the Admiralty will hear the details of our meeting?"

"Yes."

"Oh rods of scorpions and whips of steel which conscience shakes!" Adams wailed. "Not sharp revenge, not hell itself can find a fiercer torment than a guilty mind!"

Folger placed his hand on Adams's shoulder to quell his angst. "I will be sure to tell England of the good Christian people here on Pitcairn's Rock too."

"Piety has been my penance. And these children should not be made to atone for the sins of their fathers." Eighteen years of exile was a harsh enough punishment for his crime.

As they returned to the village green, Adams's wife waved them over to the banyan tree where the older women and their daughters were beginning to gather bushels of fresh provisions for Folger to take back to his men.

"I do hope this request is not misconstrued as ill-mannered, as I am very grateful to have indulged in your bounty: Might there be a token less perishable—proof—I could carry back so that when I recount your story to those at home they do not think I've gone mad in these remote waters?" Folger turned to Adams, who then disappeared into the darkness of his house. He promptly reemerged with two items: a small wooden box containing a rusting azimuth compass, and a Larcum Kendall marine chronometer that looked like a silver pocket watch. He handed the gifts to Folger. "We have no use for these as we never plan on leaving this paradise."

Stone by stone, Folger followed Thursday October back down the mountainside, with the younger oarsmen close behind carrying the baskets of fruits and vegetables for his languishing men. As they launched the outrigger into the twilight, he could hear an evening prayer from above, a madrigal sung by the children of castaways.

> *Father! Let our supplications*
> *Find acceptance in Thy sight;*
> *Free from Satan's foul temptations*
> *From the perils of the night.*
> *Oh, preserve us,*
> *Till return of morning light.*

ON THE BOW of the *Topaz*, Captain Folger stared back at the redis-
covered island. Adams's campfire had been snuffed out and was now
nothing more than a pyre of smoldering embers. Folger dangled the
Bounty's chronometer by its chain, twirling it on the tip of his finger. The waxing moon had eclipsed most of the starlight; its beams
flashed against the metal of the timepiece as it spun around.

From deep within his coat pocket Folger produced not a skinning
knife but the delicate hibiscus flower from the young girl. He plucked
the petals from the bulb, pressing them tightly between the last two
pages of his logbook until they stained the parchment red. He un-
scrolled his nautical charts and let his plume bleed a single droplet
of ink where Pitcairn properly stood—25°02'S 130°00'W—righting
Captain Carteret's erroneous markings from over forty years ago. A
smile crept across his face as he chronicled the events of the day. He
had inadvertently solved one of the greatest nautical mysteries of all
time. Racked with anticipation, he tongued the interior architecture
of his mouth once more.

When the morning light returned, the ship turned east into the
rising sun and toward South America, over three thousand miles
away. The day felt auspicious; the seas were finally calmer and the
winds favorable. Little did Folger know, however, that the *Topaz* was
sailing directly into hostile territory. Six weeks later, the ship would
be pummeled by gunfire from the Spanish fleet, and the story of
Fletcher Christian's fate locked away in the bowels of a naval prison
along with Folger and his men. His only proof of the encounter—
the chronometer and azimuth compass—was seized as contraband,
never to be returned to the captain.

It took a haggard Folger over fifteen months to finally arrive in
Valparaíso, Chile, where he reported his findings to the Royal Navy.
And a second year passed before his logbook reached the Admiralty
in Britain. Navy officials promptly buried the transcript under bu-
reaucratic rubble, devoting their attention to the ongoing war with
France instead.

In 1813, a full five years after his faraway encounter, Folger vigorously penned a letter from his new home in Massillon, Ohio,

attempting to solicit the interest of the Admiralty once more. But it wasn't until 1814 that the news finally spread, when two ships sailing in tandem, the HMS *Briton* and the HMS *Tagus*, happened upon Pitcairn not knowing of Folger's discovery. With the Napoleonic Wars drawing to a close, Britain finally acknowledged the blemish on its naval record. The *Bounty*'s fate quickly filled the pages of periodicals around the globe, igniting the imagination of millions.

But which of Fletcher Christian's comrades was John Adams? Could Adams have been Christian himself, so reviled by the British Crown that he adopted an alias during his eighteen years of solitude? And, more importantly, was Adams's account of his time on Pitcairn and the fates of the other fugitives even true? The real identity of the mysterious mutineer would remain hidden. But secrets are like water—they always have a way of trickling out . . .

CHAPTER 3

ARTOCARPUS INCISA
AUGUST–DECEMBER 1787

William Bligh penned his correspondence with polite precision. "My dear Sir, I have heard the flattering news, that you intend to honor me with the command of a vessel to go to the South Seas." He showed no trace of the bitter disappointment he harbored. "After offering you my most grateful thanks, I can only assure you I shall endeavor, and I hope, succeed, in deserving such a trust." He added one last flourish of his quill—the slashed strokes of his autograph, meticulous yet grand—before folding his note in half.

A short time later, the letter arrived in London's Soho Square, at a lavish town house filled to the chandeliers with oddities and artifacts collected from every corner of the known world: feathered headdresses, jade pendants, and long canoe oars that once stroked the surface of foreign oceans. Over the last decade, the home of Sir Joseph Banks—president of the Royal Society, England's academy of sciences—had become an unofficial museum, a mad scientist's lair where tens of thousands of botanical specimens had been dutifully dried and logged with detailed renderings.

Banks had become a fixture of polite society after traversing the globe with Captain James Cook on his first round-the-world tour aboard the HMS *Endeavour*. The official mandate of the mission was to observe the transit of Venus across the sun, and thus be able to measure the distance between the Earth and its star through solar parallax. But secretly the Royal Navy had also hoped to find a much-mythologized southern continent in the heart of the Pacific. Banks personally funded the inclusion of his elite entourage on board—four distinguished scientists and four servants from his estate—and turned the voyage into an ambitious attempt to document all the world's living wonders. He recorded over 1,300 new species of plants—sketching bougainvilleas in Brazil and giant *winika* orchids in New Zealand—and excitedly wrote about the unique leaping abilities of a never-before-seen "kangaru" creature in Australia. But it was the spirited recounting of his time on Tahiti—"the truest picture of arcadia"—that propelled the hobbyist to fame after the three-year journey was complete.

The mere knowledge of Tahiti's existence seemed to subvert the word of God. While visiting the island, Banks readily partook in all of its locals' pursuits: fishing, naked dancing, attending strange rites of human sacrifice, and "making gifts" of the beautiful women sent to his tent—abhorrent vices by Christian doctrine. And under his exaggerated macaroni fashion, Banks hid a constellation of small tattoos. Although the Tahitians knew no temperance to their carnal pursuits, they were also blissfully free of the lust for power and possessions that etched canyons of disparity between Europe's prosperous and poor. The perfect escape fantasy from greedy, rainy London, Tahiti quickly became a mainstream obsession as well.

But of all the oddities stashed in the cargo hold of the HMS *Endeavour*—and of all the titillating tales told at the banquets and balls that followed—the one item that most captured Banks's botanically inclined imagination was a fleshy orb that weighed down the branches of the Tahitian mulberry: *Artocarpus incisa*, known colloquially as breadfruit for its starchy consistency and toothsome bite. Supposedly, with eyes closed, one could not discern the difference between a morsel of the baked wedge and a crusty loaf fresh from the oven.

The plant's magical properties—hyperbolized like Tahiti's other virtues—also excited the imagination of several wealthy landowners in the Caribbean, including Duncan Campbell, who ran a large plantation in Jamaica and a fleet of private ships that indiscriminately moved convicts and cargo across great oceans. Triangle trade was booming—rum and sugar zipped between continents—but the management of African slaves had become a costly prospect. Perhaps the introduction of breadfruit to the West Indies could be a more efficient means of feeding the landowners' human capital?

Campbell tried to solicit a merchant vessel to undertake the procurement of some breadfruit seedlings, but the project was deemed too cumbersome and costly for a trader to turn a worthy profit. So Campbell called on Banks to help inspire a bit of benevolence from the Crown. The Royal Navy soon agreed that a voyage to the legendary island was a worthy investment in the prosperity of England's slave trade, especially after losing its new-world colonies during the recent American Revolutionary War.

"One hour's negligence may at any period be the means of destroying all the trees and plants which may have been collected," instructed Banks. A special ship would need to be outfitted to ensure the mission's success. The Royal Navy thusly purchased the *Bethia*—which happened to be one of Campbell's mercantile cruisers—and spent a small fortune remodeling the craft. First came a protective copper plating to safeguard the hull from both woodworm and Tahiti's tropical waters, which threatened to turn the ship's well-worn timbers into rotted mush. Then, a sprawling greenhouse took up half the lower deck in the only area on board with windows, and a special stove was installed to help regulate the temperature of the plant cuttings as they drifted through different climates on their eventual journey from Tahiti to Jamaica. The ship measured almost ninety-one feet in length, weighed just over two hundred tons (around half the volume of Cook's *Endeavour*), and had three decks and three small tenders for shoreside ferrying. The only item on board that remained untouched was the thirty-foot figure of a woman in full riding habit that adorned the ship's front under the long reaching arm of the bowsprit.

Newly refitted, the *Bethia* was the Royal Navy's strangest little watercraft and, in honor of its equally unusual mission, was duly renamed: His Majesty's Armed Vessel *Bounty*.

The *Bounty* now needed a captain, and at Campbell's suggestion Banks urged the Admiralty to offer the job to William Bligh. Bligh had helmed one of Campbell's merchant ships in the West Indies; he also happened to be married to Campbell's niece.

As kings crowned their princes, so, too, was the calling in of familial favors an implicit part of everyday life in England. But the Age of Discovery had begun to close the gap between the nobility and the other classes; the ocean was an arena in which ambitious commoners played war games alongside the sons of dukes and earls. Bligh was one such gentleman who sought to climb the rungs of society all the way to the upper decks. He inherited his frosty blue eyes from his peasant mother, who died when he was a child, and his tight curls of black hair from his father, the head customs officer at the Royal Navy's dockyards, which gave a teenage Bligh an advantage when signing up for a life at sea.

Slightly shorter than the average man, and with the white skin of a porcelain doll, Bligh—now just shy of his thirty-third birthday—may not have looked the part of sea captain, but his experience did in fact make him a worthy choice to lead the mission. Like Banks, Bligh was one of the few Englishmen to have witnessed the fantasies of Tahiti firsthand. Eight years earlier he served aboard the HMS *Resolution* on Captain Cook's third and final voyage around the globe, a fateful journey that ended abruptly for Britain's most celebrated navigator when he was pelted with stones and stabbed to death on the island of Hawaii by its indigenous inhabitants. After returning to England, Bligh was the only member of Cook's inner sanctum not to receive a promotion—likely due to the lack of distinction in his pedigree—so he sought work aboard private trading ships instead.

In his concise letter to Banks, Bligh expressed his gratitude to the scion of scientific discovery for offering him a return to the Royal

Navy with his first command posting, but a half-size vessel filled with shrubbery was not what he had in mind.

And there was more to complain about besides the large amount of space he would forfeit to the delicate breadfruit: He would receive a reduced salary. With space for a crew of only forty-six (again, roughly half the size of Cook's *Endeavour*), Bligh would have to double as the ship's purser, responsible for balancing the vessel's expenses. He would, however, be allowed to skim the coffers of any funds not spent on rations or repairs—a system the Royal Navy regularly implemented to incentivize accountants not to overspend. And as the mission was of a scientific nature, the usual marine marshals—dispatched for disciplinary purposes—were replaced with a botanist and gardener, meaning Bligh would also moonlight as the *Bounty*'s only security detail. He had hoped these command caveats would earn him an appeal to his vanity with a formal promotion from lieutenant to captain, but his repeated requests for an advancement were categorically denied—such honors were only bestowed during wartime.

After the botanist and gardener—and the usual assortment of warrant officers, like a carpenter and sailmaker—Thomas Huggan joined the *Bounty*'s ranks as its surgeon, despite his reputation as a bumbling old drunkard. Once again Bligh waved his quill, sending a spate of politely incensed letters to the Admiralty demanding a more suitable doctor. His appeals were unsurprisingly ignored, but Bligh was allowed to staff the rest of his crew with sailors of his own choosing, starting with the midshipmen (young officers in training).

Bligh had finally ingratiated himself into the upper echelons of society, and now its members came calling for favors. His desk was stacked with correspondence: requests from influential acquaintances hoping to place their teenage sons and nephews aboard his ship so that they may break into a career at sea. The Royal Navy recommended hiring two such apprentices. Bligh chose six, and a few extras that he crammed onto the ship's decks under different titles, honoring a handful of flippant promises made to friends of his wife's family, since he, too, found himself painted onto the *Bounty*'s register by the light brushstrokes of nepotism.

In September, the fledglings left their nests, traveling from every corner of Great Britain to gather on the docks at Portsmouth, the same piers on which Bligh's father had worked, surveying the arrival of imported goods from all over the world.

"I heard Mr. Bligh watched Captain Cook die at the hands of murderous savages."

"I heard Cook's limbs were ripped apart, his body torn into pieces—one for every continent he discovered."

John Hallett and Thomas Hayward came from prominent middle-class families, whose new money afforded their sons the full battery of etiquette and elocution lessons to smooth their unrefined behavior into pastiches of perfect gentlemen—their pubescent propensity for gossip and self-righteousness notwithstanding, blemishes on otherwise polished facades, like the pink peppering of mild acne that freckled their cheeks.

"Yes, boys, it's true," Bligh interrupted. He had arrived unnoticed, startling the circle of teens during their rapturous exchange of rumors. They quickly tugged at their jackets to shake out any unwanted wrinkles and craned their casual posture into awkward at-attention poses.

"And had I been in command of the landing party, instead of watching the hideous display from a rowboat," Bligh continued, "I guarantee that James Cook would still be alive and well today."

Most men would have been deeply affected by witnessing such a massacre, but Bligh was haunted more by the circumstances of that fateful day than the torturous dismembering of his mentor. The landing party was disorganized, its sailors easily spooked, "not a spark of courage or conduct was shown in the whole business." He was sure that if he had been in charge of the mission, he would have been brave enough to stand his ground against the sudden ambush by the Hawaiians.

Bligh squinted at his midshipmen, trying to estimate how each one would soon fare on the open seas. Their dark blue coats and rippled black hats looked more like costumes than uniforms. They seemed younger than the descriptions offered by their esteemed contacts—the families and friends who had secured their tenures on the ship. A few were not yet sixteen, boys emerging from the chrysalis of childhood knowing only of the vast world through the books that lined the libraries and salons of their families' country estates. Even the debauchery of nearby London was just as much of an abstraction as the monstrous jungle vines of faraway lands newly drafted in Banks's botanical journals.

As the group continued to exchange formal pleasantries, another man joined Bligh's side—not too much older than the boys, but already toughened by a sea voyage or two. He was tall, verging on lanky, and his olive skin—perhaps tanned in warmer climes—starkly contrasted with the milky hues of the delicate youths. It would have been easy to assume he was of Spanish or Portuguese extraction if it weren't for his eyes—like two pewter coins that hinted at a Norse or Celtic heritage instead—and his prim British cadence: "Pleasure to meet everyone. I'm Fletcher Christian."

"Mr. Christian was once a midshipman like yourselves," Bligh added—the two had twice sailed together on mercantile missions in the West Indies—"and it is by my own special request that he joins us on this, a most ambitious of scientific missions."

At twenty-three, and with a promotion to master's mate aboard the *Bounty*, Christian was well on his way to captaining a ship of his own in ten years' time, like Bligh, though a naval career seemed like an unusual prospect for a young man with such a distinguished pedigree who had once shown great academic promise.

"Fletcher Christian of the Whitehaven Christians? It's a privilege to serve aboard the *Bounty* with you. I'm Peter Heywood. I hail from the Isle of Man." He was the most boyish of his rank, and although he had grown taller than Bligh, his features were still childlike—rosy cheeks and sandy blond hair that had been carefully combed just the way his mother had taught him, save a sprig of a cowlick, untamed without the benefit of a mirror.

"Well, we must be cousins then!" Christian had a knack for turning strangers into kin. He was the tenth child of a prominent family from the Lake District who indeed traced their royal roots back to the Isle of Man—they were also direct descendants of William the Conqueror, England's first Norman king.

Bligh's wife was Manx as well, an acquaintance of the aristo-cratic Heywood family who helped the young man earn a spot on the ship's roster—an act of favoritism that Bligh would not soon let him, or any of the other gentlemen-to-be, forget, especially if Bligh needed to curry favor for a more prestigious command in the future.

"And by the way, the carnage in Hawaii was far worse than your whispered depictions," Bligh snorted, pulling the attention back to himself. "The heathens of the South Seas are quite practiced at chucking their spears and stones."

Having stunned the midshipmen into silence, he began to walk away—"Now get to work!"—but paused to field a final question.

"Lieutenant Bligh?"

"It's *Captain* Bligh."

It wasn't.

"What's Tahiti like?" Edward Young was the oldest of the mid-shipmen; at twenty-one, he had already completed an extensive ed-ucation in biblical and classical studies. And although his father was the patriarch of a noble English family, Young was born from a West Indian dalliance on the island of Saint Kitts. His mixed lineage hampered his social standing, despite his first-rate schooling, and made him the least favorite of Bligh's new disciples.

"Well, Mr. Young," Bligh turned around, "they are an unenlight-ened people who know no modesty in their divinity, sobriety, and most certainly in their sexuality. They worship rocks, eat until they vomit, and they copulate for sport. And yet, rather than punishing their moral decay, our good and gracious God has rewarded their hedonism with warm sun and plenty of fresh food—even bread, apparently—which grows wild on the trees' branches."

Bligh paused. "I imagine you'll like it quite a lot." He then de-parted, leaving dozens of crates for his new crewmen to load onto the ship.

BLIGH'S FIRST ACQUISITION as the commanding officer of the *Bounty* was Captain Cook's logbooks: navigational aids that he'd follow in the South Seas and rationing recipes to sustain his seamen during their journey. Cook never had a single scurvy death aboard all three of his round-the-world expeditions, and Bligh sought to maintain a flawless track record as well, ordering the usual biscuits and salted meat, plus a cocktail of powdered soup stock, malt, wort, vinegar, sauerkraut, and mustard to help ward off the skull-crushing effects of the mystery ailment that so often plagued those who spent too long at sea.

"We must find some seamen to carry these victuals on board." Hallett had no intention of scuffing hands that had only ever borne the weight of a book.

"Yes, good idea. We'll supervise," added Hayward, also ignoring the request of his superior. Apparently laziness was another attribute that new money afforded.

Christian chuckled, lifting a large wooden parcel stuffed with bouillon sachets. Heywood followed suit. "Pardon my ignorance, but I've failed to appreciate the humor of my fellow midshipmen's reluctance to follow orders," he shyly wondered, unloading a pallet of wort and malt.

"Oh, cousin Heywood, at sea it doesn't matter who you are or to whom you're born. Everyone shits through the same hole in the bow." Christian flashed a smile at Heywood, who didn't quite seem to get it.

The last lot of crew members on the *Bounty*'s roster were its able seamen, the lowest-ranking on board, a motley assortment of hardened sailors saved from more pitiful existences on land.

"And what do we have here?" Matthew Thompson was skulking in his berth when he noticed Hallett and Hayward enter the lower deck looking for a place to hang their hammocks. Almost forty, Thompson was one of the oldest men on the ship's roster, and he had picked up every bad habit from a life lived at sea: he swore profusely, he drank obsessively, and fisticuffs had gashed his hands and jaw. His skin was dark and leathery from furling sails in the hot sun, and his teeth were rotted through after years of a deficient diet of dried biscuits and cured ham.

"Who are these little ladies?" voices taunted, as more sailors emerged from deeper within the windowless deck. Some grimaced with sallow faces cratered by smallpox scars; others wore burly muscles that rippled and flexed as they approached. All together they looked like a ragtag group of pirates depicted in the storybooks of Hallett and Hayward's childhood. The two midshipmen stood paralyzed, unsure of what to say or do.

Thompson lunged at Hallett, yanking his trousers down to his ankles. "Ah! As smooth as a lady!" Cackling laughter echoed through the room as Hallett tried cupping his hands for modesty. Hayward inched back, bumping into another seaman who hinged the crook of his arm under Hayward's neck and lifted him off the ground.

"Hellooo lassie," Charles Churchill cooed and hissed in Hayward's ear as he choked him. Churchill was the tallest of the sailors on board and sprouted not a single hair on his shiny bald head.

"Put him down at once!" Hallett scrambled to pull up his pants but tripped face-first after a hardy kick in the back from Thompson.

"Oh yes, he'll do quite nicely," Thompson stepped one foot atop Hallett's bare buttocks, pressing him flat against the floorboards. "And what about the other one?"

Hayward tried to yell for help, but Churchill tightened his chokehold.

"Alright gentlemen, that's enough for now," Christian ordered as he walked in. "We'll play after we finish stocking the foodstuffs for our journey to Gravesend." Thompson took his leg off of Hallett, and Churchill let Hayward go.

"You know they're only joking, right?" James Valentine helped the two young men collect themselves. "They won't make women out of you. They're just excited to leave for Tahiti." Usually—and especially during times of war—the Royal Navy would have to force men into duty to fill the lower ranks of a vessel, but Bligh found many eager applicants for the *Bounty*'s journey, all bewitched by tales of Tahiti's exotic women and eager to taste their forbidden fruit.

As preparations for the voyage continued apace, Valentine, soft-spoken and strikingly handsome, became one of Bligh's favorites.

When works of art would be commissioned to lionize the successful delivery of Tahiti's breadfruit to Jamaica, Bligh thought to himself, he'd have Valentine pose for the painting as the heroic mariner heeding the words of his valiant commander.

In early October, four small swivel cannons were installed at Gravesend before the *Bounty* moved to the naval yard at Spithead to load several farm animals—goats, chickens, and a dog—and the final crates of cargo: 1,000 pounds of nails, 100 pounds of glass beads, 168 mirrors, and a variety of other trinkets—fodder for barter in a realm where little metal coins stamped with the face of British kings held no interest or inherent value.

With the *Bounty* fully stocked, Bligh curtly wrote to the Admiralty once more, impatiently imploring his superiors to confirm the sailing orders that would dictate the specifics of his route as he crossed the Atlantic and sailed down the coast of South America. Any delays would jeopardize his ability to pass Cape Horn, the doorway to the Pacific, which was only open between December and February—the warmest months of Patagonia's otherwise impossibly frigid and squall-ridden year. But winter arrived earlier than expected in England—mythic sheets of ice and hail, a harbinger of the biting winds and clawing seas that would soon pummel the passageway at the bottom of the New World—and Bligh's attempts to navigate the November storms were rebuffed like his many requests to the Admiralty. The *Bounty* made it as far as Saint Helens on the Isle of Wight—a mere dozen miles offshore—before having to turn around for repairs.

Back at Spithead, a few of the able seamen had disappeared with their salary advances, which came as no surprise to Bligh. He quickly scoured the dockyards to find their replacements, hiring a half-blind fiddler named Michael Byrne to boost morale with his music and two strapping sailors in their twenties, William McCoy and Matthew Quintal—both fit enough to pose alongside Valentine for that commemorative painting, thought Bligh, too wrapped up in his own ambitions to be a proper judge of character.

Only one member of the *Bounty* quietly relished the mission's postponement. Christian had received word that his older brother

Charles was soon returning from sea; the extra weeks stuck at Spit-head would afford them a brief reunion before it was Christian's turn to venture into the horizon. Charles was the surgeon aboard the *Middlesex*, a merchant ship for the East India Company that had spent the last year and a half trading goods and wares in Madras (Chennai, India).

"This brawny man is a stranger to me!" Charles squeezed Christian's arm, hardly recognizing his brother from the memory of a gangly teenager he kept.

"I delight to set the men an example!" Christian rolled up his cotton sleeves, flexing a bicep. "I not only can do every part of a common sailor's duty, but am upon a par with a principal part of the officers."

"He makes toil a pleasure, strict but playful!" Charles had heard only praise from his cohorts aboard the *Middlesex* of the affable ways in which Christian inspired fellowship from younger sailors.

The two brothers retreated into a pub near the dockyards.

"Oh Fletcher, I went on this ship as a tree in a state of promising blossom, full of life and vigor, and left as one withered with blight, disappointed, dispirited and full of heart-damping trouble." Charles had returned to England a fragile man. He had borrowed £500 to scour the fabric markets of the Far East but came home owing an insurmountable debt, unable to source a single scrap of merchandise. And there were troublesome circumstances aboard the *Middlesex* that deeply weighed on his conscience as well. Charles wasted no time recounting them to Christian: "When men are cooped up for a long time in the interior of a ship there oft prevails such a jarring discordancy of tempers, and conduct—repeated acts of offense—to change the disposition of a lamb into that of an animal fierce and resentful."

Two weeks prior to the *Middlesex*'s return, Charles had been involved in a mutiny born from months of rising tension between several crewmen and their captain. Such crimes were punishable by hanging in the Royal Navy, but as the uprising had occurred on a commercial vessel, Charles would instead be barred from the trading service for two years. He had no regrets—"from a humane sympathy sprang my sudden ebullition of passion at seeing cruel usage exercised towards one who is deserved a far different treatment by the capricious orders of tyranny influenced by a hollow sycophant."

Tipsy and tired, Christian left the pub at dawn, heeding his older brother's careful advice for the journey ahead, so that he, too, would not return home a shell of a man: "Beware of whom you speak, to whom, of what and where. Give every man thine ear, but few thy voice."

Stumbling back to the *Bounty*, he found a homesick Heywood sitting on the upper deck unable to sleep and confided in the young midshipman of the disturbing stories his brother had recounted. Charles was not the only Christian facing debtor's prison—the entire family had fallen on hard times and was quietly grappling with the preservation of their prominence and honor. Heywood's family was broke too, foisting their teenage son upon Bligh, where he'd eventually earn a decent wage after rising through the ranks of the Royal Navy.

"We must do everything in our power to protect our reputations," Heywood insisted. "Be it the pound sterling for us Manxmen, or these shiny beads and mirrors for the Tahitians, nothing is in fact more precious than our honor." Maybe Heywood wasn't as naive as he looked.

Under charcoal clouds—a brief respite from the perpetual storms—the *Bounty* trundled away from Spithead on December 23 as dark waves slashed its bow. Two days later, a special roast, plum pudding, and extra rations of grog were dispatched from the galley as a consolation to the sailors who had hoped to spend Christmas with their families. But the mission could not afford even one more hour's delay. By Bligh's estimates, they would arrive at Cape Horn in mid-March, weeks beyond the ideal time frame to ensure safe transit through to the southern seas of the Pacific.

"Next year, on Christmas Day, we'll be in Jamaica, or maybe even back in England!" Bligh stepped up onto a small armory chest to toast his crewmen, who had all gathered on the upper deck. "To the breadfruit!"

"To the breadfruit!" everyone cheered back. As Byrne played the fiddle—a mix of navy chanteys and carols to which the sailors drunkenly danced—Bligh quietly knew it was a promise he could never keep. He wondered what other misfortunes would befall his little vessel before returning to England. Perhaps the ceaseless onslaught of torrential weather was an omen that terrible things would happen if the *Bounty* were to snake its way across the South Seas and snatch the fruit from Tahiti's paradisiacal garden.

CHAPTER 4

DISCOVERY IN THE AGE
OF THE SUPERSTORE

2017–2018

There is no better monolith to globalization than the superstore: the windowless, could-be-anywhere, big-box hypermarket that lends a pallid sameness to the towns and cities it inhabits. There is a lot more to lament about the superstore too, but consider for a moment that perhaps it is a miracle of our modern times, aggregating all the world's things in one convenient place—like Sir Joseph Banks's townhome in London's Soho Square, filled with goods gathered from practically every continent on his journey with Captain Cook.

·Today, it's almost impossible to comprehend the disconnectedness of Cook's world when he and his contemporaries were filling in the final blanks on the map. Back then, a pineapple—for example—was worth more than gold. They couldn't grow in the cooler climes of Europe and had to be precariously imported from far away. The sweet tropical fruit became such an important status symbol that, for many years, it was used only for display at parties—even rented out to poorer families to showcase in their homes for an evening or two—before being devoured by its owner when it had all but withered and rotten.

Equally as inconceivable was William Bligh's journey aboard the *Bounty*, that a man and his crew would be asked to forfeit two whole years of their wretchedly short lives (and millions of pounds from the Admiralty's coffers, adjusted for inflation) for what was essentially a grocery run—a task that today would take a laughably quick fifteen minutes at a superstore and require not much more than a few nickels and quarters.

Still, I often daydreamed about what it would have been like to voyage aboard a tall ship during the Age of Discovery. I'd brave the scurvy, sickness, and maggoty sea biscuits to sail back in time—to drop anchor in an uncharted bay and make contact with an unadulterated culture—since now, I figured, there was nothing left in the world to discover.

But then, trapped in my New York City high-rise one gloomy winter afternoon, three short sentences materialized in my inbox, challenging that very notion and quickly setting into motion a journey across the sea to a place where the flooding tide of globalization had yet to come crashing down:

> I want to send you to an island no one's ever heard of.
> Call me? It's far.
>
> —Ally

I immediately picked up the phone.

Ally and I had known each other for years. She was a marketing executive who helped fledgling countries break into the travel industry. She cut to the chase: "Have you heard the story of the mutiny on the *Bounty*?" I knew right away that she was talking about Pitcairn.

I had spent over a decade researching and visiting emerging destinations for guidebooks and magazines (my best attempts at modern-day exploration). After a hundred countries visited, my geographical interests had veered sharply toward the obscure.

Pitcairn was a name I couldn't un-hear, and the story of its founding—a series of events sparked by the *Bounty*'s legendary downfall—was so disturbing and surreal that it ran like ticker tape in the back of my mind. I had started to notice its influence everywhere: Samuel Coleridge's "The Rime of the Ancient Mariner"—the "water, water everywhere" poem—was inspired by Fletcher Christian; the original *Star Trek*'s Leonard "Bones" McCoy was named after one of the mutineers; *The Simpsons* spoofed the *Bounty*'s hijacking in an episode; even the Mars chocolate company had a Bounty candy bar with coconut palm motif on the wrapper.

Additionally, Clark Gable, Marlon Brando, and Mel Gibson had all played Fletcher Christian in three separate major motion pictures. In Gibson's 1984 version—a slightly more faithful representation of the true events that went down—there's a block of text that appears on the screen at the end of the movie before the credits roll: "The mutineers' fate remained a mystery for 18 years until their island was discovered by an American whaling ship. . . . What happened to Fletcher Christian remains uncertain. . . . However, his descendants live on Pitcairn Island to this day."

There were still castaways living on this godforsaken rock over two hundred years later. This was the first thing I knew about Pitcairn.

Incredibly, this community—no greater than fifty people, as Ally explained—had been largely subsisting on the profits of postage sales for several decades, hawking reams of their obscure stamps to eager collectors who gladly paid a premium for the novelty of having little bits of paper sporting breadfruit and *Bounty* drawings from the far side of the world. But with philatelic interest on the decline, the island—a tax-exempt adjunct of the United Kingdom—was now enlisting Ally's help as it eyed tourism as a possible new revenue stream.

The second thing I knew about Pitcairn was that it was far. So far, in fact, that at one time it was considered the most remotely inhabited place on the entire planet—a superlative that both intrigued intrepid travelers and filled them with pangs of frustration, as not a single form of commercial transportation links the island to the rest of the world.

"So how will I even get there?"

There was a freighter, she explained, that sustained the islanders on a supply run undertaken once every three months, and a berth had been made available on board in a year's time so that a single journalist—Pitcairn's first visitor welcomed under this new tourism initiative—could spend a couple of weeks on the island while the vessel shuttled a few passengers to French Polynesia for medical care before definitively departing until its next seasonal run.

In total, the trip into the unknown would take a full month, from New York City to Los Angeles, then on to Tahiti to wait for a puddle-jumper to fly me a thousand more miles to a distant atoll deep in the South Pacific, where the cargo ship would pick me up and ferry me across a final three hundred miles of cruel and unpredictable ocean. And then, of course, I'd complete the difficult journey in reverse to get back home.

I knew then that the trip would never be financially viable—thirty days away from my desk with no access to phone or email. Plus, none of my lifestyle magazine editors would ever commission a glossy travel story on a destination without a single hotel, restaurant, or any other semblance of infrastructure, let alone an actual way of getting there that didn't involve shipping oneself as human freight aboard a merchant vessel. But I couldn't pass up the opportunity. Living in the Age of the Superstore, this felt like my last shot at the discovery I so yearned for.

"I'm in."

After twelve months of careful planning and anticipation, suddenly I was roaming the extra-wide aisles of the Target near my New York City apartment in search of all the things I wouldn't be able to find on Pitcairn: candles for the nightly power cuts to the island's generator; cooking spices (gifts for the islanders welcoming me as their homestay guest); protein bars for extra sustenance should the food options be woefully poor; a waterproof camera case to document the world's largest marine reserve (over 325,000 square miles of protected reefs enrobe the island); and an expedition-grade medical kit with bug repellant, sunscreen, bandages, disinfectants, anti-inflammatories, and hydration sachets to combat the inhospitable elements. One by one, I dutifully checked each item off my list—my packing list for the end of the world.

CHAPTER 5

A SCORE OF WORLDS
January–October 1788

I n the not-too-distant past, when the sea became the back door
to exotic lands once deemed too perilous and far, a Portuguese
sailor lined the hull of his caravel with casks of wine from the island of Madeira, which he planned on trading for spices and tex-
tiles more vibrant than the dull medieval senses could fathom. But
when he arrived in the East Indies, there was little interest in his
liquid gold; his other metals, however—copper and lead, the al-
loys of future civilizations—proved a much more compelling barter in these realms ruled by weather and wood. The vats remained
unopened—extra ballasts to help steady the sailor's return journey
through rougher waters—but when he arrived home, ready to drink
his losses, he made a discovery more galvanizing than the new cot-
tons and potions his crewmen had off-loaded into the mercantile
mansions of their sponsors: the wine was richly flavored, warm
mouthfuls of toasted fruit that usually took decades to develop. It
seemed the sloshing of the barrels under the glow of other suns had
bent the properties of time, maturing the vintages well beyond their
years through some kind of modern alchemy only the crossing of the
planet's parallels could yield.

The accidental experiment was tested again over several subsequent sailings, and with similar success. *Vinho da roda*—round-trip

wines—quickly became an indulgence as coveted as the incense and opium brought back from the other ends of the Earth.

"When this crosses the equator—and comes back again—it will be a fully realized liquor." Bligh hoisted a small cask of wine onto the table with both hands. "Don't touch it!" He slapped away the fingers of his midshipmen who had gathered for dinner; they were not to open the barrel. The round-trip journey to the mythic blue continent far beyond the East Indies would have the same effect on the callow teenagers he had collected through the usual nepotism of the haut monde: they'd sail down all of Earth's latitudes and return home as gentlemen, matured by a year's worth of experiences garnered between two Christmases. Or so he hoped.

In January, the *Bounty* had anchored at Tenerife in the Canary Islands, a popular stop where passing vessels could replenish their provisions and mend leaky caulking or tears in their sails before moving on to newer worlds. After a series of winter storms, Bligh had already penned a long list of repairs, and for his first diplomatic act as captain he sent Christian out to meet with the Spanish governor, remaining on board like a king in his castle.

Christian promptly returned with all the men and materials needed to refurbish and restock the *Bounty* anew, including several barrels of that tantalizing wine from Madeira—only two days' sailing away—now rolling around in the ship's hold, save the one small cask on the table.

"I'm changing the watch rotations," Bligh announced to his midshipmen as they gorged on cheese and fruit, fully aware that their next feast of fresh produce would likely be in Tahiti. "Starting tomorrow we will have three shifts instead of two, and Mr. Christian will take charge of the third." The ease with which Christian had tended to all of the ship's needs on Tenerife was of no surprise to Bligh—he had long seen a captain in the making. Christian possessed all of the refinement, implicit in his patrician upbringing, to effortlessly contend with the different dignitaries at foreign ports. Bligh believed himself to have also mastered these aristocratic airs—his a careful imitation instead of an inborn trait. But while Bligh felt as though he was owed the admiration of lesser men—his crew unequivocally obliged to follow the orders of their leader—Christian merely desired to be well-liked, garnering fellowship through camaraderie instead of his title. Christian's ardent sociability puzzled Bligh—great leaders were never preoccupied with such things, he felt—but it ensured him a modicum of loyalty from his newly promoted officer, lest they fall out of favor.

The following week, Thompson and Churchill came hollering through the berths, tearing down snoozing crew members from their hammocks. "Pollywogs on the upper deck, now! It's time to cross the line!" They were corralling the younger sailors for the more traditional method of minting new men at sea. Sailing across the equator—the most famous of latitudes—gave more hardened sea dogs the right to haze their shipmates through the guise of pomp, initiating them into the fraternity of shellbacks. The men unanimously tapped Christian to play the presiding King Neptune, wrapping a tattered sail over his shoulders like a royal cape that reached all the way to the floor. He entertained the other *Bounty* members, balancing musket barrels atop both of his palms, then called for all of the ship's novices to present themselves for their shaving: a messy rite of lathers and blades. Tars and ointments were gathered to ease the stroke of sharp objects as the sailors scalped the junior crew members of all their hair. Thompson and Churchill took great pleasure in wrangling Hallett and Hayward first, who tried unsuccessfully to bribe their way out of the ritualistic balding. Christian mercifully swished a clean cutlass across Heywood's head, sparing him the nicks and sores of a blunter blade.

"Now you look like proper babies!" cheered the older sailors in the crowd.

The crew's morale remained high as they diagonaled across the Atlantic, passing a merchant vessel, the *British Queen*, which offered a final opportunity to send correspondence back to England before they followed the jungles of Brazil down to lower latitudes.

"I am happy and satisfied in my little ship," Bligh wrote to Joseph Banks. He had changed his mind, finding his stewardship of the breadfruit and the *Bounty* to be less perfunctory than he initially anticipated. It was a good opportunity to mentor his coterie of young aristocratic sailors on board. He issued Christian an acting order to lieutenant—third in command of their vessel, announced in front of the entire crew—and practiced his navigation skills for what he hoped would be a commission of far greater importance when he returned to England.

"We are now fit to go round half a score of worlds," Bligh added, before slashing his signature across the page. But he wasn't naive to the perils that were waiting for him at the bottom of the planet; the *Bounty*'s delayed departure promised wicked storms and walls of wind and ice that would test even the finest captain in the fleet.

BLIGH ALWAYS LEFT the door open to his quarters, even when he slept. His cabin was unusually small for a captain. When the *Bounty* was the *Bethia*, the commanding officer slept in a sprawling, window-lined room that now sat empty in anticipation of the breadfruit stocks and seedlings that would need the tenderest of care on their journey from Tahiti to Jamaica. The open door also allowed Bligh to better eavesdrop on the minor goings-on around the ship.

"You know, dogs can smell land before man can spot it," Quintal mused within earshot, climbing the ladder up from the hold where he had been feeding the ship's animals.

"Hogwash!" McCoy traipsed behind, his wet shoes squeaking on the waxed floor.

"Goats too—they're feral but they're cunning as hell," Quintal added as he and McCoy slinked by Bligh's room.

"Who told you this nonsense?"

"It's true! They can smell fear—like when those gentlemen twits send their hounds on a fox hunt because they're too cowardly to catch one on their own." Quintal grabbed the next set of rungs, lifting him up toward the higher deck.

"So our goats and dog are sensing fear. Is that right Quintal?" McCoy followed closely behind, his tone growing more skeptical with each sarcastic rebuttal.

"I . . . I suppose so!"

"And what, pray tell, are they afraid of?"

"Your fucking face!" Quintal let out a pop of laughter. The two friends had already reached the upper deck, but Bligh could still make out the punch line and Quintal's sharp cackle, which dropped through the floorboards like the chomp of a hatchet.

Bligh disregarded the brief distraction and returned to his work, scrawling lengthy notes in his log—his manifesto of good captaining, an instruction manual for future leaders filled with the haughty remarks of the Royal Navy's newest prodigy. Today, March 11, 1788, Bligh would congratulate himself on the successful implementation of a third shift on board. After two months, the watch rotation had proved even better than anticipated; although his men were forced to work more diligently—and in smaller groups—while on duty, the newfangled system generally allowed for more sleep and plenty of time for their uniforms to dry in the now unflagging sunshine, which meant no one had to work a shift in soggy clothes. And Christian, who promptly took the helm at 4 a.m. every day, met Bligh's high expectations, molding his teenage shipmates—like Heywood, a most loyal pet who heeded all of Christian's commands—into promising officers.

Another fit of laughter pecked its way through the ceiling from upstairs—longer this time—causing Bligh to once again lose focus. This was the most loathsome part of a seafaring career, he remembered: being stuck aboard a small vessel with every class of man, including the dregs of society necessary for maintenance, mast rigging, and other menial tasks unfit for a gentleman. Although all of the *Bounty*'s crew had mustered of their own free will, Bligh kept a running tally of those he deemed "hard cases." Quintal was now at the top of the list.

Punches were exchanged as commonly as foul words on the lower deck of the ship, but Bligh wanted to know nothing of it, unless it affected a crewman's ability to work. Thompson and Churchill were the most likely culprits as two of the oldest and largest men on board, their bulbous knuckles permanently calloused after years of brawls. But there was something different about Quintal—he was coiffed and clever, and not at all thuggish like the others. If he had been born into a good family, instead of under a moist stone, he might have been a rake, his raw bouts of emotion mollified by the mannerly facade that a moneyed upbringing afforded. But his impulsive outbursts disturbed Bligh. They sparked up almost instantaneously like a flash of lightning. And then came the roll of thunder: fits of giggles or vicious, vulgar rage. And McCoy—just as handsome if he shaved his thick beard—was Quintal's enabler, stoking the bolts of fire before clapping them out.

John Fryer, the *Bounty*'s sailing master, came screaming through Bligh's open door, his eye bludgeoned, swollen and purple. "A flogging for Mr. Quintal at once!"

"Well, fuck." Bligh didn't care about the specifics of the incident. He was annoyed because an assault against the ship's second-in-command warranted logged disciplinary action. Horseplay was easily left off the books, but Fryer would undoubtedly cite this offense in his journal, tarnishing Bligh's notion of a pristine record. To him, a slap of the whip meant he wasn't an exemplary sea captain; he couldn't control his crew.

"For insolence and contempt to the master, I hereby order two-dozen lashes to be delivered down on Able Seaman Matthew Quintal," Bligh announced to the entirety of the *Bounty*'s complement, crowded on the upper deck. A heavy metal grate—used to help ventilate the lower decks with fresh air—had been heaved from the wooden slatting and leaned upright against the mainmast. Quintal's ankles and wrists had been tied each to one of its four corners, and with his shirt removed, his bare back lay exposed, waiting for retribution.

The weather had turned suddenly colder after a month of beaming tropical sun. A few of the men clenched their jaws to hide a fit of shivers as Bligh performed a thorough reading of the Articles of War, the code of conduct for those who served in the Royal Navy. A long black whip was then exhumed from the armory, and Bligh stepped back, retreating into his thoughts as the boatswain raised his right arm high. The first dozen lashes came quickly—and each with a little snicker from Quintal—leaving the singeing red scratch marks of some ferocious feline streaking across his spine. The cool air between strokes felt like the rough lick of a cat's tongue. Then the second set of lashes came swinging down, each one more severe, tearing off tiny flecks of skin. Bligh looked away, repulsed, but could still hear Quintal's chuckling, which steadily crescendoed—"HA! Hahahaha. HA! Hahahaha."—on the downbeat of the whip until it swelled into a wailing exclamation of laughter and rage.

A few days later, the last current of warm air swished through the *Bounty*'s sails; a shawl of haze flapped through a colder sky. The goats and dog were grunting. Quintal was right; the Falklands were hiding in the brume. Lower and lower the little ship sailed, and with each passing latitude the seas continued to swell and the clouds grew more menacing until they finally broke into a punishing squall.

"It's a higher sea than any I have seen before." Bligh stared into the black abyss that had swallowed Cape Horn as a battery of hail rattled the upper deck. The storm was wicked, almost calculating in the way it brought down the *Bounty*'s crewmen one at a time. Doc Huggan was thrown across his clinic, his shoulder torn out of its socket. Young then fell from the yardarm, knocking out most of his front teeth. The ship's cook cracked a rib against the stove as he hastily prepared the daily porridge. And Churchill scalded his hand after taking over the necessary galley duties. A hot breakfast, steeped in sugar and butter, was the most important defense Bligh could conjure, an attempt to stave off seasickness with full bellies and provide enough energy for the constant slacking, shortening, and furling of the sails. The sleet continued to whirl at different angles around the besieged vessel. Wheat-y chunks of vomit were now unnoticeable in the sailors' snow-caked beards, save the putrid smell.

A wave of crippling fever and congestion then ravaged the trembling crew as gallons of seawater filled the hold, drowning some of the ship's animals. The berths were flooded too, but no matter—it was impossible to tell day from night; everyone manned their stations at all hours, constantly bailing out the rising ocean and scraping off the tiles of ice that had hardened the sails.

In the perpetual storm that raged under the world, April went by unnoticed—Hallett, Hayward, and Heywood's hair had grown into thick locks encrusted by ice; the ropes of scabbing on Quintal's back somehow seemed a lesser punishment than the lashing of the gales that had cracked ribs and shattered teeth. The weather continued to worsen, and with half the crew ill—and the other half hastily ridding the ship's bowels of rising seawater—the *Bounty* had no more fight left in her.

"Turn the helm aweather and bear away for the Cape of Good Hope," Bligh finally surrendered, pointing his half-ruined vessel east toward the southern tip of Africa. And although his men heartily cheered, Bligh was very much aware that the necessary course change would add over ten thousand miles to their journey. The winds would finally be in their favor, but there were many more worlds—and a new set of impossible obstacles—that awaited the commander and his crew before they'd reach Tahiti.

———————

DEATH HID IN the unkempt corners of a ship when it sailed across the Roaring Forties, the endless blue banner that wrapped around the planet between the fortieth and fiftieth parallels. In the far south, the continents feared nature's cruelty—they crawled their way up to the equator, leaving only a few straggling islets to break up the large swath of waves that grew more foreboding in their search for a place to crash down. With strong eastbound winds to blow a ship along, it was possible to travel almost twice the average nautical speed, but the distances were far, far greater. And that's where the specter of mortality loomed; a dirty pocket would seduce a curious rat, who brought the threat of disease, and a fully manned ship could be quickly whittled down to a skeleton crew, or—just as bad—a crew of skeletons. For months there would be no port where a ship could call for fresh supplies, leaving dwindling rations of bouillon soup, salted meat, and biscuits tinged with the crunch of half-eaten insects to sustain a waning sailor. Bligh was well aware of what lay ahead.

He had followed the same route on Captain Cook's third voyage around the world. A period of austerity loomed, as did the gradual thinning of one's faculties.

It had taken another month for the *Bounty* to sail between the two capes, floating into the Dutch-held Simon's Bay in late May as little more than a leaky mess of sails and timbers. On July 1, after thirty-eight days of extensive repairs under the shelter of the Cape of Good Hope, the little ship was finally ready for—by Bligh's estimation—four full months of loneliness, with only one planned stop to break up the journey.

A strict schedule was Bligh's strategy to defend the mind and body against the madness of monotony born on landless seas—some of his more unpredictable seamen had already started to rattle their cages. A cycle of unending chores would be the only way to safeguard against more unmanageable behavior; a clean ship begot clean thoughts. Byrne played the fiddle every day before sunset and the crew was expected to dance—their daily exercise; kicks were better than punches, after all. Christian continued to dine with Bligh every third evening, and Heywood would often tag along. It was a happy arrangement, where the captain would get updates on crew morale to supplement his open-door eavesdropping and teach his protégé everything he knew about navigation, from scanning old nautical charts and following star patterns to taking longitudinal readings using the ship's new top-of-the-line Larcum Kendall chronometer.

At the end of August, the *Bounty* sailed into the aptly named Adventure Bay, which scalloped the edges of a massive world hidden under the heavy breath of wet fog. Hardly anything was known about the area besides its name: Van Diemen's Land (Tasmania), coined by the Dutch explorer Abel Tasman, who had plotted it on a map around a century earlier. Bligh took his eager minions Hallett and Hayward to shore and wandered through a misty graveyard of waist-high tree stumps, like the toppled pillars of a ruined kingdom. Bligh wormed his fingernail through the little crevices carved into several of the half-trunks: a "WB" and the other initials of Cook's shore party from over a decade ago, kept perfectly intact since the last time he was there. Minutes felt like hours aboard the *Bounty*, on its interminable journey around the far side the planet, but time, it seemed, moved even slower here.

Bligh put Christian in charge of the efforts to restock the ship, but he still wasn't allowed to touch the *vinho da roda*, even when making room in the hold for the refilled kegs of fresh water. Christian couldn't handle the captain's library of maps either, for fear that his sweaty palms would ruin the inking. Bligh was the master of little jibes like these. Usually, they floated so lightly on the breeze that they were almost unnoticeable. But halfway through the Roaring Forties, the teeth of the wind had a bigger bite, and storms of words started to gust forth. Bligh was unhappy with the goods hauled back to the ship; the water was brackish and the logs mealy and splintered. But Christian had done the best he could between the constant spittle of hovering clouds and the damp gloss of daylong dew that helped clothe the shivering trees in mossy fleeces.

"Why do I offer you the lead when I always do a superior job?" Rhetorical questions were another of Bligh's slighting specialties.

"The quality timbers have already been chopped here—to cull wood from another forest was a task too cumbersome for the other men," Christian reasoned, knowing Bligh wasn't receptive to excuses, even when they were sound. What angered Bligh more than the measly gathering of supplies, unfit for another two months of journeying, was the abject laziness that had befallen his crew. Not even Christian—a far more likable character—could inspire his peers with a song or some humor.

"And what in God's name are these?" Bligh wiggled his fingers through a pile of beaks and feathers, pulling out a long, gangly bird by the neck. "I'd say this one resembles you, Christian—look at its big nose and bowlegs!" Bligh's overwhelming tiredness had worn away the fakery of his refinement. Christian, on the other hand, stifled his retort, heeding his brother Charles's advice to filter his words. He had used his musket to supplement their rationing with some fresh meat, but even the fowl in this realm were disappointingly lean.

On the crew's last day collecting wood and water, several silhouettes emerged from the perpetual drizzle, wrapped in the furry pelts of unknown animals. The sputter of hunting gunfire must have lured them toward the *Bounty*'s landing site. They hid behind taller trees and watched the sailors make their final preparations to depart.

"Why, they seem like the most miserable creatures on the face of the Earth," Heywood whispered, slightly frightened by the timid onlookers.

"Perhaps they think the same of us." Christian had seen his scraggly reflection in a pond when he combed the local forests for fresh supplies, the scent of pine a wonderful distraction from the stench of unbathed men now permanently baked into the ship's walls. And although he and his fellow crewmen were still able to carry out their duties, he knew that a strange anguish lurked deep within their depleting bodies. Surely the two more months of isolation that awaited would fell even the stockiest of trunks.

There was little to excite the desperate mind in September besides the discovery of some rocky outcrops—shorn of any grass or trees by the elements—which Bligh named in honor of his vessel. In mid-October, Thomas Ledward, the assistant surgeon, lightly tapped the doorframe of Bligh's cabin as the commander scrawled notes in his log about another pod of whales that had followed his ship northward through the final puffs of the southeasterly trade winds. "It's Valentine . . ."

"Yes, what about Valentine?" Bligh wondered, quill still in hand. He stopped when there was no response, just a look in Ledward's eyes of great concern.

Bligh followed Ledward across the ship to Doc Huggan's cabin, where he found Valentine—eyes closed—languishing on the surgical table, writhing his body into slow, impossible angles as though he were suffering a horrible nightmare from which he couldn't wake. Huggan was similarly unconscious, slung back in his chair with the neck of a small wine bottle teetering between two fingers.

"Why didn't anyone tell me earlier?" Bligh was furious.

Huggan sprung up. "He 'ad fever and fatigue. Gave 'im a bloodletting, but it di'n't take." He slurred his consonants, then made a vowel over the mouth of his bottle and nipped another swig.

"You drunken sot," Bligh cursed the doctor, who had been so preoccupied with self-medicating that he had let his surgical knives rust in the salty air. Huggan had poisoned the seaman with the tainted blades, and there was nothing more that could be done halfway between two continents. Valentine was going to die.

But what really sent Bligh into a boiling rage was the obvious misdiagnosis. "IT'S SCURVY, YOU INCOMPETENT MONGREL!" he yelled. "Three tablespoons of malt and wort and he would have been fine!" Bligh had avoided saying the word aloud for a couple of weeks. The disease, in his esteem, was another symptom of an unkempt crew and thus a poor reflection of his captaining—much worse than flogging. But a wave of lethargy had crashed over the *Bounty* during their final push toward Tahiti. Captain Cook had never lost a man to scurvy, and Bligh was determined not to either. He had hoped it was just low morale after such an extended amount of time without seeing land, but the violent gales of diarrhea that splashed against the sides of the ship were an undeniable indicator of its onset.

Even as a corpse, Valentine was more handsome than some of the seamen that still haunted the *Bounty*'s decks. Bligh put his young midshipmen—Heywood, Hallett, and Hayward—in charge of the body; he thought it the perfect task to harden them into future sea captains. He sent Quintal and McCoy down below to ransack Huggan's cabin of every last bottle of alcohol the doctor had been smuggling. The ship's sailmaker sewed Valentine into his hammock, placing two cannonballs at his feet and cocooning the fabric all the way up to Valentine's face, where he pushed the sewing needle through the rubbery cartilage at the tip of the dead sailor's nose—a final check to make sure he was definitely dead before his body would be committed to the sea.

"The death of Able Seaman James Valentine comes as a surprise and shock to me. This poor man was one of the most robust people on board," Bligh spoke to the entirety of the *Bounty*'s crew, who had gathered around Valentine's shrouded body on the upper deck. He then thumbed through his Bible to an earmarked page he had hoped never to use:

We therefore commit his Body to the Deep, to be turned into
    Corruption,
looking for the resurrection of the Body—when the Sea shall
    give up her dead,
and the life of the world to come, through our Lord Jesus Christ;
who at his coming shall change our vile Body,
that it may be like his glorious Body, according to the mighty
    working,
whereby he is able to subdue all things to himself.

Bligh clapped the Bible shut with both hands. The funeral was over—a gathering much shorter, and with far fewer formalities, than Quintal's lashing several months earlier. Thompson and Churchill hoisted the sewn-up hammock—now uncomfortably heavy with the added weight of the stitched-in cannonballs—and dropped the body over the railing. It plummeted down into the trenches of unknown depths.

That was the risk of the *vinho da roda*, and why a bottle was far too dear for any commoner's enjoyment: you were likely to lose a cask along the way due to the inevitable perils of long-haul ocean travel. And sometimes, under the most extreme circumstances, an entire reserve could end up at the bottom of the sea if, say, a ship foundered, sliced through by the pernicious hands of waving coral that gripped an unseen barrier reef.

Bligh had successfully navigated many more worlds than the half-score he had bargained for, and was furious he'd have to register such an unnecessary blemish—a foolish oversight by his incompetent doctor—on an otherwise pristine record. They were so close to Tahiti too; the dog and goats had started chuffing in their cages again at the smell of land.

A few days later, the *Bounty* steered around Mehetia, a perfect, pyramidal volcano clad in luscious greenery; Tahiti was less than seventy miles away. In the early evening, after sailing over twenty-eight thousand miles, the crew spotted the spiking crags and cliffs of their long-awaited destination, backlit by the setting sun. But it was late October now—ten months had passed since they'd left England—and storms were soon heading for Tahiti as well, the beginning of its season of rains. Bligh knew before they landed that he'd have to protract their breadfruit mission by several months—far more time than the handful of weeks other explorers had spent on the blue continent since its discovery—in order to avoid a situation similar to the insurmountable squalls that almost sent the entire *Bounty* crew to a watery grave at Cape Horn.

But what happens to casks of Madeira wine after they've rested under the perpetual warmth of the Tahitian sun, shaded only by palms and never by the veil of winter? Bligh wondered. It would be the longest amount of time any batch sat stagnant in the tropics before resuming its long swim back across the latitudes, swishing in the *Bounty*'s basement once more on the journey home. Would it be ruined? Its delicate color would inevitably darken and varnish—tan like the sun-kissed skins of the men and women who would greet them in one day's time. Would the wine become too unrefined to return to England?

CHAPTER 6

THE THREE LEGS OF MAN
OCTOBER 1788–APRIL 1789

There were no clearly defined trails beyond the fringes of the gushing brook. In fact, there were few places where nature yielded to the intentions of man—every step crinkled leaves or cracked twigs underfoot as two men crept through the patchwork shade under pandan pines and wind-tussled casuarinas.

"Careful or she'll hear you!" John Millward waved wide strokes, clearing cobwebs and thistles as if he were swimming through the overgrowth. With strong muscles and a hulking torso, he was one of the more brutish piratical archetypes among the *Bounty*'s able seamen. Thomas Burkitt, two tentative steps back, embodied a more ghoulish version—a memory of smallpox had scarred patches of reptilian scales across his grimaced face. They had exorcised the specter of scurvy only a few days prior, after their arrival on Tahiti; colorful fruits grew abundantly and indiscriminately here without tending or care. The men were eager to shed their starched cotton tunics too—fabric woven for British temperatures—but at Bligh's insistence they were to dress themselves in heavy layering despite the tropical humidity. Millward and Burkitt had unbuttoned their shirts as a compromise, and the blaring sun stained their pale chests cherry red.

The stream they followed carved a corridor all the way up to the top of Mount Orohena, where its cleft peak tore through the only tuft of weather that loomed. Millward paused, forgetting for a moment his purpose, and admired the view in both directions. Dramatic scenery had lain hidden behind thick clouds throughout the entirety of the *Bounty*'s ten-month journey to Tahiti, but now the island laid everything bare for its new visitors to see—including its women.

"There—there she is!" Millward blurted to Burkitt with the hoarseness of a half-spoken whisper. He darted behind the thick trunk of a tree and peered excitedly just beyond its perimeter.

"Ah, she's as pretty as you promised!" Burkitt pressed himself against a neighboring palm and watched in silence, mouth agape, as a young woman emerged from the river as if she were born of its froth and foam. She reached for a pleated bolt of swan-white cloth and slowly dabbed her face, as her bare body, now supine, dried in the warm glow of the rising sun.

Burkitt's heart clanged against the bars of his ribcage as his imagination laid himself on top of the nubile bather. He let his hand graze the fabric of his tightening pants—back and forth—then glanced at Millward, who had already unbuttoned his trousers to fully give himself over to his fantasy of the girl. Burkitt clacked his tongue against his lips and followed suit.

"What in the Lord's name is going on here?" A roar from the darkness of the glade startled the two men. Burkitt fumbled with his fastener, trying to tuck himself back into his uniform. It was Young, in full midshipman garb, sent by Bligh to wrangle the sailors who were already shirking their duties.

"Fuck off Young!" Millward swore with unrelenting disdain.

"Stop, you vile animals!" Young's chiding yells caught the ear of their prey, who quickly swaddled her tapa cloth around her hips and squinted her saucer eyes to sharpen her gaze. Millward shivered, lurched forward, then started a new streamlet through the grass.

"I . . . I'm so sorry for this . . . for their behavior," Young stammered as he nervously tiptoed toward the woman—a teenager, definitely too young to remember the last time British sailors had left their mark on her island home. He angled backward, noticing that Millward and Burkitt had run away, then continued his rambling apology before cutting himself off when he realized neither one knew the other's language.

"I'm Edward Young," he spoke deliberately now, as though she'd understand him if he parsed out each syllable. "Neddy." He tapped his navy jacket and flashed a toothless grin. "You can call me Neddy."

"Ne-ti," she repeated, smiling.

Young flung his arms around with exaggerated motions, trying to act out his shipmates' indiscretions so she'd absolve them of their wrongdoing. "They were touching themselves while watching you bathe!" She giggled at his awkward pantomime, then grabbed his hands to spare him from more embarrassing gesticulations. Perhaps she knew the men were there, coveting her body from behind the trees all along.

Young was dressed far more formally than his comrades, with a large felt hat, which she carefully removed to pet the texture of the unusual fabric. She then drew her attention to the gilded clasps that studded the center of Young's shirt from his waist up to his gusseted cravat, and she fussed with each button until they separated from the seam. She ran her fingers along his taut chest and stomach as though it were another swatch of unusual material. To their mutual delight, the tanned tones of his mixed heritage seemed strangely similar to the caramel color of her skin.

She grabbed Young's hands and placed them on her bare breasts. He flinched, swelling with shame—consumed by the same lustful thoughts as Millward and Burkitt—then launched into another bumbling monologue: "Like Aphrodite herself down from Olympus!" But as she pulled at his trousers, Young realized that he was in fact the object of her desire as well.

Sex had always seemed a fraught pursuit for men, Young thought. The women who had let him up their dresses back home only begrudged him a few pokes. But now, lying on his back in the grass with the young bather on top, he was beginning to appreciate the vast, unspoken differences between England and Tahiti. She held his hands against her gyrating hips; her knowledge of the carnal arts rivaled Young's mastery of biblical and classical studies.

"Jesus. Fuck!" It was regrettably quick. Young's arms fell from her waist, flopping backward into the grass. He never took the Lord's name in vain, nor did he ever swear, but the sheen of politeness was easily worn away by such visceral pleasures, especially after a year among crude company aboard the *Bounty*. The young woman grabbed his hand once more, and used his fingers to amplify her enjoyment.

Afterward, as Young carefully rearranged the various trappings of his uniform, the teenage girl returned to the river for another bathing session. Young watched, breaking the extended silence with a smile: "Susannah." He hadn't been able to decipher her name, but he wanted to call her Susannah—the Bible's beautiful maiden from the book of Daniel, preyed upon by two lustful voyeurs who sought to tarnish her virtue.

"Tu-ta-na," she echoed, the tip of the tongue tapping three times on the teeth. The Tahitian language only had a few consonants in common with English, but one day soon, they would understand each other. He vowed to find her the next day, and the day after that. He wanted to know her beyond their strangely similar skin.

HUNDREDS OF OUTRIGGERS had met the *Bounty* when it crossed the threshold of deeper water into the clear lagoon at Matavai Bay. Up from the Tahitians' *vaa* canoes—some as long as the weary ship itself—came gifts of neon fruits, feathers, and elaborate wreaths that crowned the heads of the British sailors, roused after months of quiet deprivation by the hearty anthems of welcome.

Bligh wasted no time setting up an encampment on shore, a nursery for the seedlings and tents for the handful of men selected to tend to them. He chose the exact location where Captain Cook had landed to perform his mission's astronomical measurements: Point

Venus, named for the transiting planet, though Young and the other sailors were quick to appreciate the moniker's double meaning.

Within a few days, the ship's gardener was already counting a collection of potted cuttings. "Sixty, sixty-one, sixty-two . . ." William Brown's gentle demeanor made him somewhat of an outcast on board, furthered by his botanical zeal. A childhood scar ran down his face from the corner of his eye across his cheek, accentuating an earnest smile that calmed concerned Tahitians when they came snooping.

A fib had been concocted to shroud the true purpose of the *Bounty*'s endeavor when inquisitive islanders asked why a vessel would sail squarely around the world in pursuit of a plant: it would be a gift for their king back home, George III, who so loved the breadfruit's taste that he wanted to grow an orchard of his own. There was a second secret to keep as well, one so important that those with loose lips would pay with all the flesh on their backs, so warned Bligh: no one could know that Captain Cook was dead. The Tahitians had come to revere Cook and his sorcery; an arsenal of cannons and guns that evoked wonderment and fear. The goodwill toward the British sailors largely hinged on leveraging the influence of "Tu-te," as they called him. Bligh was to be seen as Cook's envoy, an untruth that served his own delusions rather nicely.

"Sixty-three, sixty-four, sixty-five," Brown continued as Bligh barged into the encampment. The commander's mood had returned to a more convivial version of arrogance now that they had safely arrived on Tahiti. He had just completed his first act of official business: negotiating the continued cutting of breadfruit saplings with a six-year-old chieftain who cared far more about the magic of Bligh's pistol than about the felling of a few wildly growing trees—it was a resounding success.

Unlike the monarchies of Europe, Tahiti and its neighboring islands were divided into small clans, each led by a different—but often related—chief from the ruling *arii* class. To Bligh's surprise, the desire for absolute power had never been considered among the complex ecosystem of regional rulers, who were revered as demigods, so sacred that their attendants were forced to bury their plucked hair and clipped nails—even their feces—lest mortals use them to cast spells upon their families. All that the feet of a chieftain touched instantly became his possession, so servants were also expected to carry around their chosen *arii* until the day he produced a suitable heir to pass along his divinity.

"Sixty-six, sixty-seven, sixty-eight . . ." Brown had resumed his counting when another seaman swished through the tent flaps. "Even the mouths of these women are not exempt from gratifying beastly inclinations!" Alexander Smith's cheeks were flushed, rosy florets accentuating the nicks and cuts notched from bar fights, clumsy attempts at shaving, and a mild case of smallpox. A faithful customer of London's whores, Smith had indulged in the women of Tahiti with the same alacrity that Doc Huggan had for the bottle.

"Bugger you, Smith!" Brown lost count. The other men in the tent laughed and made lurid motions with their fists. Heywood, however, didn't quite understand the reference.

"Follow me," Christian instructed. The two men left the enclosure of their camp and walked toward a circle of seated women enjoying the shade of a nearby tree. Christian reached into his pocket and produced a long copper nail, handing it to Heywood. "Here."

Heywood examined the rivet; it had grayed in the salty air. "What's this?"

"A key."

"To what?"

"To anything your heart desires." Christian pulled out two more nails and offered them to two of the Tahitian teenagers, helping them up off the ground. A third girl stood up and approached Heywood, taking the nail from his pale palm.

"Beware these Circean blandishments!" came a voice from behind. It was Bligh, warning Heywood that Christian had a history of being easily beguiled by women.

Christian disappeared into the jungle with his two girls, and Heywood boarded the *Bounty*, climbing down into the darkness of the lower deck, the young Tahitian following closely behind. As he made his way to his berth, he passed the shadows of Churchill and Thompson, panting and grunting like the ship's goats against the recipients of other copper nails.

When Heywood reached his hammock, the young woman touched his flinching shoulder. It tickled; he was nervous. She knelt on the floor in front of him and unbuttoned his trousers, showing Heywood the meaning of Smith's excited exclamation.

Back in the breadfruit tent, Brown had finally completed his preliminary tally of the new seedlings and surmised that he'd need to extend his harvest to nearby territories in order to garner enough samples.

The next day, a visit to the neighboring clan ruled by a man named Teina was arranged, and this time Bligh took Christian along, plus thuggish Churchill and Thompson to provide some intimidation. Bligh had remembered Teina from his visit with Captain Cook. The chief was exceptionally large, a full ten inches taller than Bligh and well over three hundred pounds.

While the breadfruit grew wild without tending or care, Tahiti's human population was cultivated with careful precision. The perpetuation of the ruling *arii* class was a closely guarded affair ensuring two key traits: tall height and pale skin. Newborn children were smothered without remorse if they seemed unfit to preserve the physical qualities that distinguished the island's holy leaders from its commoners, and pregnancies were terminated if there were any indiscretions between strata.

After the *arii* were the *raatira*—an intermediate caste of landowners, artisans, and minor nobles who bore similar features to their chiefs. The *manahune*—laborers, farmers, and servants—made up the majority of Tahiti's population. They were of a noticeably stockier stature with darker pigmentation after generations of forbidden intermarriage.

The strict unspoken codes of behavior governing the relationships between societal tiers also dictated how Tahitians could interact with their visitors. The men of the *Bounty* were quick to appreciate the sexuality of the island's women—a pastime or hospitable offering more than a consecrating act—but they hadn't grasped that a rigid code of conduct had made grades of their own ranks too. The *manahune* could engage with the able seamen and similarly stationed crew, the *raatira* associated with the officers like the midshipmen and lieutenants, and the chief's wife was specially reserved for Bligh.

"Is it true? Could Mr. Bligh be more enchanted by a tree's fruit than of my own sweetness?" Teina's wife, Itia, sarcastically traced the curvatures of her face and body with exaggerated gestures, then repeated herself in Tahitian for the benefit of her laughing entourage. "Perhaps he needs to be examined. He may not have the proper hoe and plow!" Itia bested her husband in height and girth, and she relished being the center of attention as Teina reclined under his thatched pavilion, quietly considering Bligh's request for breadfruit cuttings.

All subjects who appeared before the noble couple—or any *arii* chieftain—were expected to bare themselves completely from the waist up as a sign of respect. Bligh remained buttoned to the chin—tipping his hat as a compromise—but Christian, Churchill, and Thompson eagerly obliged, if at the very least to unglue themselves from their tunics, which had been stuck to their sweaty chests since landing at Matavai Bay. Itia and the others marveled at the undressed men: below sunburned faces hid skin the color of the ivory seashells that washed up on the island's beaches. The sailors stared back with similar wonderment: almost all of the Tahitians in Teina's retinue had elaborate decorations adorning their bodies. With fine instruments of tooth and bone, they had tapped the ash of an oily nut through the flesh. Animal and plant motifs coiled around their arms and legs as though they wore their skin like clothing.

The brandishing of a pistol did not charm Teina as it had the six-year-old chieftain who governed the land around Matavai Bay. And Bligh's lack of wit and dressed-down deference made Christian the more amiable liaison of the group, who quickly instructed Churchill and Thompson to start passing out gifts—mirrors and glass beads, examined by Itia and the others as though they were the most delicate of artifacts. Christian spoke of how, in only a week's time, Tahiti had already begun to feel like home.

A deal to harvest Teina's breadfruit was easily struck. "Titreano," the chieftain called Christian, "I know already that we'll be lifelong friends."

———

IT RAINED THE day Doc Huggan died, a slow patter plunking the fronds like piano keys. Ledward, the assistant surgeon, found his lifeless body and alerted Bligh, who remained wholly unfazed at what had seemed an inevitability since the outset of their mission. The doctor had drunk himself to death.

Bligh sought to arrange a funeral as perfunctory as Valentine's burial at sea, but to his surprise, hundreds of Tahitians showed up to pay their respects to a man most had never known. They sobbed and wailed over his shallow grave, tears watering the garlands they laid over the upturned earth. Uninhibited in their pursuit of pleasure, the Tahitians—it seemed—knew not how to swallow their sorrow either. The scene unnerved the British men, who were more disturbed by these hysterics than by the loss of their comrade. One mourner caught Christian's attention—she was tall, like the mainmast of a ship, and had a white gardenia balancing on her ear, her smile an indelible memory from his recent visit to Teina's court, though now she wept openly with a chorus of other grieving teenagers. Christian envied her release of raw emotions. He tamped them down the way a boy of a certain stature should, hoarding every misfortune—every gibe, even—like the *Bounty* amassing its seedlings one by one. A single breadfruit was practically weightless, but a thousand would drop the ship dangerously close to the ocean's surface, or maybe below.

The rain didn't stop; bad weather had found the *Bounty* once more. Its anchorage at Matavai Bay now proved untenable under the afternoon downpours of December. At Teina's insistence, Bligh packed up his encampment and its 774 potted breadfruit samples and moved his ship around the coast to Pare, which fell under Teina's domain. To honor his strengthening ties with the British, the chieftain sought to organize a *heiva*, a grand ceremonial gathering. The timing was convenient; Christmas had arrived once more, and Bligh hoped the fanfare would distract his men from his half-hearted promises to have the *Bounty* back in familiar waters by the end of the year.

Four blasts from the *Bounty*'s cannons kicked off the festivities as the citizens of Pare mingled with the British sailors on the beach. Byrne squeaked carols on his fiddle, "Joy to the World" and "Hark! How All the Welkin Rings." Melodies that once echoed through the transepts of stone cathedrals now sounded peculiar with the percussion of crashing waves, particularly "Coventry Carol," a favorite of Henry VIII, the father of the Royal Navy, whose legacy of wifely beheadings proved too grisly a tale when recounted to the gathered Tahitians.

Only one woman seemed unbothered by how far the Tudor king had gone—starting a new religion separate from the Catholic Church—to bed another woman. She was captivated by the story's backdrop instead: the towers of brick rising like Mount Orohena above cobbled streets. A local man named Mai had once sailed all the way to England aboard a ship similar to the *Bounty*, returning years later with stories of banquets and balls hosted by Joseph Banks at the Royal Society. Perhaps one day she would visit as well. Smith introduced her to the other sailors as Jenny.

"My name is Teehuteatuaonoa." Her English was competent after two months of practice.

"See that's why I call her Jenny!" Smith snorted, showing off the "A.S."—his initials—tattooed on her shoulder.

Young had brought Susannah. Her real name was Mataohu, meaning "rounded face," describing looks that transcended both the Tahitian and British paradigms of beauty, but she had started to take a liking to her English nickname. Susannah's friends had become regular fixtures around the breadfruit camp as well, and tonight she added another member to her clique: the tall woman from Teina's court who had caught Christian's attention at Huggan's funeral. Her name was Mauatua—Teina's niece.

The next evening at sunset, Teina invited everyone to gather at his family's *marae*—a ceremonial platform of sacred stones, the portal between mortal and celestial realms littered with the skulls and femurs of human sacrifice. Everyone ringed around a blazing pyre as a band of men and women—all swaddled in bleach-white cloth and covered in tribalistic tattoos—emerged from the jungle, singing and gyrating as they crept through the crowd. They were the cult of the *arioi*—disciples of Oro, the god of rain and war—an esteemed and mysterious sect exempt from the stringent castes of Tahitian society. They were the bards of Polynesia, called upon during special *heiva* to rivet audiences with their provocative performances. To the pounding of sharkskin drums, they began to chant while unraveling their clothing. A few of the naked performers galloped over to Bligh, winding their gossamers around his uniform; the others danced themselves into a writhing mass of twisting limbs that culminated in a feigned orgy. Heeding the call of the instruments, Churchill and Thompson jumped to their feet and tore off their tunics as well. Millward and Burkitt quickly joined them around the hearth—Smith, too—and with arms waving wildly above their heads the men showed off the new tattoos that hid beneath their uniforms: stars, fish motifs, and battling spears. Long sheets of rain suddenly began to pour down on the naked men as though their trance-like heaving had awoken mighty Oro and opened the heavens. Christian kissed Mauatua on the cheek and sprang up as well. To the Tahitians' delight—and Bligh's horror—he showed off the most elaborate of adornments: his entire buttocks had been inked black. Then Heywood stood and stripped, revealing a large triskelion emblem on his thigh, a pinwheel of kicking feet that dazzled the onlookers with its intricate design. It was the symbol of his homeland—the Three Legs of Man.

As the torrents of water showered down, the men carried on; their grinding and spinning as crazed and debauched as the acrobatics of the *arioi*. Bligh, however, was suffocating under the ceremonial bark cloth that cinched his woolen jacket tight. He stood up, shooing away the attending Tahitians, and—as he tried to move back from the hot breath of the bonfire—collapsed onto the muddy earth, smudging his face on extinguished embers.

THE SAILORS WOULD not put their shirts back on, sporting only their navy-issued trousers as they traipsed barefoot through the swampy heat to chop down different breadfruit trees. The rainfall continued unabated, shrouding Mount Orohena behind storm clouds. Bligh hid himself aboard the *Bounty*. Christian was now the de facto leader of the landing party, decamping to Teina's village to be with Mauatua when he wasn't surveying Brown's growing nursery. In fact, hardly any of the crewmen spent the night in their hammocks, having forged their own bonds with various *taio*—blood-brother-like friends—all along the coast from Pare back down to Matavai Bay. They were now fully indoctrinated in the Tahitian way of life, and some crewmen never wanted to leave.

In early January, as Hallett struggled to stay awake during his 4 a.m. watch, Churchill and Millward slyly lowered one of the *Bounty*'s tenders into the water and slid away. On the advice of their many *taio*, they sailed to a confusing maze of nearby atolls known as Tetiaroa, hoping Bligh wouldn't have the chance to find them before the last parcels of breadfruit were transplanted onto the ship. During times of war, abandonment was an offense punishable by death, but with the ship's departure imminent, the men chanced their escape.

Churchill and Millward's disappearance was an affront to Bligh's ambition and stoked the flames of his temper, unseen since the harrowing four-month slog across the Roaring Forties. He would stay in Tahiti a hundred years if it meant ensuring his return to England with his full crew. Whippings and scurvy were slights to his captaining that he could bear; losing men outright was an insurmountable embarrassment, he thought.

With the help of Teina's men, it took a full two weeks for Bligh to track Churchill and Millward down; torrential flooding had smoked them out of their hiding place on Tetiaroa. A crowd of

Tahitians gathered—similar in size to Huggan's funeral—with the *Bounty*'s crew to watch the runaways get tied up spread-eagle for their crime. The onlookers wailed with cries of sympathetic pain each time the whip clacked against the seamen's backs—first Millward, then Churchill, who joined the choir of howling voices as his flesh peeled away in ribbons. His nightly shrieking thereafter—the muggy heat chewing at his scabbing—was a poignant reminder that naval law remained in full effect despite their distance from England, but it wasn't enough to deter the other sailors from further insubordination. Bligh had lost control of his men.

Alone in his cabin, Bligh furiously logged a litany of other transgressions committed: a dozen lashes for Thompson's disobedience, another dozen for Smith's indolence, nineteen lashes to Isaac Martin for striking a native, and a flogging for John Mills. Hallett would spend eleven weeks locked in chains for allowing Churchill and Millward to disappear on his watch.

Bligh dropped his quill, distracted by the desperate cries of pain coming from down the hall. Even those who were spared the lash had found suffering.

"WHAT IN FRESH HELL IS GOING ON?" Bligh emerged from his room to find a handful of sailors impatiently waiting their turn in front of the surgeon's quarters. He pushed past the gathering crowd and swung open the door to find Heywood sitting on the medic's table, howling as Ledward burned off his venereal sores.

"It's Doc Huggan's final revenge!" Ledward turned to Bligh. "He may be in the ground, but I am the one in hell—my face buried in the crotch pox that have plagued our men." Bligh was quick to remind Heywood that he had warned him of the perils of promiscuity, but it was in fact the Europeans who had first spread syphilis and gonorrhea among the pristine islanders many years prior. To infect the *Bounty*'s sailors was an act of carnal retribution.

Susannah had caught something too; she could sense it. She searched for her maid, Tevarua, but couldn't find her—perhaps she had spent the evening with one of the *Bounty*'s sailors—and told Obuarei, another of her family's servants, that she was off to Mauatua's hut.

"When was the last time you bled?" Faahotu, Mauatua's trusted attendant, was a *taata* healer who knew all of nature's secrets—the right plants to boil for medicinal teas and how to rid the body of an unwanted visitor.

"Three months, I think," Susannah replied without much concern.

"It's too late for the herbs then." Faahotu instructed Susannah to lie on her back, then slowly dug the heel of her palm into her abdomen. Her massaging motions were gentle at first, but they soon dipped deeper as she pummeled Susannah's stomach. Mauatua knelt beside them and anxiously watched; a mixed-race child could topple the delicate balance among the castes. But other changes had already started to ripple through the strata of society like stones dropped in the lagoon, blurring the water's clarity. Jenny, a *manahune* serf, had long admired Susannah and Mauatua, both daughters of the aristocracy; she now sat beside them as a friend and confidant, part of a new circle of women—the consorts of the British sailors. Even shy Tevarua, Susannah's maid, had caught Quintal's eye.

Within a few minutes Faahotu was done, just as Tevarua walked in. "Obuarei told me you were here. Is everything alright?"

"What happened?" Mauatua immediately shifted the conversation, noticing a red mark across Tevarua's face. Her cheekbone was swollen.

Tevarua hadn't seen her reflection, but she felt the throbbing pain. "It's nothing," she brushed it off. "An accident," a fit of Quintal's excitation during an evening of drunken revelry the night before. Mauatua had witnessed the irony with which the British used bodily injury to punish instances of physical harm. She wanted to tell Bligh and hold Quintal accountable, but Tevarua was desperate to find a topic of conversation that did not pertain to the follies of excess.

Bligh also sought retribution for the injustices he suffered; a crime worse than Churchill and Millward's abandonment had occurred on Hayward's watch—the *Bounty*'s azimuth compass was gone, and without this most necessary of navigational tools he would never find his way back to England. Bligh chained Hayward next to his pal Hallett, then marched toward Teina's pavilion, each step more fervid as he seethed at the shortcomings of Christian's unchecked leadership. There were twinges of jealousy too. Bligh would never allow himself to acknowledge it, but it irked him how Christian had been so wholeheartedly welcomed as kin.

"You've lavished my men with the finest fruits and meats but THEY ARE ALL SCOUNDRELS!" Bligh began to unravel. Teina and Itia were rapt by the most flagrant display of emotion they had seen from any of the British men. "Even my midshipmen shirk the easiest of duties! Heywood, Hallett, and Hayward are NOTHING BUT DISOBEDIENT DOGS, Young is a useless WRETCH, and Christian—your dear 'Titreano'—a WIMPISH BIRD!"

Teina's guards and attendants gathered at the sound of the yelling, including Christian, who had been idling with friends nearby. To Bligh, Teina's consummate hospitality had become a slight against the special reverence he believed he was owed, and he could think of only one way to reaffirm the deference he desired: telling the Tahitians that he was the son of Captain Cook.

The words felt like hot daggers to Christian, who winced at the abject lie. But he had no recourse. Hamstrung by the promise to perpetuate Cook's legacy, he desperately wanted to silence the gasps of wonderment that were spreading among the gathering crowd. Bligh promised death to the thief of the instrument should Teina find him; to defy the *Bounty*'s cardinal rule and expose his commanding officer as a liar could mean a similar fate.

"KILL HIM." TEINA boarded the *Bounty* with the missing azimuth compass and a young Tahitian man, the culprit, bound in chains. It had taken almost a month, but the chief kept his word. Thievery was a foreign concept on an island with a more fluid notion of property ownership—dozens of items had been innocently pilfered from the *Bounty* already—but the taking of the gilded timepiece seemed like a purposeful act of sabotage. Perhaps a *taio* had been tasked by his British blood brother to further delay the ship's departure. Teina had watched how Bligh curbed insolence with searing slices of the whip and knew an instigator of the worst of crimes would pay for the wrongdoing with his life. But Bligh's temper had cooled as the crushing humidity softened into milder gray days. A hundred lashings were ordered instead of execution—a final warning to both his men and the Tahitians that nothing would stand between him and Jamaica's plantations.

The storm clouds finally lifted off the top of Mount Orohena—laying Tahiti's splendor bare for its visitors' enjoyment once more—and on the first of April, with a final count of 1,015 breadfruit samples on board, the *Bounty* was ready to depart. But before the ship could leave, Bligh ordered everyone onto shore so a clowder of hungry cats could rid the decks of rats, roaches, and other vermin in anticipation of the many-month journey ahead. It was also an act of unusual, unclenched benevolence on Bligh's behalf to allow his men to enjoy a final few evenings with their favorite Tahitians before dark and treacherous oceans would separate them forever.

The sailors dispersed throughout the island, spending their last days at the homes of their *taio* and all promising to return to the ship lest they face punishment worse than the lashings given to the robber of the azimuth compass. One large group gathered around a bonfire on the soft sands of Matavai Bay near the exact spot where they had excitedly made landfall almost six months earlier—a final sunset with their Tahitian friends and lovers, wrestling, dancing, and marveling at how fast the time had gone. The mood was light despite their impending departure; thoughts of England were still too distant, as the *Bounty* had to bring the precious breadfruit to the Caribbean before they could properly make their way home. The route advised by the Crown was a long, tiresome path around the wrong side of the globe, similar to their extended transit en route to Tahiti after being unable to break through the wind and ice around Cape Horn.

"Do you think Captain Bligh and Queen Itia ever . . . ?" Heywood sheepishly wondered with a smirk.

"Wha? Tickled the gizzard? Definitely." McCoy finished the thought between guzzles of rum.

"Never! Bligh wouldn't even take his hat off in front of her," Mauatua added, annoyed that the *Bounty*'s leader had little regard for her customs.

"No, they definitely did! And could you imagine? She's almost twice his size. She probably flattened his little pinky prick." Smith wasn't one to shroud his crassness with metaphor.

"*Mamoo*—shut up!" everyone jeered in their newfound patois of Tahitian and British words, which, after a half year, allowed for easy banter. "*Ae*! What a hideous thought!"

"I don't know. I saw how he ogled those naked *arioi* dancers at Christmastime," Young added. "It's probably why he fainted!"

"Neddie, you never told me. What happened to those two spying men?" Susannah swung her long black hair over one shoulder and combed it with her fingers as it lay across her chest like a sash.

"Which spying men? Millward and Burkitt?" Young was confused.

"No, not them, the two men from your Bible of God, the ones who watched my namesake Susannah bathe in her garden."

"Oh, they were punished for their crimes. Executed, hanged." Young responded with a matter-of-factness—as though their fates were obvious—which stunned the other women in the circle.

"Killed for appreciating the feminine figure? The British are so barbaric." Susannah exaggerated her response for dramatic effect but voiced the collective disapproval of her fellow islanders. A shared propensity for lewd humor had acted as an easy bridge between cultures, but more serious matters remained frightening and arcane to the other: the British men's deep-seated guilt and shame and the overly callous means of punishing dissent were as unsettling and bizarre to the Tahitians as their unspoken taboos and practices of human sacrifice were to the men of the *Bounty*.

"And what does my name mean?" Jenny turned to Smith, the glow of the bonfire spotlighting the "A.S." branded on her shoulder. Most of the Tahitian women now had English nicknames, given to them by their British companions after lazy attempts to pronounce their Tahitian titles. Jenny had started to take a liking to hers, much like Susannah had. The *J*, absent from the Tahitian alphabet, lent her a worldly flair, she thought.

"Jenny? Dunno. Sounds pretty, that's all." Smith slurped another swig of his grog.

"A female donkey, jenny is," Young chimed in with the earnestness of an academic.

"What?! An ass?!" McCoy burst into a fit of cackles, and the other men joined in. There was no such animal on Tahiti, but the hee-hawing of the miming sailors was a clear clue that perhaps a donkey was not the most elegant of creatures.

"I think a jenny is also a kind of small bird," offered Christian consolingly, his words overwhelmed by the laughter and braying.

Smith, embarrassed that he had quite literally given his woman an asinine name, piped up again. "Why do you women even like Young, anyway?" He tried to change the subject. "The poor bloke has no teeth!"

"Oh but teeth are of little importance," Jenny spoke up, turning her mortification into spite, "when one has a capable tongue!" She aimed her snark at Smith for having saddled her with what turned out to be such an ungraceful moniker. Of all the *Bounty*'s men, it was Smith who had given away the most copper nails. She never felt special, and Susannah still garnered unwavering affection from even the sailors too lowly ranked to bed her.

"But he's a half-breed mongrel! Enlighten us please!" Quintal couldn't help but tinge his curiosity with vindictive words. "What charms does this beastly mutt possess that has so riveted Tahiti's women?" By English standards, Quintal was far more attractive than the bookish sailor, and he knew it.

Susannah snickered, eyeing the other women in the group as though they had all taken a turn with Young. "It's like the man has three legs!" Giggles quickly crescendoed among the Tahitians.

"So Jenny's a donkey and our Young is a stallion!" McCoy added, inciting a swell of belly laughter from the men as well.

When the bonfire dimmed—now a few crackling cinders—the group quietly splintered off into couples. Christian followed Mauatua back to her hut, where the two had spent many nights together since Christmas. With everyone else asleep, it was as though they had her familial garden all to themselves. Lying on their backs, they watched as the moonlight illuminated the top of Mount Orohena.

Christian sighed; he didn't want to leave. He had begun his time on Tahiti with a colonialist's gaze of otherness, ascribing a less-than quality to a group of islanders who possessed no cathedrals, castles, or courtly attire—hallmarks of British modernity. Any similarities found between the two civilizations were little miracles, glimmers of promise that with some guidance they, too, could evolve. But now, after what had felt like a lifetime—and an alternate life—Christian clung to the tenets of Tahitian culture, values that Europeans had forsaken in the name of perceived progress and the pursuit of material things.

A custodian of Tahitian tradition, Mauatua had also mindfully observed the behavior of the visitors. But for her, it was the differences between societies that proved surprising and provided insight into the British point of view. The Christian notion that not all the world's people were like-minded legitimized the exploitation of others, and although her society was deeply stratified—and also featured forms of servitude—the well-being of one person was never categorically leveraged at the expense of another, like in Europe. But what disturbed Mauatua even more was the idea that someone could be wholly bad. Mana—the life-force essence of Polynesia—ebbed and flowed with curling currents of positive and negative energy, but when Young and the others spoke of their Bible it was always in the strictest dichotomies: heaven and hell, God and the devil, the saved and the damned, even the bather and her depraved voyeurs. She wondered, as a result, if the design of Christianity spawned purely evil men—souls bankrupt of any virtue. Quintal, for example, always wove harmful epithets in his humor, and he had struck Susannah's maid Tevarua, the softest of creatures. She voiced her theory to Christian, who dismissed the notion as conjecture. "Quintal doesn't think, he just acts. And besides, aren't good people capable of bad things?" It seemed—perhaps by osmosis—that Christian had come to appreciate the shades of gray with which the Tahitians painted their spectrum of humanity.

"But Quintal laughs with his mouth but not with his eyes," Mauatua continued to build her argument. "Those bright blue eyes . . ." While the Tahitians admired the light skin of the British sailors—a trait purposefully bred among the upper caste of the island—they were wary of their blue eyes. The Tahitian iris was chestnut-brown, even blackish—the color of the earth, solid and stable. Blue was the surrounding ocean: fickle, amorphous, and always changing.

"Captain Bligh too. He has the same eyes," added Mauatua, implying a certain untrustworthiness of his character as well.

Christian took a long contemplative breath. "There's something I have to tell you, but no one else must know or Bligh would have my head."

Mauatua sat up with anticipation.

"Captain Cook is dead."

"Oh. I know," she lay back down as Christian now sprang up, surprised. Rumors of Cook's death had circulated around the island long before the *Bounty*'s arrival, and although it seemed that the Tahitians venerated him—some even deified him—they were afraid of him too. The esteemed explorer's first two visits had been amiable, but something changed the third time he sailed into Matavai Bay. He had grown tyrannical—too accustomed to subduing "savages" with his superior weaponry—and demanded obedience instead of dealing in diplomacy. On one infamous occasion, Cook ordered the humiliation of a local chieftain who didn't fall into line; he had his head shaved and ears ripped off. The Tahitians may have remained consummately hospitable, but the Hawaiians a few months later were not. They clubbed Cook in the head, then stabbed him to death after he brazenly tried to kidnap one of their leaders.

"And what about me?" Christian, still kneeling, thought about the explorer he had long admired. He didn't want to be that man anymore. "What do my eyes tell you?"

"They are gray like metal," Mauatua assured him. It was the most powerful of elements—the protective sheathing on the hull of the *Bounty*, the bullets that whizzed out of guns, and the nails exchanged for company.

Mauatua hopped away, returning quickly with a gift, which she draped around Christian's shoulders. Over the last few months, after Christian and his comrades had stopped wearing the top halves of their uniforms, she had slyly taken his shirt and replaced its buttons with dark pearl shells that shimmered like little tar slicks in the moonlight. "Here, they match your eyes." Christian slid his arms through the sleeves, then opened the lapels and wrapped the flaps of fabric around Mauatua, drawing her in.

Unable to sleep during the last hours before dawn, the lovers stared at the stars one final time together. Stems and stalks, as Mauatua explained, grew into a celestial canopy full of her gods and ancestors—including the great Maui, with his giant hooked weapon, who helps guide seafaring Tahitians across the vast expanses of open water, much like the *Bounty*'s azimuth compass. Christian didn't have the heart to explain to Mauatua that tomorrow he'd begin a journey to a destination so far away that its dome of night had almost none of the same heavenly bodies.

In the morning, Chief Teina, his wife Itia, and hundreds of Tahitians gathered on the black sand beach, sobbing and wailing as the *Bounty* glided away—a funeral for the British sailors they'd never see again. On board, the crewmen were donning their navy uniforms once more, buttoned up to the neck. Their demeanors were equally formal, but knots of sadness tightened their throats as they hauled in the anchor and whipped open the sails.

Of all the souvenirs the crew wished they could take home from Tahiti—the weather, the water, and the women—it was the insipid breadfruit that weighed the ship low against the waves instead, slowing an already protracted journey back to England via Jamaica.

On the upper deck, Christian took his last glimpses of Mount Orohena, now in the distance, and wondered about his brother Charles for first time since he had arrived in Tahiti. Was he still a shadow of his former self after his eighteen-month trip in Asia? It had been almost eighteen months since the *Bounty* departed

England, and what remained of the voyage was its most loathsome of legs. Christian would be trapped within the cramped confines of the dark, creaking ship for months on end, but this time, instead of the promise of paradise at the end, the inhibitions and pressures of drizzly, diseased England now awaited.

"Lieutenant!" Bligh snapped Christian out of his meandering thoughts. "What an unfit officer you are," the commander said, mocking his attire. Christian was proudly sporting the new pearl buttons sewn onto his officer's uniform, but he was quickly ordered below deck to swap out his shirt for one of Valentine's old tunics.

As Christian rummaged through the ship's supplies, he could hear the goats and dog rattling their cages. This time, however, they weren't sensing land. They wanted to break themselves free of their shackles.

CHAPTER 7

THE LAST GRANDE DAME OF TAHITI

2018

On a gloomy afternoon in 1918, James Norman Hall stopped to buy a copy of William Bligh's *Bounty* logbook from a dusty antiquities shop in London on his way back to America. A journalist by trade, Hall was working as a foreign correspondent in Europe covering the Allied air brigade during the First World War when he resigned his post and signed up for the French Air Force. Later, as a captain in the Army Air Service when the United States joined the fray, his airplane was gunned down over enemy lines.

"Many years from now, when this narrative is placed in your hands, you may wonder why I should have written it, with you in mind, long before any of you were born," began Hall, thirty-one and unwed, in a letter to the grandchildren he hoped to one day have, written while he was held captive in a Bavarian castle as a German prisoner of war. He had befriended fellow inmate Charles Nordhoff, and after their release—Hall dreading the return to the tedium of his native Iowa—they moved to Tahiti, inspired by the grand adventure to the far side of the world that Bligh had detailed in his log.

Hall married Sarah Winchester, the daughter of an American sea captain and his Polynesian wife, and together they had two children.

He continued his writing career with Nordhoff as his partner, and in 1932, the two men coauthored the first in a trilogy of novels that would catapult their bylines to international success: *Mutiny on the Bounty*.

During the last decade of the eighteenth century, the story of the *Bounty*'s seizure had riveted audiences as each successive plot twist made front-page headlines the planet over. And the mutineers, who commandeered the little breadfruit-filled vessel after its departure from Tahiti, were the most wanted and notorious criminals in the entirety of the British Empire. But like all yarns spun through the loom of the news cycle, the true tale of the *Bounty* and its men had eventually faded to gray as other dark tales of the industrializing world soon spread across the globe.

Over a century later, Hall's reimagined version of the events aboard the *Bounty* had stoked a refreshed interest in the subject matter. Soon, a legion of historians were delving back into Bligh's logs and the journals kept by the other officers on board, to more properly decipher what exactly had happened in the deep of the South Pacific, three weeks after Mount Orohena had slunk below the waves.

Some academics found evidence that Bligh had quietly loaned Fletcher Christian some money during their stay in Cape Town en route to Tahiti, which had caused an ever-growing rift in their camaraderie. Others speculated that the two men had become homosexual lovers and tensions flared when Christian sought out relations with several Polynesian women. But it was Hall's romanticized version of the events on board—narrated by a fictitious crewman named Roger Byam (based on little Peter Heywood)—that would ultimately form the foundation of what most *Bounty* enthusiasts know today: a spat between Bligh and Christian over stolen coconuts that would send the young lieutenant over the proverbial edge, forever wrecking his naval career that was once so full of promise.

Like any good novelist, Hall dialed up the interpersonal drama as well, recasting Bligh as a sadistic and maniacal dictator instead of a haughty and hot-headed navigator. If there was ever a debate, Christian was now the unequivocal hero. His connection with Mauatua was largely exaggerated too—a grandiose romance between star-crossed lovers that would further contribute to the *Bounty*'s undoing.

Hall's legacy—and the *Bounty*'s popularity—would continue to ascend well after the author's death when, in the early 1960s, Hollywood eyed his *Mutiny on the Bounty* as the source material for its next blockbuster movie, casting Marlon Brando as the lead. Although it was the fourth film to immortalize this most famous of nautical events, the Brando version, made by MGM, managed to add yet another layer to the mythos with its over-the-top production budget (the biggest in the industry to date, lavished on an exact replica of the ship) that became even more bloated when the shooting schedule was—like the real *Bounty*—hampered by severe rain delays. Also, like the real Christian, Brando began a widely publicized courtship with Tarita Teriipaia, the actress who played Mauatua. He would remain in the South Pacific after filming to embrace the castaway lifestyle as well—the two eventually married and had children.

The biggest impact of Brando's *Bounty*, however, was its lasting effect on Tahiti's tourism. The purpose-built complex that housed MGM's production crew was later turned into the island's very first resort, and the panoramic vistas captured on celluloid entreated audiences to come visit at a time when commercial air travel was really taking off, so to speak. Tales of Polynesia's majesty had followed American soldiers home from the Pacific theater after the Second World War, and a surge of interest in tiki culture swelled with Hawaii's statehood in 1959. The advent of long-haul flights shortly thereafter was the final piece of the puzzle to permanently position Tahiti as the ultimate tropical fantasy.

It's rather fitting that the resurgence of interest in the *Bounty*'s story spawned our modern-day fetishization of Tahiti as holiday wonderland, because, in many ways, it's a reverberation of the news of the actual mutiny back in 1789, which is largely responsible for solidifying the island-as-paradise narrative we know today.

There are no mentions of a tropical island in the Bible—Eden was a garden, not an isle, of course—so the perception of paradise in the

Judeo-Christian canon does not necessarily match our modern-day concept of palm-fringed beaches. Thomas More wrote of a perfect society on a faraway island in *Utopia* in the early sixteenth century, but it wasn't until two centuries later—when French and British sailors made landfall in Polynesia—that the notion's prevalence really came into being. In their logs, the explorers detailed an exciting and upside-down world relative to their own back in Europe. The warm Tahitian sun and cool lagoon breezes soothed their sea-addled bodies; the fresh fruit, plucked from practically every branch, cured their ails. Louis Antoine de Bougainville—the French contemporary of Captain Cook—dubbed Tahiti "New Cythera," after the birthplace of Aphrodite, and wrote what was essentially an erotic tale of a pristine realm, bare-breasted women and all.

His account, along with many others, beguiled the upper classes back in Europe. They threw lavish parties with licentious Polynesian themes, pored over Joseph Banks's detailed volumes of exotic findings, and displayed totems of the tropical world—like the pineapple—in their mansions for all to see.

Then, word reached the Old World that a group of young sailors were so moved by their extended time in Tahiti that they chucked their captain over the side of his ship in a desperate attempt to stay in Polynesia forever. And this—the frenzy aboard the *Bounty*—galvanized the synonymity of islands and paradise forever as news trickled down the rungs of society, captivating the world whole.

———

MY TIME ON Tahiti, however, had been anything but paradise thus far.

Traveling on a freelancer's dime, I had opted for a rented room in a local home instead of an overwater bungalow at a resort while I waited to link up with Pitcairn's freighter. Raiamanu charged me 15 euros a night for what turned out to be a cot in the corner of his living room, cordoned off by a long, hanging sheet draped over a string like drying laundry. The "you get what you pay for" adage had never rung so true.

But it was the rain that bothered me more—the hot, chunky rain that bore down on me like marbles, drooping the fabric of my dollar-store umbrella and rusting its metal spokes. This was not the dainty off-season afternoon drizzle that was touted in the online brochures. No, the rain was slowly drowning me with its perpetuity. The walls of Raiamanu's house felt soggy and damp, as though mold or moss might suddenly flower out of its concrete pores. And the dull, cloud-ridden light hid all of the island's wonders from view. Matavai Bay had been stripped of its silvery gloss, and Moorea's green cathedral across the lagoon was shrouded in haze, its nave of palms and rocky spires—usually spotted from Raiamanu's porch—were nowhere to be found.

On the third straight day of unabating storms—toes pruning in my sandals—I heard the squeak of a tin-can Peugeot as it inhaled the wet gravel up Raiamanu's driveway. Kate Hall had come to rescue me from my Tahiti-on-the-cheap experiment gone horribly awry.

Through a long chain of friends of friends, I had managed to connect with James Norman Hall's granddaughter—the eventual recipient of his future-thinking letter penned in war-torn Germany exactly a hundred years prior. Our spirited conversation over email had turned into an invitation to join her on her family's private island, Motu Mapeti, before my imminent departure to Pitcairn. "It'll be like castaway practice," she joked as I climbed into her car.

In the backseat was a pink carry-on suitcase with wheels, which didn't quite jibe with her tomboyish persona. Kate was a California surfer chick—slender, with sandy blonde hair and a permanent red smudge on the tip of her nose from too many years at the beach. She was in her fifties but could easily pass for much younger. Now living in Texas, Kate was the custodian of "Papa Hall's" legacy, as she called him, and happened to be in Tahiti for a short week to deal with some estate logistics.

We slowly arced our way along Tahiti's shoreline, getting bogged down by island traffic in Papeete, the capital. In Papara, we stopped at the fresh tuna market for provisions. "They know me here," Kate announced emphatically as she slid through the door, though I could sense in her insistence that she wanted to belong to Tahiti more than she actually did. It endeared her to me, in a way, as someone who also grew up in a far quadrant of the former French Empire's wilderness—Quebec. But I had left Canada at age fourteen and, like Kate, often clung to cultural touchpoints that were maybe no longer mine.

Inside, Kate was heckling the fishmongers, jockeying for the local price instead of the tourist fare. She cooed her gallic vowels and trilled her *r*'s just like the heavyset Tahitian *mamies* beside her who were vying for their turn at the counter. Kate did a double take when I chimed in too, equally surprised to find that French also hid under my veneer of American English.

Further down the island, Kate tucked her Peugeot under the shade of a large tree. The Halls owned the sliver of mainland adjacent to Motu Mapeti and had built a modest home for its caretaker, Terii, who came to greet us with a demure smile and a *tiare* flower drooping over her left ear. Kate briefly clicked back to English as we entered the home where Terii's husband was watching TV in his wheelchair, gauzy bandages wrapped around his swollen ankles. "Diabetes has become a plague in Tahiti. He's waiting for a liver transplant too."

Terii had already carried our belongings down to the wooden dock in the backyard, which pointed directly at the island: a perfect little circle, like the tittle on a lowercase *i*, so close to shore that one could easily swim.

Ten minutes in a metal dinghy ushered us across the channel. We hoisted our belongings out of the boat, and Kate fidgeted with the zippers on her luggage. She soon exhumed what I would consider to be the single most random item one might pull out of a ratty pink suitcase on a sand trap in the middle of the Pacific: an Academy Award—its shiny bald head glistening in the sliver of sunshine that had managed to creep through the clouds.

"Wanna touch it?" Kate dropped the award in my carefully cupped hands. It was much heavier than I had imagined. "I seriously don't know how those twig actresses can hold one of these up while giving their acceptance speech," she chuckled as I read the inscription: *To Conrad L. Hall*—Kate's father, James Norman Hall's son.

Conrad had enrolled in filmmaking classes after trying unsuccessfully to follow in his father's footsteps. "He got a D at USC's journalism school," Kate divulged. Eventually, he became one of Hollywood's most acclaimed cinematographers, earning a total of ten Oscar nominations and three wins (the one I held was awarded posthumously for *Road to Perdition* in 2002). But first, while working his way up the ranks, Conrad had served as an assisting cinematographer—responsible for all of the sweeping panoramas of Tahiti's splendor—on Brando's *Mutiny on the Bounty*.

"Back in the 1960s, Motu Mapeti was only used for picnics," Kate explained. "But Marlon loved to spend his time here in between shoots." In fact, it was Motu Mapeti that enchanted Brando into buying an island of his own: nearby Tetiaroa (which incidentally was Churchill and Millward's hideaway when they were trying to escape from Bligh).

Years later, in the early 2000s, Kate got a call out of the blue. "Hello Katie, this is Marlon Brando speaking," she recounted, dropping her voice a husky octave to imitate the matinee idol. "I swear, I thought it was a friend pulling a prank on me," she laughed. "Poor Marlon, no one ever believed it was him when he'd phone them." Brando wanted Kate to help him find an engineer. He was going to build a lavish ecolodge on his island.

"That call began my year with Marlon Brando," she explained. "He rang me every single day after that. He'd even show up at my doorstep to take me out to dinner." Their relationship was purely platonic and, strangely, Brando never brought up his hotel aspirations again, preferring to discuss topics like Afropunk music instead. He died not long after.

Eventually, in 2014, a luxury resort was fully realized on Tetiaroa that rivaled the honeymoon bungalows of Bora Bora. Aptly named the Brando, the property quickly became a beacon for the jet-set elite; Barack Obama is said to have written much of his presidential memoir in one of the beachside villas.

Motu Mapeti, however, has remained a cherished secret of the Hall family, with very few luxuries or comforts. It has four flimsy huts and an open-air shower in the middle (read: a hose dangling down from a tall tree), just the way Kate's father liked it.

And like her father, Kate had built a career in the entertainment industry, working mostly in documentary television. She moonlighted as a fixer for *Survivor*, saving the series when, following the 9/11 terrorist attacks, plans to shoot the program's fourth season in the Middle East were scrapped.

"An hour after the Twin Towers fell, I was on the phone with Mark Burnett—the show's creator—suggesting that we reorient production to the South Pacific." Kate was busy preparing our dinner of *poisson cru*, dicing raw tuna into small cubes, then adding salt, onion, cucumbers, parsley, and a generous amount of lime juice. Terii sat nearby on a strange piece of burnished furniture shaped like a giant tortoise: four wooden legs and a rounded blade with serrated teeth where the head ought to be. She scraped a halved coconut against the metal spikes as white shavings snowed down into a bucket below. With a cheesecloth, Kate then separated the coconut milk from its pulp, pouring it over the browning fish and tossing the contents with her hands. "When you really think about it," she continued, "there's no better spot than a small rock in a big ocean to capture *Survivor*'s awful duality of claustrophobia and isolation, right?"

She wasn't wrong.

The "outwit, outplay, outlast" credo of *Survivor*'s interpersonal drama had riveted millions of viewers in the show's first few seasons. The game seemed ill-suited to the pure of heart—apparently nice guys did finish last—but it didn't necessarily reward those who were patently evil either. A new character archetype had emerged in the American zeitgeist, challenging the good-versus-bad duality that had long driven Hollywood's plotlines. Antiheroes like Richard Hatch nabbed the title of sole survivor instead, not unlike the mysterious John Adams—the *Bounty*'s last mutineer, who outlived his comrades in a real-life version of *Survivor*. But the men and women of Pitcairn did things far, far worse than vote each other off the island.

The rain was holding out despite the overbearing grayness of the sky, so we took our dinner outside and sat on chopped logs. As the evening's darkness set in, Kate gathered scraps of ironwood for a campfire, and from a single wick swiped from a soggy matchbook, the kindling burst into flames.

In the morning over cups of coffee, Kate finally broached the subject of Pitcairn. "It's cursed you know. The place has bad mana, bad energy, bad vibes." Interestingly, no one in the Hall family had ever visited the island. James Norman Hall's only attempt ended in tragedy when his vessel was shipwrecked off Temoe atoll, some three hundred miles away. Kate seemed convinced that the *Bounty* cursed the souls that touched its story, and she began spouting off the evidence to support her claim. Brando's life was plagued by tragedy after filming in the South Pacific. His portrayal of Christian was critically panned, sending his career on a decade-long downward spiral as he put on weight, saved only by turns in *The Godfather* and *Last Tango in Paris*, both in 1972. His marriage to Tarita soured as well. Later—and worst of all—his half-Tahitian daughter was maimed in a car accident; she then hanged herself in her midtwenties after another of Brando's children murdered her boyfriend in cold blood. Even MGM's functioning replica of the *Bounty* carried bad luck in its sails; it had sunk off the coast of New York City during Hurricane Sandy in 2012, killing two crew members on board.

With more storm clouds closing in, we quickly made our way to the island's beach and snorkeled in the graduating shallows to look for what Kate called "carrot shells," like swirling unicorn horns coated in a pearlescent sheen. Home to a mollusk, as Kate explained, they hid under the ocean's sandy floor. We swam the ten feet down to the bottom and returned to the surface each with a shiny shell in hand. Mine, however, didn't seem to have a snail living inside, which Kate found slightly strange, as they usually became dull and brittle when abandoned. "A gift from Motu Mapeti, I suppose." She encouraged me to keep it. Back on the beach, I placed the shell inside my snorkel mask's plastic casing.

THE NEXT DAY, curled up on my cot in the corner of Raiamanu's living room, my phone dinged with a new text message. It was Kate: "I told my aunt Nancy that you were heading to Pitcairn and she wants to meet you before you go. Do you have time?"

Like a moth to a flame, Conrad had sought out the bright lights of Hollywood, but his sister Nancy—James Norman Hall's daughter—had stayed behind. She was now the doyenne of Tahiti. At fourteen she had met her husband, Nicholas Rutgers, while he toured the Pacific during the Second World War; she married him at 16. "Nick," as she called him, was the heir to part of both the Rutgers and Johnson & Johnson fortunes. Kate had warned me, "Nancy lived a very, very charmed life."

Her childhood home—the Hall family's residence—was a breezy bungalow in the Arue precinct, down the road from Point Venus and Matavai Bay. As an adult, Nancy had purchased the sprawling acreage of hills just above it and constructed an elaborate estate overlooking the rest of the island. The original house down below was now La Maison James Norman Hall, a museum dedicated to her father's memory that contained a trove of priceless artifacts including his desk, typewriter, a graft of an original *Bounty* breadfruit cutting destined for the plantations of Jamaica, and that hundred-year-old letter Hall had written to Kate without having known her name, framed near the entry to the gift shop. Often when Kate would visit, she'd bring along one of Conrad's Oscars for temporary viewing.

The museum was about a twenty-minute walk from Raiamanu's house. I carried an extra collared shirt in my tote bag, fully knowing that the one I was wearing would be drenched with sweat and rain before I'd even arrive. Nancy had arranged a private viewing of her father's keepsakes—books, belongings, and photographs—after which I was invited up to her mountainside palace for lunch.

I threw my other polo over my shoulders in the museum manager's car as we trundled up a serpentine path deeper into the compound. I felt as though I had finally reached the Emerald City, and yet my trip to Pitcairn—my *real* journey—hadn't even begun.

We drove by an empty in-ground swimming pool—its tiles cracked and claimed by weeds—and a nearby tennis court full of fallen palm fronds. Nancy had plenty of staff to ensure her property's care, but in her late eighties she was interested in little more than eating, napping, and enjoying the views from the lanai. Her husband, Nick, I was told, had passed away less than two months prior, and I had begun to feel as though I would need to sing for my supper in an attempt to distract her from her newfound loneliness. They had been married for over seventy years.

"So you're the Pitcairn boy," Nancy, clad in a floral caftan, announced as she entered the parlor where I had been politely waiting. I immediately sprang to my feet.

"Sit! Sɪᴛ! There's no need to stand!" She pointed to a wicker chaise angled at a coffee table stacked with picture albums. For a while we admired dozens of black-and-white photos of a time gone by. Nancy was constantly hosting soirees over the decades, including the MGM film crew in the 1960s. "I used to give away black pearls as parting gifts," she laughed. There was something about the directness with which she spoke, as though, at her great age, she no longer had the time to decorate her words with politeness.

When Nancy grew tired of reminiscing, she called out "Lᴜɴᴄʜ!"— like Veruca Salt wanting her golden goose now—and an older Tahitian woman soon appeared in the doorframe to escort us over to the patio.

"This is Mele," Nancy introduced us, "my daughter-in-law. Because," she continued, "when your son diddles the maid and gets her pregnant, you make him marry her." It wasn't clear if Mele could understand her English, but I was nevertheless sure she knew exactly how Nancy felt.

One of Nancy's younger attendants brought us each a halved avocado topped with minced shrimp slaw, served on bone china with a pewter teaspoon. For the greater part of the next hour, Nancy grilled me on my upbringing, schooling, and how I had—like her father—become ensnared in the *Bounty*'s trap.

"Do you want another one?" Nancy offered, tapping her hollowed-out avocado peel with her utensil.

"Oh, no I'm fine. Thank you though." I thought a main course was about to round the corner from the kitchen, but that was it.

"I don't like to eat very much anymore since my bones don't allow me to do much moving around," Nancy explained.

I grinned, famished.

"Well I think that'll be all for this afternoon." She cocked her head back and yelled "NAP!" into the air. Somewhere on the property, I imagined, there was a timid maid scurrying toward her bedroom to fluff the duvets.

Built-in shelving flanked the hallway connecting the manse's public and private spaces, and before I departed, Nancy invited me down the passage to better admire her collection of books—all copies of James Norman Hall's work. She pulled a pen out of her caftan, and each time she took a book down, she'd flip it open to its title page and sign it, as though she were her father's proxy: *To a dear young gentleman on his most excellent adventure.*

I thanked her profusely but was quickly interrupted. "ONE MORE!" She reached for a paperback volume that was noticeably thicker than the others and plunked it on top of my growing stack of titles.

"*The Far Lands*," I read the cover out loud.

"It's a collection of myths and legends from all across the South Pacific," Nancy explained as she watched me turn the first few pages.

I started reading from the prologue: "The sight of any remote land in whatever latitude, though it be no more than a bare rock, still gives me something of a boy's feeling of wonder and delight—"

Nancy cut me off once more, "And you're going to the farthest land of them all."

CHAPTER 8

MUTINY ON THE *BOUNTY*
APRIL 1789

Christian and five other sailors floated toward the shore in a wooden cutter to collect fresh water and dry wood. Nomuka was an outcrop belonging to what Captain Cook had dubbed the Friendly Islands; it would be a half mile from the beach to reach the lily-padded lake in the center of the island, according to Cook's old navigational logs. Usually, when the *Bounty* arrived at a new destination, the island's population would launch a fleet of outriggers to welcome the ship to shore with garlands and gifts. Here, a gang of ominous islanders mobbed the sand as the boat made landfall. Quintal dragged the grapnel through the turbid tidewater, readying their boat to disembark, but Christian hesitated. Cook's moniker seemed terribly wrong—this island was not at all friendly.

Neither excitement nor fear showed on the Nomukans' faces. Their eyes were hollow, their bodies covered in blights and sores. Quiet murmurs crept out of their cankered mouths as they swarmed Christian's landing party to pet the sailors' cotton uniforms and burrow curious fingers into their beards. With tentative steps, Christian collected the barrels and axes needed to garner supplies, exchanging shy glances of dread with his men as they continued to be dissected by scabrous hands. The islanders were stricken with some kind of plague that had turned their figures—perhaps once as appealing as the Tahitians'—into leprous apparitions. It was impossible to tell which deformities were the effects of their malady and which were the ritualistic attempts to rid themselves of it. Both the men and women had torn large clumps of hair from their skulls and burned scars over their dripping wounds. The disease spared no one—not even the children, whose dangling limbs and catatonic stares were the most disturbing of all.

Christian split his men into pairs: one would guard their boat, one would chop wood along the coast, and Quintal would follow him into the heart of the island in search of the potable source. But a charcoal haze—smoke from dozens of funerary pyres—made it difficult to find the way, and a mob of wraiths slowly traced behind holding wooden spears. When they reached the inland lake, these shadows began to hiss; louder voices would awaken the resting spirits of the recent dead. They swung their weapons at the sailors, a taunting ballet of macabre mimicry danced so silently that Christian could still hear the glugging of the water that filled their half-drowned casks.

"Mr. Christian . . ." Quintal had the sharpened head of a spear pressed against the tender flesh between his neck and jaw. For a man who seesawed between manic fits of laughter and drunken bouts of rage, his sallow stare—eyes wide—made Christian drop his kegs in fear. This was the end of Quintal; he was being pulled toward an old mossy *marae* hidden under a heaping pile of rotting corpses. They were going to sacrifice him to their Polynesian gods as a desperate attempt to cure themselves of their hideous sickness. Christian hurled his barrel at the aggressors; the wooden slatting flew out of its copper ringlets as it shattered across the ground. "LET'S GO!" He and Quintal dropped everything on their frantic dash to join the others on the beach, the chorus of specters in close pursuit.

Another band of Nomukans had cut the anchor that moored their little watercraft. It was adrift, teasing the sailors as it rolled slightly forward then swished farther away in the ebbing waves.

"We need to leave—NOW!" Christian yelled as all of his men converged, swinging axes at the growing mob and flopping into the water in a panicked attempt to recover their getaway boat. One by one they hoisted themselves into the tender and hastily dunked their paddles—"Row!" Christian commanded—trying to distance themselves from the rush of islanders that had taken to the shallows to chase them down. No one chanced a look back to shore until they had safely reached the *Bounty*.

Tramping straight off the cutter, Christian collapsed his outstretched body along the planks of the upper deck, slowing his labored breath as the sun dried his uniform.

By midafternoon Nomuka was out of sight but not yet a distant memory. It was the first time Christian had received a menacing welcome in the South Seas. He'd seen despair—poverty and sickness—on other continents, even in his home country, but after six months in Polynesia he had become willfully naive to the possibility that there were dark corners of the blue continent too. Were there no unsullied pockets in this wretched world?

It had been three miserable weeks since the *Bounty* had left Tahiti, and now the suffering and hostility on Nomuka had awoken a more visceral angst within Christian. He needed to leave the ship and could construe no other solution but to take one of the tenders and be gone in the night.

Off the bow, Christian began to tear out the contents of his journal. He watched as the breeze carried each page over the railing and thought about following his folio overboard, but a large group of seamen had started to crowd the upper deck. The *Bounty* was approaching the next of the Friendly Islands, Tofua, which smoldered ocher and orange as flames started to burst forth from its turreted crown.

Christian skipped his usual evening meal with Bligh, feigning illness, and instead tucked his Tahitian curios into the belongings of Heywood, Churchill, and a few other friends, keeping only his pearl-button shirt, which he wore. From his hammock, he could hear the rousing shouts of wonderment from his fellow sailors upstairs as the Earth continued to shoot molten ribbons of lava into the night sky. Christian ignored the spectacle and started gathering a week's worth of rations and some copper nails to barter for favors after drifting ashore somewhere far away.

It was well past midnight now, and Christian began to replay Bligh's scornful words—triggered by memories of Cook's grisly demise at the hands of the Hawaiians—after he had failed to return from Nomuka with fresh water and wood. Never mind that he and his fellow seamen had almost been murdered on sacrificial pyres; Bligh's insults had become even more derisive and cruel since they had begun their journey back to England. Christian despised how Bligh compared his junior officers to dogs, capable of nothing more than simple obedience and worthy of a slap when they misbehaved. How could a man so concerned with cultivating a polished persona possess such a vile and unhinged mouth, a hell hatch unleashing obscenities with the same fiery fury as Tofua's volcano?

There were meaner insults too. Bligh knew exactly how to find someone's vulnerability and throw salt over their wound. For Christian it was to imply that he was undeserving of others' admiration. Bligh had slowly eroded his confidence like the methodic splashing of the waves that stripped the *Bounty* of its luster. A week before arriving at Nomuka, Bligh had accused Christian of ungentlemanly crimes like petty theft. The captain found every opportunity to call him a cowardly rascal or mock his thin, avian physique in front of the crew. The disastrous supply run on Nomuka further confirmed Bligh's narrative that Christian was not only an incapable leader but a gutless bird too.

At 4 a.m., Young and Heywood came down from the upper deck to rouse Christian—it was his turn to man the watch—and found him wide awake, doused in heavy sweat that had soaked through the coarse material of his bedding.

"Dear Mr. Christian, you haven't slept a wink!" Young offered to cover Christian's shift so he could slough off whatever waking nightmare was plaguing him.

"I'll be fine. Duty calls," he replied, patting his clammy palms on his pants before finding the dimly lit passage that led upstairs.

Back on the upper deck, Christian muttered to himself under his breath as he paced across the ship. "I am *not* a milksop!" He was an animal twice caged: chained to this vessel that plied the loneliest of seas and a prisoner of emotional restraint forced to swallow Bligh's

words like poison. And now he had become a creature fierce and
resentful, as his brother Charles had warned. Oh how Mauatua wept
so openly at Huggan's funeral. Even Quintal was somehow worthy
of envy for his hiccups of raw emotion. Christian was breaking free;
he'd take a million slaps of the whip over another tongue lashing
from his captain.

One by one, Christian approached the other crewmen on duty—
first Churchill, then Quintal, Mills, and Burkitt—and spoke to them
in muffled words, as quiet and sinister as the Nomukans' whispers.
Together, they cracked open the armory, pulling pistols, muskets,
and a cutlass out from the wooden chest, then marched down the
ladder and straight through the open door of the captain's quarters.
It was Bligh, not Christian, who should leave the ship.

————————

THE SUDDEN WEIGHT of heavy hands woke Bligh from the stillest
of dreams. He could make out the silhouettes of four men in his
cabin: two at the foot of his bed, one blocking the door, and one
hovering over his head pointing the metal flourish of a cutlass at his
neck—it was Christian.

"Murder! It's a murder!" Bligh could barely breathe the words;
Christian had pressed the blade so forcefully against his throat, he
could no longer swallow his fear.

Bligh's eyes quickly adjusted in the blackness that filled his quarters. Churchill and Burkitt tore away the thin sheath of linen that
protected the captain from his aggressors and forced him out of bed.
Christian yanked both of Bligh's arms behind his back. "Hand down
a seizing, quick, or I'll play hell with you too!" he barked at Mills,
who had barricaded the doorframe with his broad, imposing figure.

"Murder!" Bligh tried again. He could see the crazed look in
Christian's eyes as he wound some fishing line around Bligh's restrained wrists.

"Not another word or death is your portion." Christian slid his
small sword back under Bligh's clenched mandible.

Bligh desperately flopped his body toward the trousers folded over his desk chair. He had worn only a light tunic to bed, which ruffled just above his waist. If he was going to be killed, it would at least be with some semblance of courtesy. But Burkitt thrust his open palm against Bligh's face, bashing in his nose as he straightened the captain's stance. Dagger against the windpipe once more, Christian was ready to march Bligh out of his cabin.

A gauntlet of conspirators awaited in the hallway, and again Bligh started shouting for help, hoping there remained at least one loyal officer on board. His pleas devolved into shrieks—"MURDER!"—when he saw Fryer, his second-in-command, trembling at the ladder that led to the upper deck. Smith had bound Fryer's hands, and Quintal pointed a loaded pistol at his head.

The cadre of mutineers forced the two men onto the upper deck, where the moonlight shone on Bligh's disturbingly wan figure, untouched by the tropics. His men had sought every opportunity to lose their shirts on Tahiti and had become as bronzed as their islander friends, while Bligh held steadfast to his own version of buttoned-up manners. He lamented the indignity; after six months of not shedding so much as a hat in the pervasive humidity of the monsoons, he'd meet his end in a nightie with his bottom half exposed: two trunks of ashen oak and a wiry black briar patch that had never once enjoyed a day—or night—under the Tahitian sky.

"Lower the launch!" Mills and McCoy furiously unspooled a tangle of cabled ropes, hoisting the twenty-three-foot tender—the largest of the *Bounty*'s three ferrying boats—into the air. The plan was to cast Bligh and his loyal followers adrift. Christian would have preferred to give up the ship's smaller dinghy or cutter, but the number of sailors marked for an uncertain fate—rounded up by the mutineers, or leaving of their own volition—was quickly increasing.

As Bligh was tied to the mizzenmast by Smith—and with Christian's knife on his jugular—he watched the chaotic unraveling of his crew. Some scurried to grab their belongings, while the others, toting muskets and swords, frantically hunted them down. There were now a dozen men in the launch, including Ledward the assistant surgeon and Bligh's uppity boys, Hallett and Hayward, who pleaded with Thompson to let them back on board.

"Is this treatment a proper return for the many instances you've received of my friendship?" Bligh knew it would soon be his turn to go over the ledge.

Christian paused, conjuring up a gale to howl in Bligh's face: "I AM IN HELL!" He filled his lungs with another gust of wind. "I would rather die a thousand deaths than bear this treatment any longer!"

Millward held a restrained Fryer nearby, nudging him toward the railing, ready to toss him into the tender with the others. Christian approached the bound shipmaster as Burkitt volunteered to guard a speechless Bligh. "Let me be his sentinel!"

"Wait! Consider what you are doing here!" Fryer pleaded, hoping to convince Christian that all would be forgiven if he would simply call off the mutiny.

"Bligh has brought this upon himself," Christian said somberly before walking away. Millward tightened his grip around Fryer's wrists.

"You'll never succeed in steering this ship!" Fryer yelled out, spurring Christian to swivel around. He lifted his weapon and rammed it against Fryer's shirt. "Not another word or I'll run you through."

"SEND HIM AWAY!" Churchill yelled out, and Millward hurled Fryer headfirst into the launch. There were now eighteen men, still loyal to Bligh, who nervously waited to be cast out to sea, cramped between whatever personal effects they could muster—clothing and journals—and the bulky drums of rations and water that would weigh the boat down to within inches of the ocean's surface.

The time had finally come for Bligh to go overboard. Christian called out to Burkitt to untie the captain from the mizzenmast and walk him forward. "Come Captain," Christian chose his words carefully, which he delivered with unsettling stoicism. "Your officers and men are now in the boat and you must go with them." The frenzied rush of confused deckhands had subsided. The two dozen sailors who remained on board gathered around to witness Bligh's last moments on the *Bounty*. Resigned, Bligh gestured at Heywood to join him in the launch, but the young sailor strode back from the ship's edge instead.

"Ah. Bitten by my own hound, I see."

With one leg teetering between each vessel, Bligh made a final attempt to reason with Christian. "I have a wife and four children back in England. You have even danced them on your knee. Please!"

Christian did not speak. Churchill aimed his pistol at Bligh's head, tickling the trigger with his finger. Bligh committed his second foot to the small boat.

An orchestra of strings—tethers and levers—lowered the launch into the rollicking waves, accompanying a choir of dissonant voices from the *Bounty*'s decks. "Remember me! Witness me!" a handful of seamen still loyal to Bligh were testifying to their departing captain—they had not abetted this treasonous crime. The others cheered and hollered, "Huzzah for Tahiti!" while unhooking the cables from the launch and chucked the prized samples of breadfruit overboard, which plunked into the ocean like cannonballs.

"I'll do you justice when I reach England!" Bligh made one last threat, which rang in Christian's ear just as the swollen sea separated the two vessels forever.

CHAPTER 9

THE BACKWATER EMISSARY
May–September 1789

The melon scent of jasmine wafted over the *tiare* flowers, crystalizing into droplets of perfume the next morning. Mauatua could hear the chirps of excited songbirds heralding the new day, but it was the cooing of conch shells—three long puffs in spirited succession—that coaxed her eyes open.

"They're back!" Faahotu was scampering toward her bedside. Mauatua rose to her feet and plucked a bulb of dewy white petals from her garden, placing it over her left ear.

By the time they walked down to the seashore, the *Bounty* had already lowered its anchor back into Matavai Bay and was surrounded on all sides by wooden outriggers. She found Susannah—perfectly manicured with three red feathers in her hair—alongside Tevarua, Jenny, and a dozen other women keenly waiting to be reunited with their respective sailors. It was strange, though. The ship, once buckling under the weight of a thousand breadfruit cuttings, seemed to no longer have a single plant on board, and only a handful of crewmen, all carrying pistols, were alighting in their dinghy. Christian led the landing party, wearing his linen shirt that Mauatua had reupholstered with the shiny pearl ornaments. They tenderly touched noses. As Christian spoke, she quietly fidgeted with the top button, still perfectly matching the dark opalescence of his eyes. "I need to speak to Teina," he said.

Mauatua led Christian by the hand up to her uncle's thatched pavilion, where he explained to the confused chieftain the reasons for the *Bounty*'s unexpected return: "Our dear Bligh has been reunited with his beloved father, Captain Cook, on the island of Aitutaki." What was once such a divisive and cunning lie now served as Christian's perfect alibi. He continued, "It has been decided that they will build a colony atop fair Aitutaki's fertile soils, where they've already replanted the breadfruit seedlings. And I have been dispatched by my noble superiors to collect the other essentials to help their paradise flourish."

Teina did not hesitate to accommodate his friends' needs, ordering an ark's worth of animals to be rounded up. Within ten days, over three hundred pigs, dozens of goats, a handful of street dogs, and a cow—Cook's own, brought to Tahiti many years ago—were loaded onto the *Bounty*. The chief's enthusiasm even kindled the spark of discovery in some of his devotees; almost twenty men and boys, and nine women—including Mauatua and her friends—were eager to join the new adventure as well.

On the evening before the *Bounty*'s second departure, Christian paused his frantic loading of the ship to indulge in one quiet evening with his mainmast, Mauatua. They visited her family's private *marae*—laying ceremonial blossoms down on the rolled stones of the sanctuary—before retreating behind the vine-draped palisades of her home. Never did she think that she'd welcome Christian back into her private garden, yet there they were, limbs intertwined like the hedges of wild vanilla that cloistered them from view under a blanket of starlight.

"Tell me where we're *really* going." Mauatua knew the story Christian had recounted to her uncle was a lie—he had already confided that Captain Cook was long dead. Christian smiled, summarizing the last six weeks of events that had inspired the *Bounty* to turn around. Mauatua listened while continuing to stare up at the stars—patterns she had memorized like the freckling on her lover's arms and legs—wondering if tomorrow she would journey to such a faraway land that it slept under a sky filled with different celestial bodies.

They were leaving for a place called Tubuai, "a beautiful paradise not dissimilar to Tahiti, just smaller in size," Christian explained. He had assumed command of the ship following a disastrous supply run on the island of Nomuka, and, after moving into Bligh's quarters, used his library to find a suitable location for an outpost of the British Crown. Aitutaki was indeed a real place—they had discovered it upon their departure from Tahiti—but Tubuai was more ideal. He had already surveyed the little island, where, upon their arrival, they had encountered a ferocious band of tribesmen at the mouth of the reef who were easily subdued by the sailors' weapons. The clash was an unintentional show of strength—a dozen Tubuaians were shot—but it would not deter their colonial efforts when they returned.

"And Bligh is waiting for us on Tubuai?" Mauatua wondered.

"No. Bligh . . . Bligh's gone." Christian drew in an uneasy breath, soothed by the scent of the night jasmine.

———————

It was as though Maui, with his celestial hook, had lobbed the top off of one of Tahiti's conical crags and plunked it down in the middle sea some three hundred miles away. Tubuai had the same misty green mountains and black sand beaches that Christian had promised Mauatua, and a sprawling ranch of coral that protected its cyan lagoon from the dark waves of the deep. There was only one small break in the reef where the *Bounty* could glide closer to land: "Bloody Bay," as the mutineers had named it, where they had clashed with a band of hostile tribesmen who were now wearing the spent bullets as jewelry around their necks. The Tubuaians were hardly adorned otherwise—unlike the Tahitians they bore no tattoos, and their small swatches of modesty had been dyed a pale, buttery yellow using local stones or clay.

Like their attire, Tubuaian politics also seemed much simpler than Tahiti's vast ecosystem of clan-held territories and rigid social order. The seventeen-square-mile island was neatly divided into three parts. Its large, westerly domain surrounding Bloody Bay fell under the leadership of Tamatoa, who had already dispatched dozens of outriggers filled with fruits and garlands toward the arriving ship. Christian was relieved at the much friendlier welcome this time around. It seemed having a sizable party of Tahitians aboard eased some of the anticipated tension, and it took only a few sentences for Mauatua to tune her ears into the local dialect.

Christian brought Tamatoa onto the *Bounty*, offering bolts of European cloth as gifts. Mauatua's coterie of Tahitian women— preened by Susannah with colorful flowers and feathers—danced for the chieftain. Tamatoa then reciprocated, inviting Christian to his *marae*, where he performed a special rite of friendship. Christian had Mauatua follow along as his trusted translator and tapped Heywood to join as well, hoping to mold him into a future leader—like how Bligh had handed him the diplomatic reins on Tahiti.

Over ceremonial cups of yava root, doled out in coconut husks, Christian made his intentions clear. He was looking to settle on Tubuai, and he showed the local leader his ambitious plans, scrawled on a blank page in one of Bligh's unused logbooks: a fort measuring fifty yards square, with walls eighteen feet wide and twenty feet high, embellished by turreted towers in all four corners to house each of the *Bounty*'s cannons. An eighteen-foot moat would ring around its walls, and a large tract of turf would be cleared just beyond where Brown, the ship's gardener, could plant an array of taro and other root vegetables to sustain them.

Tamatoa obliged, walking Christian and Heywood down the coast in search of a suitable site while the other mutineers loosed the *Bounty*'s farm animals on shore—a stampede of clomping hooves that sent the villagers screaming into the jungle.

"They're more afraid of our hogs than they are of our guns!" remarked Heywood. Until the mutineers' arrival, the biggest beast most Tubuaians had seen was the native rat.

Although Christian had become fast friends with Tamatoa, he also hoped to broker relationships with the island's other two leaders for good measure. However, Tinarau, who governed the south, was still seething about earlier events; it was his men who were pistoled by the mutineers at Bloody Bay. He had no interest in civility, as made clear by his dispatched brother who—with a warrior's bearing, waving an axe—marched against Christian and Heywood when they tried to invite themselves onto Tinarau's land.

The north was ruled by Taaroa, who welcomed the mutineers with as much pageantry as Tamatoa. Christian and Mauatua duly returned the sentiment with more gifts and dancing. Although it was the smallest chiefdom on Tubuai, the area was more arable than the western half of the island, which was riddled with marshes and swamp. It was quickly decided—with Taaroa's consent—that the *Bounty* would permanently dock on his land, setting up its colony right along the beach, where dozens of sea turtles nested. Christian had Heywood ready a surplus of goods—animals, spirits, and tools—to barter for his desired real estate. Taaroa, however, had his eye on only one thing: "He wants the three red feathers that Susannah wears in her hair," Mauatua explained.

"That's it?" Christian was surprised.

"That's all."

"Well, then, make it so!" He sent Mauatua to cajole a reluctant Susannah into giving up her ornaments and Heywood to Tamatoa's village in the west with news that the *Bounty* would lower its sails in the north after all.

Within two weeks, the foundations of the sprawling citadel were secured, and Christian led by example, rolling up the sleeves of his pearl-buttoned chemise and using every minute of daylight to dig the surrounding moat. He named the future colony Fort George, after the king of Great Britain, His Majesty George III—an attempt to rebrand his mutiny as a mere coup d'état instead of a full-on act of treason against the Crown—and planted the *Bounty*'s large Union Jack where he hoped the drawbridge to his imposing fort would one day unfurl.

And then the raids began. After such a warm welcome, Tamatoa had cut all ties with Christian, interpreting the construction of the colony on his neighbor's land instead of his own as a wicked abuse of his largesse. But it was the southern chief, Tinarau—still bent on revenge for the murders at Bloody Bay—who started terrorizing the mutineers while they were out in the jungle collecting coconuts and firewood. Heywood took a stone to the brow, scraping a scar across his face; Thompson was hit in the chest, bruising his ribs. Petty attacks soon escalated into small spear-wielding war parties warded off by musket fire, and in late August the *Bounty* sustained its first casualty: one of the Tahitian men was concussed by a thrown boulder and slowly bled out from the wound. Taaroa offered his northerly *marae* for the funeral. Besides language, it seemed the only thing the Tubuaians and Tahitians had in common was the way they honored their dead.

After another week, news came from Taaroa's younger brother Tetahiti that someone was killing the *Bounty*'s free-roaming animals, which had started trampling through the island's villages rooting for food. Christian wasn't overly concerned about losing a dozen hogs, but they only had one cow. He pulled four of his most trusted men—Churchill, Millward, Burkitt, and Smith—away from their construction duties and sent them into the brush to bring back their heifer.

Churchill took the lead, crisscrossing through dense tracts of jungle. Perhaps their bovine had wandered into the island's interior in search of shade.

"We should have put a bell on her," mumbled Millward, tired after several hours of wandering. They had scoured all of Taaroa's land and moved south into Tinarau's domain. Churchill signaled to his complaining cohort to keep quiet—he heard a rustling in the branches up ahead. Suddenly a boulder came hurling through the overgrowth, clunking Churchill in the stomach and sending him stammering backward.

"Shit!" he screamed in pain. It was another ambush. "That way!" Churchill pointed down a thin path that led toward the reef. They'd have a better chance of retaliation along the beach after drawing their assailants out from the shadows of the brush. There would also be less ammunition—fewer rocks—for their opponents to throw along the sand. A hailstorm of stones showered down on the four men as they ran toward the clearing, cursing intermittently as they were struck in the head and shoulders. When they reached the shore, their attackers emerged from the jungle: a small group of young Tubuaians—warriors in training—had been deployed on another of Tinarau's missions to harass the mutineers. With fists hardened by years of bar brawling, the sailors began throwing brutish punches at the slender adolescents, bloodying their noses. The Tubuaian gang began to disperse, retreating to their village, but Churchill wasn't done. He dragged one of them down like a lion pouncing on a lithe gazelle, then straddled the upturned teenager, who gasped for air between thumping blows to his face and splashes from the rising tide. Churchill pulled him deeper into the lagoon and plunged his head underwater. The young man frantically windmilled his arms, trying to release himself from Churchill's unwavering grip.

"Stop!" Smith yelled out. The others had successfully rid themselves of the band of troublemakers and had turned their attention to the harried splashing. "He's just a boy!"

But Churchill wouldn't relent, holding the young Tubuaian's head below the surface, his anxious flailing now desperate clawing as he scratched his nails down Churchill's forearms. His hands then flopped back into the water, his eyes—filled with piercing dread—drifted out of focus, and his body became unsettlingly light.

"Let this be a lesson to Tinarau!" Churchill lurched back onto the beach, leaving the lifeless body floating in the shallows.

"He deserved it," scoffed Millward.

Burkitt agreed. "Shark bait."

Smith didn't speak as they resumed the search for their missing cow.

As the fortification's walls continued to go up, the social structure of the colony began to crumble. Christian was the only one invested in a long-term island dream and had to continuously gratify his men with their vices in order for work to progress. Initially, he meted out the alcohol rations as though they were at sea and required everyone to sleep on the *Bounty* to better yoke his ragtag group of sailors under his authority. He made an example of Quintal—putting him in irons—when he disappeared for a night in search of trouble.

"You command only this ship. You are not the captain of my soul. If this is indeed our new home then I am free to disembark as I would back in England." Quintal had a point, and Christian relaxed the rules, allowing two men a night to find comfort on land. The only problem, however, was that the patches of swamp that pocked the island bred vicious swarms of mosquitos and lice that ravaged the mutineers with fever and burrowed into their pale, hairy bodies. Until Fort George was finished, the *Bounty* proved a much more appealing place to camp out, catching wisps of wind on the reef to shoo the insects away and soften the overbearing humidity.

Furthermore, the Tubuaians did not embrace free love as readily as the Tahitians, and they were not keen to let the British share in their wives. The imbalanced gender ratio on the *Bounty*—there were only nine women in Mauatua's brood for over two dozen sailors and a sizable lot of Tahitian men—endlessly frustrated the mutineers, who tempered their obsession in different ways. Thompson's fits of rage had the more waifish sailors spitting out their teeth. McCoy broke into the liquor locker, blurring his misery with Quintal. Martin found Brown to be quite capable with his whole hand and not just his green thumb. And others, like Smith, remained in relentless pursuit of a Tubuaian tryst despite their better judgment.

Jenny mocked Smith's constant lechery; she thought about adding a second *S* to the "A.S." tattoo on her shoulder, if only the Tubuaians practiced body decoration. But she was secretly grateful that he had chosen her as his consort. On Tahiti, Jenny would have never associated so closely with women of a higher caste. It bruised her ego, however, to see her new friends garnering such adoration from their respective men. She considered herself to be just as beautiful, but perhaps there was a beguiling quality belonging only to upper-class women that she did not possess. So she focused her attention instead on caring for the *Bounty*'s dogs—they freely wandered the island like the boars, but each night they would reliably come back to camp to feast on the scraps she had prepared.

"Smith's gone," Brown came running toward Christian from the muddy flats of the taro patch. "He followed a Tubuaian girl into the forest and now I can't find him."

On Tahiti, Christian regularly caught Smith bouncing young women on his lap, half-hidden behind a tree. He'd even pleasure himself on his hammock aboard the *Bounty* while other sailors watched. It wasn't in Smith's nature to wander off for the sake of discretion; he must have been taken by force.

Christian called upon Heywood; they would hike south to Tinarau's house and negotiate Smith's release. He needed some brawn to tag along just in case, but Thompson—assaulted by the constant onslaught of insects—was bedridden with scabs and sores. Quintal and McCoy would do the trick should diplomatic angling devolve into intimidation tactics.

Armed with pistols, the four men combed the jungle for a possible ambush until they finally arrived at the chieftain's home. Smith, wearing only a shirt, had been bound and gagged using a spool of sturdy cordage stolen from the *Bounty*. Tinarau and his bodyguard brother were nowhere to be found. Christian and Heywood tore at Smith's shackles as Quintal and McCoy began dismantling a large reliquary of sacred carvings, chucking the elaborate pieces onto the ground.

"Wait, wait, wait!" Christian called out to Quintal and McCoy, who had unbuttoned the tops of their trousers, ready to desecrate the artifacts. "No, don't. We're taking those with us"—collateral to finally confront Tinarau after so many furtive assaults by his men. With the wooden totems in hand, Christian set the house on fire. The dry thatching of the roof incinerated almost instantly.

As anticipated, the next morning Tinarau approached Fort George demanding the return of his ancestral idols, but he wasn't irate. Instead of weapons, his warriors brandished fruit and plenty of yava poured into various gourds. It appeared to be a truce, but

Mauatua wasn't convinced. The cloudy brew looked different than Tamatoa's welcome cocktail and the funerary beverage served atop their respective *marae*.

"I think it's a trick," she whispered to Christian. "They've poisoned the drinks and will return at night to attack when you're too sick to defend yourself."

Christian knew his refusal of the token of amnesty would lead to retribution, but he heeded Mauatua's warning.

News quickly came from Tetahiti once more that Tinarau was on a rampage to poach the island free of the *Bounty*'s livestock. Additionally, after his recent visit to Fort George, Tinarau had grown suspicious that the large circular ditch—the battalion's defensive moat—was an empty grave ready to be filled with more bodies of his men.

Christian was exasperated. He had affected every version of polite British diplomacy—and even tried a few less gentlemanly ploys—to reestablish his friendship with Tamatoa in the west and put an end to Tinarau's unceasing belligerence, "and everyone's names sound the same!" How could Christian ever hope to broker a truce with people who were more afraid of his pigs than his pistols in a backwater society that preferred a few colorful feathers to money, livestock, or tools? There was one last currency he would try to exchange: brute force.

Christian knew little about war tactics, but was keenly aware that his magic—gunpowder—gave him a major advantage over Tinarau's attacks. He divided the entire complement of the *Bounty* into two cadres: one would guard their ship and fort, and the other would march into the jungle to launch an assault on their enemy. Christian led the charge through the canopy with Burkitt and Thompson on either side. Suddenly, a spear came whirring through the hanging leaves, as if instantly materializing between Burkitt's ribs. He dropped to the ground. The fight had begun. Christian was expecting a skirmish, but Tinarau had launched a war. Hundreds of men began to appear between the trees wearing bright red sashes over their yellow tapa kilts, an army led by a burly warrior sporting a helmet of long black plumes. With each successive war cry, the legions of screaming tribesmen drove the mutineers farther and farther back until they reached the muddy gardens that flanked Fort George's half-built ramparts.

Once in the clearing of his pastures, Christian could better see his attackers. The man sporting the feathered headgear was Tinarau's brother, who promptly dispatched twenty of his spear-slinging warriors at the ragtag battalion of mutineers and Tahitians. A clattering round of musket shots muffled the Tubuaians' hideous war cry, and through the gray haze of gun smoke their leader unleashed another rank of twenty fighters, sprinting beside them, hatchet in hand. The sailors sprayed more bullets, which tore indiscriminate holes through their charging enemies' tawny musculature as they all fainted to the floor. The rest of Tinarau's army, staying safe along the tree line, no longer dared to venture into the dell, even as a few of the fallen men—one bullet not sealing their fate—called out for help.

Christian then ordered his men to reload and advance. Some of the mutineers silenced the groaning Tubuaians haplessly lying in their taro patch, the others kept their barrels and bayonets aimed forward. Thompson's steps were deliberate as he maneuvered his way to Tinarau's brother, who had been shot through both thighs and was inching toward the jungle on his elbows. He tore the feather helmet off the man's head then kicked him in the stomach, flipping him onto his back and releasing his hatchet. Thompson grabbed the weapon and swung it high over his head. He'd had enough. Enough of the tribesmen's constant harassment—SLASH. Enough of the feckless mosquitos that tormented him at night—HACK. Enough of building this ridiculous fortress—CHUNK. He cleaved the warrior's chest until his torso matched the scarlet color of his stole. Driblets of spurting blood now decorated Thompson's face like war paint as he wagged his lifted head; a primal scream heaved from his jowls—born from depths of his booze-addled belly—frightening not only the retreating Tubuaians but also his comrades.

———

ALTHOUGH IT WAS a decisive victory for Christian, he now knew that their colony was untenable; there were still too many variables that hampered its success. Beyond tribal politics—which had escalated into full-blown aggression and retaliation—he continued to face a great deal of defiance within his ranks. The handful of men who didn't have the mutiny's proverbial blood on their hands had stopped digging ditches around the fort. The gender ratios remained ever askew; his most trusted men now refused to work without the comfort of a Polynesian bride. Christian winced, tearing little critters out from under his armpits and crunching them between his finger and thumb. Yes, life was quickly becoming more miserable on this sweaty, swampy island covered in vermin than on the high seas.

"Gather Jenny and the other women," Christian instructed Mauatua. "Start loading our belongings back onto the ship." In the cool shadows of Bligh's cabin, he prepared his words, then summoned all of the *Bounty*'s remaining crew members inside. They would abandon Fort George.

"Gentlemen, I will carry you, and land you, wherever you please." They would sail for Tahiti once more, where Christian would release anyone else who wished to depart. He knew not where he was going but vowed to never again repeat the mistakes he had made on Tubuai. "I desire none to stay with me, but I have one favor to request: that you will grant me a ship and leave me to run before the wind. . . . For I have done such an act that I cannot stay at Tahiti. I will never live where I may be carried home to be a disgrace to my family."

A solemnness filled the crowded quarters, unusual among such a rowdy and perpetually contentious pack of sea dogs.

"I will follow you into the sun," Young finally said. He was overtly not a part of the core group of mutineers who instigated Bligh's disposal but had become hopelessly enamored with Polynesia and wished to stay. His biracial features were a boon on Tahiti, while back in England his "half-breed" status garnered whispers from polite society, despite his rigorous education.

"Aye!" John Mills, the oldest crewman, echoed Young, knowing his complicity spelled certain punishment as well.

"Hear! Hear!" Smith joined in.

The rest of the sailors would have a week to pick their destiny— the time it would take to sail back to Tahiti, where they could fully realize their dreams of living like kings consorting with tribal chieftains and their harems. That was, of course, assuming that Bligh had been committed to the sea. He may have been prone to childish outbursts, but he was also wily enough to steer that little launch by starlight and paddle it all the way back to Spithead if he had to. Christian never dared use a bullet to lend finality to his captain's fate—he would let the wind and waves decide the severity of the punishment—but every time he wondered whether Bligh had in fact found land, the pit of his stomach would ache with gut-twisting dread. The journey with Christian into the unknown seemed perilous and perhaps futile, but at least the mutineers would stand a chance of avoiding the Royal Navy's iron fist, which would drag them back to England and hang them for their crimes.

The next morning, as the mutineers herded their livestock back on board and stowed the rest of their possessions, the *Bounty* acquired two more passengers. Tetahiti, the loyal messenger, had requested asylum—fearful of Tinarau's revenge—and brought along his young cousin Oha, who was around the same age as Heywood.

The ship's anchor had slept on the floor of Tubuai's lagoon for around five months. By the end of the afternoon Christian was ready to crank its rode, landing the rusted iron—now covered in barnacles—back on board. The *Bounty* slowly slid toward the mouth of the lagoon, past Bloody Bay, and back into the churning waters of the deep. As Tubuai vanished into the twilight, Christian's delusions also began to fade. He was not in fact some kind of emissary tasked with the grandiose plan to establish an outpost of the British Empire. He was a fugitive.

CHAPTER 10

THE GEOMETRY
OF SOLITUDE

There was no trumpeting of conch shells to announce the *Bounty*'s arrival—its third—at Matavai Bay. The cruiser slid over the horizon in the early evening, and by nightfall it waded, motionless, close to shore.

One by one, Christian said a very permanent goodbye to most of his coconspirators; he hoped they would never meet again, as it would surely be on the gallows. First, Burkitt—not shipshape after being wounded in the battle with the Tubuaians—then Millward, Thompson, and a dozen more. Christian even bid farewell to Churchill, who had become the honorary son of his chieftain *taio* during their first foray on Tahiti and decided to remain behind.

Besides Young, Smith, and Mills, that left Brown the gardener, Martin, and Williams on board. Like Young, the three sailors were merely guilty by association and not key instigators of the mutiny, but Christian did not question their personal motivations. He was grateful to add some muscle to his skeleton crew. And then there were McCoy and Quintal—the last two men to join Bligh's *Bounty* would also be the final two sailors to consign their fates, journeying with Christian before the wind.

After most of their comrades had departed, there was plenty of room on board for the nine remaining mutineers to welcome dozens of their Tahitian friends for a final gathering. Christian liberally doled out the liquor and snuck away to escort one last sailor off the ship: Heywood.

"You've done nothing wrong, dear cousin. You can no longer accompany me on this journey," Christian instructed, feet planted in the sand. "You've only just become a man here on Tahiti, and have a long and prosperous life ahead of you. When the Royal Navy comes—and in time they no doubt will—you must surrender yourself to them immediately and avow your innocence." Christian then presented Heywood with an envelope. "And when you return to England, I beg of you to deliver this letter to my brother Charles."

Heywood did not speak. Whatever inclination he had to subscribe to the *Bounty*'s next adventure had been quashed by Christian's pragmatism. He slid the envelope down into his jacket pocket while watching his friend climb back on board and quietly cut the anchor cable, letting the ship slowly drift deeper through Tahiti's signature ribbons of tidewater—crystal, turquoise, then blue—all indistinguishable in the blackness of the night.

Although Christian deeply desired that Heywood steer his own destiny, it was with equal deliberateness that he made himself the captain of several unwitting souls. When everyone awoke the following morning, they found themselves over a mile from shore, cruising the navy waves between Tahiti and Moorea. During the night, Christian had mitigated two of the major factors that contributed to Fort George's demise: he had rid himself of anyone who might still be loyal to Bligh, and he had gathered the right ratio of women—a dozen—to finally satisfy his brood. The partygoers who had spent the night on board were now forever bound to the *Bounty*'s next chapter; they had been duped. One woman hurled herself over the rails, attempting to swim back to Tahiti. The others, fearing they would drown, openly wept on the top deck, reaching out to their mother island's coolie-hat-like peak, Mount Orohena.

In the comings and goings of the night before, four more men had also joined the ship's ranks along with Tetahiti and Oha, the faithful Tubuaians: a nobleman from Raiatea named Tararo and three Tahitians—Teimua, Niau, and little Minarii, who couldn't have been more than fourteen.

They sailed in a westerly direction, not dissimilar to the course charted under Bligh's authority when the *Bounty* first left Tahiti. On the upper deck, the mutineers were trying to calm the nerves of the taken women with the help of Mauatua and Jenny. Christian had re-cused himself to Bligh's quarters below to resolve the final issue that had caused Fort George to fail: he needed to find an island without any natives. He thumbed through the cabin's library of old nautical maps and captains' journals, searching for notations about uninhab-ited rocks or passing references to unturned stones. Bligh had taught Christian that while charting latitude was simple—using the sun's apex or the positioning of certain stars—longitude had long proven problematic for explorers. A destination's north-south positioning on the Earth could be quickly fixed to a finite dot, whereas its east-west configuration required an arbitrary meridian—a stripe down the Earth currently imagined along a line that passed through Brit-ain's Royal Observatory in Greenwich. Furthermore, time was the preferred method for calculating longitude, and until the invention of the marine chronometer, which the *Bounty* possessed, a faulty clock on board often meant wildly inaccurate point plotting when a new anomaly was doodled onto the blank sheet of the Pacific. As a result, a mythology of hidden Edens had been born from the myriad misdrawn ink spots that blemished the charts of the South Seas. Armed with modern navigational tools, Christian was determined to triangulate a new geometry of solitude.

For almost two months, the twenty-seven other members of the *Bounty* indulged Christian as he chased down ghost islands like Mendana and Quiros—named after the navigators who had spot-ted them during a fever dream. When they stumbled upon new destinations like Rarotonga that already hosted a local population, they traded goods and rations but never stayed too long. Christian considered aiming for the islands of the Marquesas but chose instead to again steer back along Bligh's original route home, sailing through those not-so-Friendly Islands once more, the haunting at Nomuka still deeply weighing on his psyche. By the time the ship reached Tongatapu nearby, everyone had grown tired of their tentative lives at sea. All of the men and women on board had now paired up, including Quintal and Tevarua, Williams and Faahotu, and McCoy and Teio, the mother of a one-year-old baby named Sully. Smith now pursued Obuarei, leaving Jenny with Martin. They were eager to disembark.

"Perhaps, there are no islands left to explore." Mauatua tried to reason with her fanatical husband, still bent on finding a hideaway so perfect that it likely didn't exist. The Tongan capital was somewhat of an ideal compromise—the land was arable, and those who greeted the ship seemed much friendlier than the Tubuaians—until Quintal drunkenly shot a young man who had climbed aboard wanting to try on Christian's pearl-buttoned shirt.

Christian's mood had swung low, worse than his darkest day on Tubuai. He had grown reclusive in Bligh's cabin, unwilling to contend with the growing dissatisfaction on board. He was sitting on the floor next to the bed when he noticed an unopened tome stuck in the crevice between the captain's table and the timber-lined wall, *Hawkesworth's Voyages*, an illustrated almanac of new territories discovered in the name of the British Crown by Commodore Byron and Captains Cook, Wallis, and Carteret. He tussled its pages until he found a paragraph that caught his eye: a fertile landmass described with such certitude that he knew it wasn't merely the mirage of a weary explorer. It was an island that appeared to have no inhabitants or safe anchorage and was "so high that we saw it at a distance of more than fifteen leagues. . . . Having been discovered by a young gentleman, son of Major Pitcairn of the marines, we called it Pitcairn's Island."

Carteret had plotted Pitcairn in 1767, after which it seemingly drifted off the face of the Earth. Christian knew that the *Swallow*, Carteret's ship, had sailed without a modern marine chronometer, so surely the island's longitudinal readings had been incorrectly deduced. Pitcairn was out there, and he was going to find it.

"Turn the ship around!" Christian came storming onto the upper deck—book in hand—underlining the promising passage with his finger. "Follow the twenty-fifth parallel!" It was their last chance for salvation.

"There are no birds here." Mauatua stared at a cloudless sky. She was lying on her back on a square of thatched matting, which did a pitiful job of softening the *Bounty*'s weathered floorboards. For over a month, after the ship swooped eastward, she had locked herself in the ship's hold. They were in the mouth of the Pacific where the continents yawned wide, and the swaying of the ocean no longer rolled back and forth but whirled in circles like the grinding gears of a clock that ticked slower and slower the further they ventured. Her head didn't spin in the dark below deck, where she preferred to retch over the smell of the penned animals—perpetually damp and riddled with fleas—than have the rest of her senses overwhelmed by vicious bouts of nausea. The women on board had begun to call her Maimiti, "seasickness."

Jenny visited Mauatua daily while tending to the rowdy dogs, bringing her scraps of bread and sometimes the bricks of dried meat the others were forced to eat. She offered updates on the other passengers too. Today's was the best—and only—good news in weeks: calm seas. Mauatua climbed the steps to the upper deck and laid her tartan of sun-bleached fronds down under a halo of tropical sun, a warming glow she hadn't felt since leaving Tahiti.

"We haven't spotted a seabird in a while," Jenny responded. "We're tacking in the teeth of the southeast trades. They would never dare fly this far from land."

Christian was delighted to find the breeze gently combing Mauatua's raven-black hair. The calming of the seas was serendipitously timed with their second Christmas in the South Pacific, an

occasion he hoped to leverage for a bit of goodwill. Under the afternoon sun, Christian planned a feast for his *heiva* and encouraged
everyone to gather around the fresh hog meat and extra spirits he
had earmarked for the holiday.

But Tahitian men and women never dined together—one of
the many taboos that still puzzled the British mutineers. "It was
more than superstition," Mauatua would repeatedly explain. "Breaking these unspoken rules would portend bad luck." At Christian's
insistence—he desired to affirm a sense of community—everyone
joined together as a new tribe with a new set of customs. The men
sang songs and hymns, the women danced, and the ship's dogs
scampered around trying to angle for morsels of pork. Bellies full
and brains soused, the little society of the *Bounty* went to bed after
dark, leaving only a small group of its citizens on the upper deck:
Tevarua, Susannah, McCoy, Quintal, Young, and Williams.

Behind the ship, Orion was low in the western skies—his shield
looked more like a bow with an arrow pointing straight down at the
waves, ready to harpoon a deep-dwelling creature and carry it back
to the heavens.

"Orion the Hunter, son of King Neptune, god of the sea." Young
reached out toward the constellation, tapping each of the three stars
in its belt. "And you can see his canines too, following just behind:
Canis Major and Canis Minor."

"Let's name *him* Canis!" Tevarua suggested, flapping the ears of
the snoring puppy on her knee.

"No, no. He's nothing but a street mutt," Quintal interjected,
nudging the lazing dog, hoping it would crawl back down to the
ship's hold. "Never name a feral animal. They're not loyal pets."

"Is Orion from the Bible?" Susannah wondered, still staring into
the night sky.

"No, if I remember correctly, he's in the *Odyssey*," responded
Young. "That's a book about a different god—well, gods—and the
great journey of a hero and his men."

"Where were they going?" asked Susannah.

"Home, I think," finished Young, who stumbled to further explain why, to him, the Bible represented an absolute truth—parables

to guide good Christians through life—while the Classics were interpreted through the passionless distance of the academic lens.

"Will you sing that Christmas song from the Bible about the dead children?" Susannah now turned to Williams. "The one your King Henry so adored. It's Tevarua's favorite too."

Young laughed. "She means 'Coventry Carol.'"

"Oh, I bloody love that song!" Quintal piped up.

"Wait, Quintal loves music?" Young teased.

"Quintal doesn't love anything besides a double ration of grog," McCoy piled on.

"Ah, c'mon!" Quintal punched McCoy in the arm. "I love it 'cause it's a fucking miserable tune. It's exactly what Christmas is all about."

Williams began to sing, his tenor voice so pure and delicate, hardly a candle flickered:

> *Lully, lullay, thou little tiny child,*
> *Bye bye, lully, lullay.*
> *Thou little tiny child,*
> *Bye bye, lully, lu . . . lay.*

He leaned into the final syllable—brighter than the rest of the mournful melody—then continued:

> *O sisters too, how may we do*
> *For to preserve this day*
> *This poor youngling for whom we sing,*
> *"Bye bye, lully, lul . . . lay"?*

Again concluding with an upturned note.

"Why does it get rather happy at the finish, though?" McCoy interrupted.

"It's called a *tierce de picardie*." Williams had grown up on Guernsey and trilled his French *r*'s with a British brogue. "An unexpected overlaying of a major chord at the end of a minor melody—a little reminder that even the saddest things can end gladly, maybe."

For Tevarua, however, it had never been about the song's unusual cadencing. The Tahitian ear wasn't so sensitive to the major and minor inflections of European music. She liked the sacredness with which "Coventry Carol" was sung. It evoked a markedly different feeling than the other tunes belched out by the British sailors—it was tender; it commanded the solemn attention of those who listened.

Quintal suddenly chimed in, turning the carol into a demented sea chantey:

> Herod the king, in his raging,
> Chargèd he hath this day
> His men of might in his own sight
> All young children to slay.

Susannah slapped Quintal on the shoulder, hoping he'd cease his impression of the verse's despotic subject. Then Williams sang the last part alone:

> That woe is me, poor child, for thee
> And ever mourn and may
> For thy parting neither say nor sing,
> "Bye bye, lully, lu . . . lay . . ."

The ghostly tune settled into its major key one last time, the sound of hope for the sorority of mothers now childless at Herod's behest. There was no drunken applause from Quintal or snarky remark from McCoy, as was usually expected. Everyone stared quietly off the *Bounty*'s stern. The sky had shifted; the top of Orion's arrow had pierced the waves, its shaft and fletching still visible. Maybe he was pointing the way back to Tahiti?

With a sigh, McCoy broke the extended silence. "Another Christmas of unfulfilled promises." Last year, Bligh had sworn he would have his men heading back to England by way of the West Indies, but they had only just dropped anchor in Tahiti's turquoise waters in late October, celebrating the yuletide, instead, with the perverse acrobatics of the *arioi*. And tonight would be no different—an unkept vow to land their band of mutineers on a new colony. Perhaps it was indeed time to turn the ship around.

Down in Bligh's cabin, Christian had tucked himself into bed beside Mauatua and listened to Williams's singing in the unusual stillness of the night, a lullaby that further soothed his wife's seasickness as she slept. But he could hear his comrades airing their grievances too. Mauatua had warned him: Jenny's regular visits had started to bring news of dissent as unpalatable as the scraps of moldy bread and dried meat. There was about to be a second mutiny, and this time it was his turn to be cast out to sea.

Christian looked around his quarters. The room was haunted by Bligh. His tattered books and nautical charts were scattered across his varnished desk—even his pants still hung over the chair—all amplified by the hollow starlight that shone through the open door. Maybe Bligh was right. Maybe he was a skittish seabird after all. His flights of fancy—the mutiny, the colony, and now the quest to find a fragment of volcanic shrapnel blown halfway across the Pacific—had provided nothing but increasing despair. He desperately wished that the "Coventry Carol" could be a parable for *Bounty*'s members too, and prayed for a cadence of hope at the end of this odyssey—his *tierce de picardie*.

CHAPTER 11

THE FALLOUT ZONE

2018

There are no stories of pirates in the South Pacific. While the Caribbean contains thousands of islets where marauding ships could find a sandy beach to stash their stolen treasure, the South Pacific is mostly water—punishing amounts of navy blue water. A desert of ocean, really.

Here, passing vessels never fell prey to peg-legged rumrunners. Instead, tales of moral depravity are relegated to the specks of land themselves, so impossibly far from one another—and away from watchful eyes—that only they bear witness to the bleakest forms of moral turpitude. This is where darker thoughts have their lease, where the scarcity of resources allows the rational mind to act with reckless desperation.

Early European explorers filled their journals with the grim details of cannibalism and human sacrifice, but the region's modern-day history is just as rife with disturbing accounts of torture, incest, and vanishing tourists. The deeper one travels toward the brink of civilization, the more improbable the stories become. In the 1980s, an actual witch hunt took place on the distant isle of Faaite, wherein a mob of religious zealots slaughtered six of their neighbors, whom they believed to be possessed by demons. Until as recently as the '90s, the atoll of Mururoa, more distant still, was used as a live nuclear testing site by the French government, which dropped almost two hundred bombs—some a hundred times stronger than the atomic weapons that flattened Hiroshima and Nagasaki—then tried to cover up the side effects: rampantly rising rates of cancer and deformities in eastern Polynesia.

In the shadow of Mururoa's mushroom cloud—its fallout zone— lies the final passage to Pitcairn.

———————

A WHITE VAN picked me up before 4 a.m. and shuttled me to Tahiti's international airport, where I waited for my flight to the other side of French Polynesia, a thousand miles away. Mangareva was my destination, the largest island in the Gambier archipelago—scattered remnants of an ancient volcanic blast that carve the southeasterly boundary of the region. Like Pitcairn, Mangareva was far too craggy and rugged for a runway, but a raised coral shoal nearby provided the perfect stretch of flat terrain for a landing strip.

The journey on the Air Tahiti propeller plane took four hours, including a stop halfway on a sparsely inhabited atoll where the majority of the passengers disembarked.

After landing on the thin *motu* islet of crushed shells, I was escorted to a small ferry that connected the airport (read: tarmac and shack) to the village of Rikitea, where most of Mangareva's thousand or so inhabitants lived.

The metal spars of the Motor Vessel *Claymore II* dwarfed the other structures along the bay; Pitcairn's cargo freighter was tethered sideways against the dock as it made its final preparations before departure. Built in West Germany during the 1960s, the ship was 160 feet long (almost twice the size of the *Bounty*) and lacquered in thick coats of glossy black paint in an attempt to cover up some of the rusting.

Four times a year, the *Claymore* left the port of Tauranga, New Zealand, shuttling supplies to Pitcairn on its slow crawl across the South Pacific. A detour in the Gambiers allowed Pitcairners and their visitors to reduce the length of their transit time by embarking and disembarking in Mangareva and completing the rest of the journey by airplane. Still, however, two nights had to be spent aboard the *Claymore* for the last three hundred miles of open water. There was no other way to reach Pitcairn.

The freighter wasn't scheduled to depart until the very end of the day, which gave me plenty of time to explore my surroundings.

Long before radiogenic clouds rained poison over its inhabitants, Mangareva was an unlikely stronghold for the Catholic mission, when European priests in heavy robes sailed from island to island smashing ceremonial *marae* and adulterating the Polynesian way of life. Evangelized islanders were put to work, chiseling blocks of granite and coral to build a convent and a cathedral, which, to this day, are set in stark contrast to the airy thatched huts that surround it. The lavishness of the Christian complex starkly contrasts the surrounding poverty as well.

The twin steeples of Saint Michael's Cathedral—the biggest church in all of French Polynesia—rose twice as high as the masts of the *Claymore*. Down the hill, children were kicking soccer balls on a dusty field while their fathers unloaded fish from the backs of their pickup trucks nearby.

Out of town, a ribbon of pavement wound its way up the side of the island's volcanic ridges. I followed the path through a series of hairpin turns until I came down the other side, and there, at long last—far from the rumbling storms that had seemed to permanently enshroud Tahiti—I was finally treated to the quintessential South Pacific view: ample sunshine, swaying palms, and idle outriggers bobbing in a lagoon of Gatorade blue.

At 5 p.m. we were asked to muster aboard the *Claymore* at the picnic tables in the dining mess both to receive a safety briefing and to skip our clocks forward an hour to sync up with Pitcairn (which, in a strange deception of geography, shares the same time zone as the West Coast of the United States). Then the ship's cook—a middle-aged woman more weatherworn than her fellow crewmen—ushered out a long, cafeteria-style tray of our evening meal. It had the look of a microwave lasagna but was made with beans and Mexican spices. "Fusion!" she announced, beaming with unfounded pride.

According to maritime law, the *Claymore* could carry a maximum of twelve passengers on board without being classified as a passenger ship. We were nine. There were six Pitcairners: grandparents with their teenage grandson, and a mother and father with their young daughter in braids. And there were two other visitors besides myself: a retired astronomy professor from New Zealand taking starlight measurements from the island and a wealthy German tourist who was a self-avowed *Mutiny on the Bounty* superfan. He had even made special business cards for the occasion engraved with his name, a small motif of a ship's steering wheel, and "HMAV Bounty Enthusiast" neatly typed underneath, which he eagerly handed out.

A professor, a millionaire, and a girl in pigtails; the allusion to *Gilligan's Island* wasn't lost on me. I, however, was going to purposefully maroon myself on Pitcairn after the *Claymore* departed.

Initially, I had thought the journey on the freighter was going to be a convenient opportunity to start getting to know the various Pitcairners aboard, but everyone scurried below deck and locked themselves away in their berths as soon as they finished dinner. One crewman noticed me lingering and suggested I make use of the showers before we left the dock. "Once we're at sea, you won't be doing much moving around." Even the calmest of weather forecast during the ship's passage still promised the inevitability of thrashing seas.

The first level below the main deck was reserved for the *Claymore*'s crew. Each of the eight members had their own little cabin with scuffed plexiglass portholes. The rest of us were relegated to the windowless hold one more level down, a shrewd reminder that this was not in fact a tourist transport and that, in a way, its nine passengers were cargo too. There was a benefit to being all the way down below, however; the closer one was to the ocean's surface, the less susceptible one was to its rollicking waves.

Each cabin had three beds—two small, stacked berths and a larger double mattress separated by a tiny pedestal sink that came with explicit orders from the captain: "If you're going to be sick, please do it in a bucket instead." The professor and I had been assigned to the same room. I offered him the comfort of the double bed, which he took without hesitation, and I organized my belongings on the bottom bunk, certain that I would fall from the top when we encountered rougher water.

After my shower I explored the rest of the ship. Besides the dining mess, there was only one other common area—a small lounge with a plush sofa pointed at an outdated television and DVD player. Every other area of the *Claymore* had been overtaken by stacks of imported goods. Whatever hadn't fit in the iron shipping containers on the foredeck was crammed into the various nooks and crevices on board. Even the lounge had crates of Spam and pallets of eggs stacked high next to the TV.

At sunset we began to glide through Mangareva's sapphire lagoon. I stepped out on the stern to find the ship's cook chain-smoking a pack of cigarettes. We watched as the volcanic towers of the Gambiers slowly drifted back into the horizon.

"Rippa view," she rasped with her Kiwi twang before puffing another drag.

"I could get used to this," I thought, and began to entertain the fantasy of one day retiring and sailing around the world.

I wandered back upstairs to the lounge for a final glance at the fading archipelago out the window. The ship then began to violently pitch and yaw before emitting a loud, bellowing creak from the deepest bowels of the hull. We had ventured into open water. I should have battened down the hatches like the others, but instead I languished on the sofa, grabbing bolts of its itchy polyester fabric by the fistful while I tried to hold on.

The onset of seasickness is like hearing a really terrible secret. It begins as a whisper—so faint, it's almost a passing notion—but then it starts to get louder, slow at first, but soon it's the only thing on your mind. And when you finally wish you had never heard this terrible secret in the first place, it's already too late. The thought is all-encompassing now, and you have no choice but to blurt it out— only it's not words that come up, but vomit instead.

I was suddenly reacquainted with my taco-lasagna dinner. It didn't look much different from the serving tray.

Pale and green, I sheepishly sought out the captain, who handed me a bucket even before I could muster up the energy to ask for one. I then climbed down to the lowest deck and curled myself up in my bunk. The professor was already asleep, presumably lulled into unconsciousness by the steady motoring of his own flatulence. I was too weak to look for my headphones, so I cupped my hands over my ears until I fell asleep—my dream of one day sailing around the world had become a delusion.

In the late morning on our second day at sea, I managed to extricate myself from the recycled air downstairs and took the captain up on his open invitation to visit the bridge. Out the windows, for as far as we could see, there were only waves and clouds in every direction—swollen mounds of crestless ocean and caravans of cumuli and nimbi unbroken by landfall. On the nautical charts, our journey seemed short relative to the surrounding vastness of the page. I mouthed the names of the other dots on the map—sacred oases across the void—but we would pass none of them, even within distant eyeshot, on the final push to Pitcairn.

From the captain's chair, I watched how a shoreless sea could roll even a hulking freighter on a relatively calm day. The *Claymore*'s front mast ticktocked like a metronome, as though it were eagerly trying to sip the Pacific as it swung from side to side.

Worried our dinner would be another calamity of mismatched ingredients excused as fusion cuisine, I snuck back down to the hold, tucked myself into my berth, and cracked open my emergency stash of granola bars before closing my eyes to better relieve myself of the interminable nausea.

At around 4 a.m. I awoke to the most grating sound of scraping metal, a shrill squeaking that reverberated across the vessel like a dentist's drill. The freighter was unspooling its anchor—it dropped hundreds upon hundreds of feet to the bottom of the ocean despite our proximity to land. I immediately crawled out of my bunk, climbed the ladders up to the main deck, and peered overboard to find the high beams of several blue-green floodlights shining out from the ship's hull just below the waves. They had attracted hundreds of writhing reef sharks that were basking in the glow as they hunted for tropical fish.

In the quiet of the moonless night I couldn't see the island, but I knew Pitcairn was there.

CHAPTER 12

THE QUIET

JANUARY 1790

The sails were never without wind in the loneliest part of the ocean; they flapped desperately, staccato, like a stork leaving its roost. The mutineers had given up on keeping watch. Another month had passed and only Christian manned the perch in the evenings, catatonic from too many restless nights. Down below lay a massacre of sleeping men and women, the village of the *Bounty* splayed on the upper deck and lulled into soundlessness by the yawing of the keel.

Quintal, consumed by fury, was awake. He had pulled up a piece of the brine-soaked floorboard and, with a paring knife, slowly whittled it down to a point like a knight sharpening his blade. His strokes were long and purposeful as he collected his thoughts. He must turn the ship back toward Tahiti. He'd do it by force if he needed to.

Young was staring skyward nearby, his shoulders propped up against an empty crate once overflowing with seedlings and soil. He cradled Susannah's head in his lap and watched the mainmast swish back and forth against the cosmic shield.

The quietest clatter pulled Young's attention away from the moonless night. Quintal had dropped his tools and tiptoed toward the starboard railing. They locked eyes; Quintal's were wide with anticipation and dread. He stared intensely back at Young while slowly lifting his arm; his finger, pointing overboard, pierced the indigo cloak of night and sea.

In two leaps Young had joined Quintal at the side of the ship, plunging his nails into the mush of the weathered banister and craning his neck with disbelief. He had inadvertently awoken Susannah, who groggily stumbled over to his side. "What is it?" she wondered, placing one hand atop Young's to steady herself as she rubbed her eyes with the other.

A shapeless form came into view—too large to be an earthly creature—twisting and bending as the *Bounty* continued its approach.

"Leviathan," breathed Young, in a tone so soft that the whipping wind quickly scraped it away like sea-foam. "The unconquerable monster who lives over the Sources of the Deep," he said, his voice growing stronger.

"From your Bible?" Susannah asked.

"Book of Job," nodded Young.

Susannah squeezed the top of Young's hand even harder as the seaward body began to take on a ruthlessly vertical form, a hulking torso of cliffs and stone.

"Don't be scared," consoled Young, as they watched in awe. "This is our salvation. It is foretold that the righteous will feast upon the Leviathan at the end of time . . . at the end of our journey."

"Are we the righteous?" Susannah asked.

"Ha. Good question," Quintal muttered.

Daybreak splashed across the horizon like candlelight from under a closed door, and the full scope of the island's body suddenly came into view: a long, inhospitable rock face without a welcoming arm of land reaching down toward the waves.

"MR. CHRISTIAN!" Young yelled up to their leader, napping in the crow's nest. His booming cry woke the others, who wondered if they were still dreaming as they glimpsed the lonely isle. "*Fenua maitai*," the good land, they cheered, as others wept with happiness.

Frantic, Christian fetched the ship's Larcum Kendall marine chronometer from his cabin and carried it out into the dawn. He then stared at the landmass rising in front him, reciting Carteret's log entry by heart: "A great rock rising out of the sea, not more than five miles in circumference, covered with trees with a small stream running down its side . . . and surrounded by unimaginable stretches of water." He paused, stunned into breathlessness. "It's Pitcairn—this is Pitcairn's Island."

CARTERET NEVER SET foot on the lonely rock—"It was pounded by violent unhindered surf, which made landing treacherous if not impossible"—but he got close enough to marvel at its fecundity, which had ignited Christian's ambitions.

The *Bounty* battled its way toward the island for two more days. Each time it maneuvered an approach the swells grew larger, as though some greater force was purposefully rebuffing their attempts to make landfall. The wretched cocktail of anticipation and seasickness had poisoned even the hardiest of seafarers on board. Mauatua, in particular, clung to the bow of the boat, perpetually heaving overboard.

Finally they broke through. Christian would leave Young in charge of the ship and lead a small surveying party ashore to spend three days assessing whether they could truly sustain themselves on the isle. He tapped McCoy, Brown, and Williams to join, plus the three Tahitian men—Teimua, Niau, and Minarii—to help steer the way in the *Bounty*'s dinghy and negotiate any surprises on land.

The rolling seas dropped their boat onto a jagged reef that would have easily broken up a bigger vessel. They slid into the waist-deep water and navigated a maze of boulders belched forth by a primordial volcano then rounded and smoothed by the perpetual crashing and ebbing of the tide. A skin of algae coated the outcrops, making them impossible for the sailors to grip as whips of seaweed coiled around their ankles, pulling them down into the undertow.

Finally on land, the men rested—outstretched on large dry rocks like reptiles—before attempting an almost-vertical ascent onto the island's plateau. Their first upward steps loosened the earth above, raining down red dust, and higher up they were devoured by a hot, wet tongue of rotting leaves and vicious mud.

Once they reached less precipitous ground, the seven men organized themselves into a single file. Teimua led the way, adze in hand, slashing narrow passages along overgrown paths that spread like sinuous veins. He paused under a large tree drooping with bulbous fruits and ripped one the size of his fist off from its stem, then sharked his teeth through its peel. It bled bright purple. "Guava!" he smiled, handing one to Christian behind him, who bit into the fibrous sphere with similar gusto. They laughed, savoring the puckery flavor, a huge improvement from the scraps of salted meat aboard the *Bounty*, rendered so bland after two months at sea that they no longer tempted even the rats.

They passed more fruit trees—plantains and coconuts dangled overhead—mulberry trunks, and pandanus palms. To their delight, they found yams, taro, and even sweet potato growing underfoot. Brown, the gardener, brought up the rear, dutifully cataloging the island's abundance and spouting off the flora's scientific nomenclature with glee: "*Allophylus rhomboidalis, Senna gaudichaudii, Colocasia esculenta . . .*"

But something wasn't right. There was a strange geometry to the way the fruits and vegetables were growing. Brown paused to take a closer look—yes, only the craftiness of man could organize nature's chaos in such a measured fashion—then sprang back to his feet in terror: there are other people here.

He refocused his attention back on his comrades, but they were gone—disappeared into the impenetrable brush that grew more forbidding with each step. He yelled to them without reply, then began to sprint while frantically waving his arms; branches scratched his side and cobwebs veiled his face. A surface root snagged his hurried footing and he collapsed onto the gritty mix of loam and soil that carpeted the island's floor. He desperately clawed his way back to his feet, hobbling as he ran. Surely he was being followed.

When he finally found the others, they were standing bewildered in front of a small clearing. A sweeping stone *marae* lay just beyond, decorated in glyphs and framed by bushy breadfruit trees. Brown and Christian exchanged glances. Carteret was not Pitcairn's discoverer after all. The island clearly belonged to someone else, but were they still home?

Before nightfall Christian chose a concealed spot in a small glade for their rudimentary camp. They dared not light a fire and reveal their position, as there were still too many unexplored crags and crevices where someone, or something, could be hiding. They sat in a circle, monitoring any potential danger lurking over each other's shoulders, and feasted on fresh fruit until the darkest stripe of night set in, amplified by the pervasive shade of the overgrowth.

Christian, McCoy, and Minarii kept the first watch while the others slept. Brown was restless, however, haunted by the traces of other island dwellers they had discovered earlier in the day. "It's so quiet," he whispered. The only sound was the plinking of tiny *lilikoi* seeds that McCoy spat into the center of their circle. He broke the silence. "Say, Minarii, do you know the story of Jonah and the whale?" Minarii shook his head as McCoy continued. "There once was a man named Jonah who was asked by God to go to the village of Nineveh. But Jonah refused. He had a premonition that something terrible would happen to him if he did, so he escaped to the open seas with a band of friends." McCoy paused and glanced at Christian. "But misfortune followed—rain, wind, and waves—until Jonah's friends realized that it was all his fault. They wanted to toss him overboard, but instead Jonah was swallowed by a great monster of the deep. And there he spent three long and lonely days, miserable in the bleakest, blackest pit of the whale's belly."

"What's your point, McCoy?" Christian rolled his eyes. But Minarii wanted to know more. "What happened next?"

"Well Minarii, I don't quite remember." McCoy flashed a big, toothy smile through his brambly beard. Minarii turned to Christian for an answer, but he didn't have one either.

"Shut up, McCoy." Brown added, lying on the ground trying to sleep.

On the second day, the men followed the island's spine all the way down to its thin, rocky tail—it curled landward around a small cove fed only by the occasional splash of an overbearing wave. They baptized themselves in its crystalline waters, washing away the putrid dirt that the island had spat at them while exploring. Further on, they cataloged more trees proffering exotic fruits and found the stone foundations of several toppled dwellings—the homes of the long departed. It would be here that they'd set up camp after landing the rest of their brethren.

They returned to their same hideaway on the second night, and on the morning of the third day negotiated impossible sea swells to return to the *Bounty*.

"The island has exceeded my most sanguine hopes," Christian preached to his community, both anxious and desperate, "in its fertility, its beauty, and, above all, in its inaccessibility." He spoke of arable soil, fresh water, and recounted a long list of the great plants and trees that would provide shelter and sustenance while doling out dozens of ripe fruits brought back aboard the dinghy. "The race which had planted these, ready for their use, have thankfully abandoned this little paradise."

Christian ordered the *Bounty* to the northeasterly side of the island, where it could get close enough to shore to be tethered to the trees with a rope. "We're home."

THE GRASSY SPOT where the twenty-eight souls of the *Bounty* finally touched terra firma would be known from then on as the Landing Place. They would build their camps along the ridge just above using the foundations of the ancient inhabitants' stone structures, well hidden behind a phalanx of trees. The pigs, chickens, goats, and dogs were landed with extra care, making sure that none were drowned. Even Baby Sully was put in a barrel and floated to shore. Lighter cargo—dishware, books, and seedlings for planting—came off next, followed by furniture. Finally, the sails were dropped for tenting, and some of the ship's timbers were torn from the decks and bow for additional housing construction. Their tired bodies trembled as they fought the island's punishing verticality, hoisting cargo—heavier and heavier—up what they dubbed the Hill of Difficulty to their makeshift village. Not a drop of rain quenched their sweaty brows, and the protective forest—the shield against a seafarer's spyglass—also blocked the islanders from redemptive ocean breezes.

Nevertheless, progress was quickly forged. Williams, the *Bounty*'s armorer, sharpened their tools and weapons. Jenny groomed the dogs, who squealed with excitement after months in the ship's hold. Faahotu scoured the underbrush, collecting medicinal herbs and flowers. Brown found a freshwater well and started pruning the bumper crops that had been planted hundreds—or maybe thousands—of years ago. As the others readied small garden plots and tilled a communal vegetable patch, they unintentionally excavated more artifacts from the island's past: fish skulls, spear heads, and rudimentary tools. It seemed, perhaps, that Pitcairn's original keepers had primed the land to be used as some kind of supply station between long overseas journeys. But for one reason or another, they never returned to enjoy the literal fruits of their labor.

On her knees, Mauatua was using a small trowel to loosen the earth into a more suitable plant bed when its metal tip clinked against something solid in the ground. She dug around with her fingernails and unearthed a long whalebone that had been carefully fashioned into a comb. She scrubbed it clean using the coarse tapa cloth of her dress and marveled at its ornate design—ten long prongs and a maze of spirals adorning the handle—wondering if perhaps it once belonged to a *raatira* princess like herself.

A dark hand reached down and firmly cupped the ball of Mauatua's shoulder as if she had conjured the spirit of the relic's owner, back to reclaim her possession. Frightened, she dropped the implement, its sawtooth wedges tucking into the upturned earth. It was Faahotu. She had brought Mauatua a bouquet of flowers: long green stalks, pulled up from the root, with bursts of scarlet bristles on top. "Flame ginger, to help with the dizziness." She explained how to boil them into a medicinal tea as Mauatua reached for her fallen artifact and wiped it clean.

"I don't think this island was just an outpost." Mauatua presented Faahotu with the whalebone comb. She ran her fingers along the black circular grooves etched into the ivory, then held it up to the afternoon light for further inspection. She paused, then clasped Mauatua's reluctant palm. "Come with me."

The two women walked for what felt like almost an hour, straight across the island until they could see the ocean on the other side. They stopped on a treeless knoll where the earth cascaded less precipitously down to the waves when compared to the rest of Pitcairn's cliff-ridden shores.

"What are we looking at?" Mauatua wondered, winded and wobbly from the trek.

"Wait for it," exhaled Faahotu, watching the sun glide into the golden glow of eventide. The tumbling escarpment of sod and stone suddenly lit up, revealing a glittering field of black crystals—an obsidian mine, chipped away by the ancient dwellers.

"I found it the other day when searching for wild herbs," she added while Mauatua watched the twilight bend its way through thousands of little prisms.

On Tahiti, volcanic glass was a prized commodity of unknown origin, coveted by the mightiest of tribal chieftains as tools and jewelry. Perhaps a prosperous little kingdom once flourished here, rich in goods traded for their unique, dark diamonds.

Mauatua returned to the Christian camp just as the sun dipped into the sea for its nightly rest. She started a small fire over which she boiled some fresh water in a little iron drum. When the liquid started to roll, she tore up the flame ginger petal by petal and tossed it in, creating a bloodred brew while stirring it with a long twig. Christian didn't want any—he was already lying down, lost in thought. He was pondering an issue that had plagued him since their arrival: they had stripped their ark down to its skeleton, but it remained a viable watercraft—both a lifeline for a furtive escape and an announcement of their position to passing ships. He sat up and played through a series of uncertain futures with Mauatua: What if a faction of dissenters arose? He already had trouble managing Quintal and McCoy—would they seize the ship one day and give up the location of their hideaway? He would raise his concerns with the other mutineers in the morning, and they'd put it to a vote.

Christian had no trouble dozing off now that they had found a bolt-hole, but for Mauatua the world still spun even when she closed her eyes. Every time her thoughts finally began to drift, she'd be roused back to consciousness by the incessant yapping of the dogs.

She sprang up, frustrated, and drew light tracks along the veins of her forearm with the prongs of the carved whalebone. "You know we have a bigger problem than the conspicuousness of our ship."

"The dogs." Christian opened one eye.

"Yes, the dogs. They haven't stopped barking since we arrived. You can probably hear them ten leagues away. They'll give away our position long before anyone would even see the *Bounty*!" Mauatua started pacing.

"You're right. I'll bring it up with the men tomorrow. Now come back to bed, my mainmast," entreated Christian with an open arm.

She returned to Christian's side, but was still preoccupied. "What if they never left?"

"What—who? The dogs?"

"No. The ancients," she showed him the ivory comb.

"What do you mean?" Christian examined the object in a cursory fashion. "We've found no sign of anyone else living here. They've all gone."

"No, I know. What I'm trying to say is . . ." Mauatua swallowed her fear, now indistinguishable from her sick. "What if they never left because . . . because something terrible happened to them here?"

THE DEXTEROUS TAHITIAN hand fit snuggly into the European glove of democracy. The men were Pitcairn's social architects while the women's savoir faire built its physical walls. The mutineers met each morning with a semblance of navy decorum as they ironed out a verbal covenant, delegated tasks, and voted on contentious issues like the fate of the dogs, and, more difficult, what to do with the *Bounty*. A dozen garden plots had been hoed, and seeds were planted. Now mulberry bark was culled for new tapa-cloth gowns and pandanus leaves stripped for thatching.

"First you must pluck out all of the thorns from the screw pine." Tevarua was giving Susannah her first lesson in resourcefulness, the maid and the maiden sitting cross-legged next to one another, now equals of circumstance. Tevarua's hands were large and calloused. The needles easily sluiced through her fingers as she glided them up one side of a thick frond and down the other. Susannah winced each time she pricked herself, resenting the notion that her manpower was now more valuable than her femininity. She had always taken to self-care with the same discipline that her peers applied to chores and cookery—she wasn't ready to forfeit her beauty.

Quintal suddenly emerged from the jungle with an unwavering focus in his gait. He marched straight past the seated women and their green quilt of folded fronds. "Where's my shovel?" His voice rumbled from the interior of their hovel.

"It's in the garden," Tevarua gently answered as she continued to weave the pandanus leaves into interconnecting bows. "Are you planting more taro?"

Susannah paused her work, unnerved by the mania in Quintal's cadence.

"I'm taking care of something much more important." Quintal grabbed the rusted spade and carried it like a trident. "We've traveled too far to let our country be discovered because of a few mangy mongrels," he added.

"What do you mean?" Susannah was confused, but Tevarua knew exactly what Quintal was implying. During their first few nights on the island, she had let the smallest of the *Bounty*'s dogs sleep at their feet, but he'd bark and root around in the dirt, disturbing Quintal, and was quickly sent to Martin's camp, where Jenny kept the other animals.

"Wait, please! Don't hurt them!" Tevarua desperately threw her hands around Quintal's ankle, hoping to weigh him down like a ball and chain.

"Get off me, woman!" Quintal shook his leg, but Tevarua wouldn't let go. She collapsed her muscles along the dusty earth, heavy like the metal shackles Christian had forced Quintal to wear on Tubuai. "Let me go to Martin's land and be done with this already!"

Tevarua began to sob, mustering only a whimpering, "Please . . ."

"Jenny loves those animals, you know. She'll never let you touch them!" Susannah stood up but paused before daring to take a step closer.

"Ha, she can try! She's only fond of them because she thinks she can control them. If she did a better job of it, I wouldn't have to intervene." Quintal yelled, punting Tevarua in the cheek with his other foot. She rolled onto her back, muffling a long, piercing scream with her hands. Susannah rushed to her side, lifting Tevarua by her arms so she could rest her head on Susannah's shoulder as she wept, her fingers still obscuring the pain Quintal had inflicted.

"And besides, it was Mauatua's idea to do away with these bitches." Quintal, unremorseful, stood over the two young women. They looked up at him, speechless, unsure whether to believe him. "And what did I already tell you? Never name feral things because they can't be trusted. It's their animal instinct."

"Then why'd your mother bother naming you?" Susannah spat at Quintal, who raised his shovel over her head.

"I won't waste five bullets on those hounds, and I won't dent a perfectly useful shovel to wreck your face." He began to walk away. "I'll put a child in you if you really want something to care for." Then he squinted at Susannah—"You too"—before disappearing into the overgrowth.

Susannah slowly pulled Tevarua's fingers off of her face, wincing when she saw the purple bruising.

"I'll be fine," Tevarua sniffed, wiping her nose with the inside of her elbow. "We have to keep working on these roofing palms. Mauatua is depending on us." Susannah reluctantly obliged, if only to provide her friend a distraction from the pain.

They sat quietly for a while, fixated on their toil. The constant swishing and folding of the long, dried leaves felt meditative—soothing, even—until they heard Jenny's shrieks of protest from the other side of the forest. Susannah squeezed her eyes shut, trying not to commit the sound of Quintal's actions to memory. Tevarua sang quietly as she continued to stitch and sew:

Lully, lullay, thou little tiny child,
Bye, bye, lully, lullay.

Susannah joined in, louder, to better conceal the muddled yelps and dull thudding of the dogs' slaughter.

Thou little tiny child,
Bye, bye, lully, lullay.

Never once did Tevarua look up from her latticework.

———————

SMITH STOOD ALONE on a long crest of white sand separating a turquoise lagoon—glassy and waveless—and a dewy field of clover dotted with the occasional palm. Birdsong filled his ears. It was everything he had imagined before leaving England on this misadventure, when he'd listen to sailors muse about their exploits on the South Seas with Captain Cook. But a strange apparition disturbed his placid smile. The glint of the Polynesian sun obscured its form at first, but as Smith drew closer he saw someone floating facedown in the shallows. He waded through the tidewater and flipped the body over. It was the teenage boy Churchill had so callously drowned back on Tubuai. His eyes, wide with shock, were bulging from his bloated face. How could this be? Panicked, Smith began to pull him to shore, first by the hand, then the foot, but he couldn't muster enough energy to drag his corpse onto the beach. The boy's legs were splayed on the wet sand, but his chest and head bobbled underwater as though he had been severed at the waist.

There was no time to salvage his body—a figure on the horizon was ominously approaching, waving a large hatchet. Smith couldn't escape. The powdery sand proved more viscous than he remembered, and he began to sink into a tidal mix of pebbles and shells. The faceless stalker moved faster, unaffected by the slushy consistency of the sand. Smith cowered behind his upheld hands, shaking as he waited for the mortal swing of the scythe that never came.

There was now another man walking along the beach. It was the handsome Tubuaian warrior whom Thompson had demolished with his axe, put back together again. The mysterious assailant was instead moving toward him with even more speed. Smith desperately wanted to yell out but couldn't muster much more than a whimpered warning. He watched helplessly, horrified, as the faceless man hacked the pleading Tubuaian warrior to pieces once more.

Smith gasped when he awoke. Obuarei was still asleep beside him, oblivious to the terrors of his subconscious. He sprang up from the ground, seeking something to douse his mind's fire. He repeatedly smashed a rock over a felled coconut until it cracked open; he poured its fizzy contents over his upturned face, cupping his hands over his scalp as he slicked back his long, milk-soaked hair. Wiping his eyes, Smith noticed a warm orange hue emanating from just beyond his camp. He wasn't dreaming.

There was now enough of an ambient glow to light the way. Smith followed the ridge until he reached the lookout over the Landing Place and stared down, aghast. The mutineers had yet to vote on the *Bounty*'s fate, but the ship was burning in the bay. Flames had burst through its caulking seams, feeding on the boiling tar. The forward mast came crashing down onto Bligh's former cabin. This time, Smith could scream—loudly. He saw the arsonists down below: Quintal had torched the carpenter's storeroom while McCoy cheered him on from the shore.

Obuarei quickly found Smith, having already realized that he'd wandered into the night. Then, one by one, the others joined them on the ledge until all of the *Bounty*'s souls stood together, Pitcairners newly anointed by the wicked spectacle they beheld. The upper deck collapsed through to the hold below while the glass in each window shattered, overwhelmed by fire. The ship's gilt scrolling, fanciful but long weather-beaten, warped into the illegible lyrics of some satanic prayer as it melted off the stern. No one spoke, not even to reproach Quintal and McCoy. There was nothing to be done.

A loud cracking sound echoed across the anchorage when the iron ballasts dropped through the hull's copper sheathing, snapping the ship in two as they plunged to the bottom of the ocean. Almost the entirety of the vessel was now submerged, still burning red-hot under the shallow waves as it was dragged down to hell.

The *Bounty* was gone.

THE NEXT MORNING, Christian faced not only the other mutineers but all of his fellow castaways—even Baby Sully bounced on Teio's lap—and addressed them with the same warbling conviction and pageantry that had won him their allegiance on Tahiti but faded after months of uncertainty on the high seas. He reminded his new countrymen that they no longer needed their vessel, as they had—after much wandering—finally reached the promised land.

With a long stick, Christian drew a large triangle in the dirt, a crude map of their world, which he divided into nine parcels of arable land, one for each mutineer and his consort. Christian would retain his current acreage, his house now reinforced with the *Bounty*'s timbers near a craggy spire riddled with nooks and caves. Young and Susannah, for example, would live next door. Smith and Obuarei got the land under the shade of a great banyan. Brown and his spouse, Teatuahitea, were given the gardens that hung over the obsidian field on the south side of the island. The Polynesian men—deemed more resourceful then the English—would be relegated to the difficult terrain in the east. Since there hadn't been much permanence to the initial arrangement of the encampments, Christian hoped that the creation of little fiefdoms for his peers would rekindle their loyalty.

The women wanted Mauatua, their leader, to quell their flurry of emotions. Susannah, always armed with a quip, was quiet. Tevarua hid her sorrow—and bruising—behind a thick tress of wavy hair. Mauatua spoke of the valor of their sacrifice in order to help their men realize their island dream. Something, however, was different about Jenny—she had become withdrawn after Quintal stormed her encampment, shovel in hand. Neither the *Bounty*'s burning nor Mauatua's warm words had melted her icy demeanor.

Back on Tahiti, Mauatua had long watched her chieftain uncle Teina make difficult decisions for the greater good. She had no
qualms about leading with a similar sense of unwavering duty. She
had navigated Tubuai's suffocating politics more successfully than
Christian, but perhaps on Pitcairn—smaller still, where one person's
shifting allegiance could mean a dramatic change in power—she
would think more carefully about cause and effect before committing her ideas, like killing the dogs, to words. She may have
possessed Jenny's friendship, but she hadn't garnered her blind devotion. Mauatua looked into Jenny's eyes once more—black and
expressionless—and knew that their kinship was forever broken.

And then there was the question of what to do with Quintal.
He could not be villainized for disposing of the noisy hounds. Their
fates had been mutually agreed upon by the men who hadn't yet
deliberated the *Bounty*'s destiny. But was burning the ship deeply
maligned, or was Quintal performing a misguided act of civic duty?
Destroying the last trace of their heist was the only true way to
secure their safe haven, but there was a mean streak—something
unhinged—to his vigilantism that alarmed the others. Regardless,
punishing Quintal was moot. They weren't going to fashion a brig
with their limited supply of construction materials. Besides, less op-
timistic voices argued that they were already living on some kind of
island prison.

———

INITIALLY, THE DAILY ceremony of making a bed seemed like an
unessential and overly servile task that distracted from more pressing matters, but Mauatua obliged at Christian's insistence. Perhaps
it reminded him of the home he'd never see again. There was no
such similar tedium in Tahitian culture—even the term "routine"
seemed untranslatable—but she had begun to enjoy the particulari-
ties of a custom clearly designed for a far less temperate climate. As
her husband was the *Bounty*'s captain, she had inherited all of the
sleeping accoutrements from Bligh's quarters: reams of bedclothes

and even some pillows. Every morning she'd reconsolidate the contents of their makeshift mattress, a small pile of hay over which was draped a generous swatch of the ship's mainmast sail. Then she'd perfectly pleat each layer of blanketing on top, first the thin linens, then the duvets stuffed with goose down. Christian would tussle the fabric, his body drained of its vitality by the tropical fever that ravaged him nightly, and the cycle would start anew the following morning. The entire proposition seemed absurdly lavish considering that the structure of their home wasn't yet complete, but nevertheless Mauatua feathered her nest, which she greatly preferred to the punishing rigidity of the *Bounty*'s gopherwood floorboards—now the walls of her makeshift abode—on which she had languished for so many weeks. She had finally found some rest.

Christian, however, couldn't sleep. He had stuffed more hay under the cotton sail for a cozier slumber, but the coarse material choked his clammy skin. Lying on his back, he had clasped his fingers under his head, his palms soaked through as they held the weight of his weary countenance. Even on land, his hair had remained perpetually damp; an alloy of sweat and dust had gnarled his mane into unbreakable curls. He stared up at a boundless sky made hazy by the waxing moon. The pandanus roofing on his makeshift house was days, maybe weeks, away from being finished, but it didn't matter. There hadn't yet been a threat—or hope—of rain since arriving on the island.

Christian had memorized every aster in the star field, the only constant during the last eight months besides Mauatua's inextinguishable devotion. They were the same celestial "stalks," as she had once called them, holding up the heavenly canopy over Tahiti to guide its mariners. There was Ana-mua burning scarlet, Ana-roto glowing violet, and unwavering Ana-ni'a, which he remembered from his childhood: Polaris, the compass rose.

He traced a swooping line across the cosmic garland, starting with Hokulei, the brightest bulb, and paused to remember the myths and legends—lullabies etched into the darkening sky—of each subsequent star as he blotted them out with a passing finger. While at sea he'd hum or sing to himself for solace during his evening watch—the constant thrashing of the waves was the orchestra for his lonely torch songs—but tonight he dared not make a sound. Mauatua had finally found some rest. She lay still on her side with her mouth slightly ajar as the moonlight touched the tips of her front teeth—they had lost their luster after her time on the *Bounty*; she was never able to find her sea legs. He realized then that he couldn't remember the last time he had seen her smile. She had mustered an exhausted grin when they finally found Pitcairn, but even back on land she continued to feel unwell.

From their elevated position in his new domain, Christian could no longer hear the crush of the waves. The night creatures were unusually quiet too, choked by the unyielding heat that also blanched his tongue. Not even a rat tried to scratch its way into one of the burlap sacks of salted meat; they had all scattered or drowned when the *Bounty* smashed its bow against the boulder-ridden shore. The silence weighed Christian down like the linen blankets he had already kicked off of his legs, but it was the looming foreverness that felt insurmountably heavy, as though he were trapped under the *Bounty*'s iron ballasts that now lay on the ocean floor. Could the other men truly fathom that (if everything went according to plan) they'd never return from this, the farthest of lands? There were no new stars to chart, no new songs to learn, and they'd never see a new face again, save those—God willing—of their future progeny.

And what about his forebears, the ancient custodians of this paradise? What tragedy had befallen them? An unknown terror yet to be revealed? Had Christian unwittingly condemned his disciples to a similar fate? Were they forever trapped inside the belly of the whale? He couldn't breathe. He sat up, clawing at his neck to save himself from drowning in an eddy of quietude.

"What's wrong?" Mauatua mumbled, her sleep disturbed.

"It's nothing," panted Christian, staring into the darkness, unsure if his eyes were open or closed. It was Nothing.

CHAPTER 13

THE MUSEUM PEOPLE

2018

I waited with anticipation on the main deck as the morning's first light cast a topaz glow over the brooding rock. The surrounding sea seemed unaware of Pitcairn's existence, swerving and sloshing—enlivened by the moon's gravity—as it crashed against the island's cliffs in a chaotic fit. The *Claymore* was anchored in the safety of the deep over a mile away.

A wooden longboat had propelled itself away from the jungle-draped shoreline, arcing a path in our eventual direction. After it docked alongside the freighter, a member of its crew boarded our vessel to complete the immigration paperwork on the picnic tables in the dining mess. I could hear the longboat clanging against the *Claymore*'s metallic hull as our passports were inspected and stamped. Then, back on deck, we carefully disembarked one by one over the side railing; our suitcases and small bits of cargo went over the ledge next.

The three hundred miles of open water from Mangareva posed legitimate hazards, but the final mile to Pitcairn was, on many occasions in the island's history, a deadly gauntlet of clawing, pernicious waves. Our tender was nothing more than a wide-hulled canoe; its helmsman had to anticipate every swell and know exactly when to rev and cut the engines, lest we be tossed overboard and dragged all the way down to the ocean's depths. The motor fell silent on a final crest of the surging tide. It lifted us twenty feet above the harbor before rolling us down into the safety of the Landing Place, where Christian and his comrades had found their way ashore long ago, now sheltered by a long concrete pier.

I wanted to kiss the dock's cement as I was pulled out of the longboat by both arms. The gathered onlookers briefly broke into song—"We from Pitcairn Island," sung to an early twentieth-century hymn—before hastening toward their loved ones who were finally returning to the island after three long months away.

A large, broad-shouldered woman approached me as soon as I had found my footing and wreathed a thin strand of cobalt-gray beads—shells and sun-bleached seeds—around my neck. Just over her head, a billboard affixed to the boathouse read:

> *Welcome to Bounty Bay*
> *Pitcairn Island*
> *Home of the Descendants of the Bounty Mutineers*

Finally, after what had felt like a hundred years stuck in the spin cycle of a washing machine, I had arrived.

"So *you're* the journalist?" A middle-aged man jolted me out of my daze of excitement. He had shoved his way through the hugs and smiles to accost me at the edge of the pier.

"I . . . I suppose so?" I wasn't quite sure how to answer. I had come to Pitcairn with the intention of writing a magazine feature about the island, but my pursuits were not necessarily investigative or hard-hitting.

"Well, know this now," he continued. "I don't want you talking to me, coming up to me, or even looking at me while you're here. Got it?" His words were in stark contrast to the joyful backdrop of reuniting families. I scrunched my mouth and widened my eyes to both telegraph my understanding and quietly mock the unwarranted severity of his timbre. I had been on Pitcairn for four minutes—it was way too early to be making enemies.

I reverted my attention back to the others in an attempt to discern who my homestay parents might be. With no hotels on the island, travelers are matched with a local family and given a spare bedroom and meals in their home. I had been offered accommodation with Steve and Olive Christian, the seventh-generation descendants of Fletcher Christian.

Olive lingered on each syllable before lilting to the next word: "You, must, be, Brandon." It was easy for her to pick me out from the crowd; I was the only stranger.

In her sixties—and shorter and thinner than the other women at the dock—Olive started fussing with a stubborn sprig of her wavy gray hair that had long outgrown its auburn dye job. She smiled wide as we exchanged introductions; her cheeks buttressed the drooping frames of her thick-lensed glasses.

"I saw you talking to Simon," Olive cut right to the chase. "What'd he say?"

"He told me to stay away from him during my visit," I replied, failing to pull off nonchalance.

"Oh, don't mind him!" Olive laughed. "That's just Simon Young. It used to be Yung, Y-U-N-G," she continued. "His wife is oriental. He took her conveniently similar surname and now pretends to have mutineer blood." Olive could tell she hadn't assuaged my confusion about Simon's unprovoked aggression. "Don't you worry, really. He's not one of us!"

As Olive walked toward a long line of parked quad bikes, her T-shirt billowed in the breeze—a Rutgers University tank top so stained and hole pocked it was hardly more than a wearable tatter. Her ATV was nearing the end of its use as well—cracked plastic and exposed gears were covered in the rocks and mud its wheels had pulverized as she rolled around the island.

The long, dangerously vertical path from the pier up into Pitcairn's interior was still called the Hill of Difficulty. Olive revved her engine to negotiate the climb—I sat hanging off the back, holding my luggage—and, only halfway up, as the vehicle lurched into a higher gear, I realized that I, too, was now completely covered in the island's filth.

When the road finally plateaued, Olive turned back toward me from the front of her quad bike and flashed a playful smile. "It's not the Hilton, but it's home!" There was something rehearsed about the way she spoke—as though she had tried her witty welcome out on previous guests—but then how many people had actually stayed here before? With only four runs of the *Claymore* each year, and only a couple of berths available to nonresidents, it had surely been a while since she had hosted another traveler. She seemed genuinely excited.

Steve and Olive's house was called Big Fence—"big" being the operative word. The bungalow seemed to ramble down the dirt road as more and more rooms were added on over the years. Olive parked the ATV in the shade of her portico garage. We entered through a cramped mud room ("mud" being the operative word) and into a massive living area illuminated by a far wall of oversize picture windows. Couches, loveseats, and recliners—all draped in thin bed linens—hugged the entire perimeter of the space, which had been loosely divided into zones: kitchen, lounge, dining, and solarium.

A colorful mural immediately caught my attention: whales and dolphins swimming through a vast ocean of periwinkle blue. Then my focus began to adjust to the profusion of smaller decorations that wallpapered almost every surface in the great room: aerial photos of Pitcairn; finger paintings from the grandkids; trinkets and magnets tacked onto the rusting refrigerator; a framed portrait of the family dog, now deceased; and a peculiar clock with hands that cranked backward across inverted numbers to tell time.

It was time itself that seemed most omnipresent in Big Fence's decor—palpable markers of years gone by that dented the linoleum flooring and bore leaks into the roof. Steve and Olive, and the rest of the Pitcairners, too, had resigned themselves to nature's conspiracy: to wipe the Earth's surface clean of mankind's progress. It was a battle with the elements they could not win, so no one bothered to try; the salty air had caked the island's putrid red dust into every possible crack and crevice of their home.

"Now, let's see . . . what do you need to know . . ." Olive was scanning the room much like I was, then she walked over to the kitchen. Behind a large wooden island anchoring the cabinets overhead was a row of industrial fridges and freezers that guarded three months' worth of perishables between supply ships. "Help yourself to anything." She repositioned a jar of Nescafé crystals next to her plastic kettle for convenience. "For anytime you'd like, but you know the power goes out at night, right?" I had already been warned that the island's generator shut off every evening between the hours of 10 p.m. and 6 a.m. in an effort to conserve diesel.

"Oh! And we have internet—Wi-Fi internet!" That, however, was a surprise.

It seemed the previous passing of the *Claymore* just a few months prior had landed the necessary parts to jumpstart the island's very first wireless internet connection. A few dozen Huawei smartphones were rafted ashore as well and doled out to the island's adults. Olive was already using hers as a very handy paperweight, guarding a stack of receipts from the threat of an errant island breeze.

Despite the huge technological leap forward, the islanders were perfectly content with their usual communication method: a marine VHF radio tuned into Channel 16, the international calling and distress frequency. Three shouts of a person's name would get their attention (only a first name was needed), then you'd switch to a private channel to continue the conversation (and the rest of the island would flip to the same frequency to eavesdrop). Every so often, the chatter from passing vessels would crackle into everyone's living rooms as well.

"Nana!" The young girl with braids from the freighter barged into the house through the mud room and ran toward Olive, arms outstretched. "I missed you!" She had taken the elastics out of her pigtails, revealing a short utilitarian chop that wouldn't need cutting for a whole year.

Isabel was nine and had just returned to Pitcairn with her parents after seeing her older brother off to boarding school. Education on the island was offered until the age of twelve, after which all children were sent away to Palmerston North, on New Zealand's North Island. There were currently only three children enrolled in Pitcairn's primary academy, of which Isabel was the youngest.

"I wanna go to Highest Point!" Isabel cajoled her grandmother, who quickly gave in.

"You coming?" Olive turned in my direction.

Still reeling from the interminable nausea aboard the *Claymore*, I had hoped to shower myself back to some semblance of normalcy— or at the very least brush the stomach acid off of my teeth—but I agreed to tag along, both eager to start exploring the island and not wanting to seem rude.

Isabel sat right behind Olive on the quad bike, wrapping tight arms around her grandmother's waist, and I rode on the back again, atop the flat rack meant for lugging around harvested fruit or mechanical parts. The road up to the island's apex was just as steep as the Hill of Difficulty, but the trip was surprisingly quick. Olive yanked the parking brake right beside a large signpost with arrow-shaped slats splintering off in different directions: New York 9,322 km; London 14,821 km; Sydney 7,493 km.

By the time I finished reading all of the different destinations and their extreme distances from Pitcairn, Isabel had scampered off toward a low-slung canopy of bushes and trees.

"Fruit!" she raved. "Oh fruit. I haven't had fruit in three whole months!" She reached for a yellow guava and tore it from the branches, then, with ambitious jaws, chomped off a sizable morsel, revealing its purple-pink interior.

I was confused. Surely she had come across even an apple or a banana during her time away between freighter crossings.

"Did you know that people actually have to *pay* for their fruit in New Zealand?" Isabel continued. "Only chumps pay for fruit," she snorted. "And I heard it's not even that good." She chomped another bite out of the juicy guava with a giggle, then snatched a second bulb from the tree and handed it to me for a taste. It was like inhaling technicolor.

Isabel gathered six or eight more guavas before we descended from the island's towers, dropping her off at her parents' house then trundling all the way back to Big Fence. When I walked back in, there was a shirtless man reclining on one of the sweat-stained sofas.

Steve Christian never wore a top in his home, just track shorts and a pair of green crocs.

It was uncanny how Fletcher Christian's legendary attributes decorated Steve's face: tan skin with a prominent European nose and two large eyes of gypsum and obsidian accentuated by brambly brows. Well into his sixties, Steve still had a full head of jet-black hair, slicked back with the stroke of a comb, and sprouting follicles on his earlobes. His voice conjured the presence of his mutineer ancestor too: sonorous with polite British inflections. It was easy to fathom how he, like Fletcher Christian, inspired fellowship, though Steve also possessed a relaxed confidence that made him seem unflappable.

Steve's most striking attribute, however, was his horrible limp. As a teenager he had fallen out of a tree, I soon learned, and by the time anyone could hail a passing vessel to get him off the island for proper care, his twisted bones and tendons had already begun to reset. Every crooked step Steve took was a palpable reminder of the farness of Pitcairn.

"You must be knackered. Go take a nap," Olive walked in behind me. "Yours is the last room down on the right." She was the consummate hostess, but I had already understood that Steve was in charge of the household. "Don't be shy about taking a long shower," he added. "We have a year's worth of weather in our cisterns."

The cavernous hallway leading to all of the bedrooms was covered in dozens upon dozens of family photos, like a Christian family museum honoring important moments like birthdays, Christmases, and big fish caught. From what I quickly gathered as I lugged my suitcase by, Steve and Olive had three sons (two of whom lived on Pitcairn) and a daughter, all in their forties, and around ten grandchildren including Isabel.

My room at the end of the hall had been noticeably decluttered of the knickknacks adorning practically every other surface in the house: just a bed with purple sheets swallowed by gossamer netting and two closets—one with a toilet and the other with a shower—framing the open window. At Steve's insistence, I lingered under the trickling rainwater until I felt reborn.

Later on, Isabel came barreling into the great room once again: "It's an ice cream party tonight!" Olive had invited her middle son, Randy, and his wife, Nadine—Isabel's parents—over that evening. Traditionally, on the night of the *Claymore*'s return, the Christians gorged on their fresh shipment of frozen dessert before it began its slow devolution into sugary slush, melting with each power cut, then recongealing each morning when the generator clicked back on.

"I'm what you call a luxury import," joked Nadine at the table, skimming a spoonful of strawberry from the carton of Neapolitan. Her quip seemed rehearsed as well, practiced over years of explaining how and why she, a New Zealander, had ended up on Pitcairn.

After dinner, it was Randy's turn to power down the generators, a task that regularly rotated among the island's men. And in the stillness shortly thereafter, my mind still spun as I lay in bed, as though it were a little launch cast out into the dark waves of night.

"THERE'S THE BASTARD!" Steve roared with Shakespearean vibrato. From the breakfast table we could see the bobbing *Claymore* out the window, deceptively small against an infinite sea. It was strange; the freighter was Pitcairn's only link to the rest of the world, and yet Steve clearly resented its presence.

I had woken up at 6 a.m. when the whoop of power surged back through the house's wires. Steve and Olive were awake as well. Channel 16 had been crackling all morning with plans to take the tractor down to the Landing Place and relieve the freighter of its cargo so it could begin its journey back to Mangareva.

First the diesel was off-loaded—the lifeblood of the island— followed by some of the larger personal effects ordered privately by the residents, like a new refrigerator to replace one that had kicked the bucket only days after the *Claymore*'s previous departure. Then came the nonperishable foodstuffs and housekeeping supplies for the general store.

Pitcairn's general store was the only place on the island where money was traded. Steve and Olive managed the shop: a dusty

warren of canned soup, cornflakes, instant ramen, laundry deter-
gent, tampons, and grape jelly, all heavily subsidized by the British
government. The prices were, in fact, so reasonable that most of the
items cost about half as much as they did back at a superstore in New
York City. There was no fresh produce, however. That could all be
found directly at the source with a fishing pole or machete, or dug
up at one of the communal garden plots on the hill.

The general store was only open three days a week for two short
hours, but on the day of the freighter's arrival, Steve and Olive
worked until dark unloading and stocking their new crates of goods.

I had swung by the shop offering to help Steve and Olive unpack,
but was quickly distracted by a strange handwritten sign on the wall:
Calcium bites for Miz T, $13.21. Thirteen dollars and twenty-one
cents was awfully specific, but it was the wordage that seemed more
peculiar. I hadn't heard a single "Mr." or "Mrs." uttered on the island
so far, even when addressing a respected elder.

"Who's Miz T?"

Olive was pulling bouillon sachets out of their boxes and stacking
them individually on the shelves. "Miz T is our resident turtle, a
giant Galapagos tortoise who lives out on the far side of the island."
Olive reached down and grabbed the small knife she had been using
to cut through the packing tape. "Here," she handed me the blade,
"you can have a look for her if you'd like. And take this with you if
you get hungry for a banana or a coconut along the way."

In the evening, Olive was too tired to cook after spending the
entire day at the general store; she tossed some frozen french fries
and chicken nuggets in the oven. Tonight it was just the three of
us: Steve, Olive, and me. At the dinner table, I politely rehearsed
the answers to the usual assortment of questions one receives as a
travel writer.

"We've been there too," Steve noted as I ran through my short-
list of favorite destinations. There was no pretension when he interjected, just a genuine desire to match me with his own experiences
on the road. I had assumed that people so steadfast in their desire to
remain on a remote island would know little about the world around

them, but Steve and Olive were so phenomenally well traveled that they continued to regale me with stories by candlelight long after the generator had cut its power: high tea at Buckingham Palace and banquets at the Royal Geographical Society.

The closest living relative of Fletcher Christian, Steve was a GBE—the highest appointment of the Order of the British Empire—and a man of both English and Tahitian royal lineage. For years, he and Olive had been paraded around the planet to dine in the finest restaurants and attend the most lavish events as both oddities and esteemed guests. Celebrities seemed endlessly charmed by the fact that Steve had no idea who they were, since the televisions on Pitcairn could only tune in to a single Australian channel.

As Steve got up from his chair and wobbled into the darkness, he left me with one final thought before going to bed: "We're the museum people." It seemed the Pitcairners saw themselves as the living incarnations of the most controversial and talked-about personalities from the Age of Discovery, an ongoing legend of castaways that inspired both the highest esteem and lowest pity. Printed invitations to black-tie galas would arrive on the same freighter as a charity dump of secondhand clothing from which Olive had fished out her Rutgers jersey. Either way, an odd cult of fascination had developed around them and their island, of which I was slowly becoming a member.

In the morning, I found Steve at the breakfast table staring out the solarium windows once more. A smile had crept into the corners of his mouth as he severed the yolk of a fried egg with the side of his fork.

The *Claymore* was gone.

———

THERE IS A tourist office on lonely Pitcairn—a dedicated space with maps and brochures and souvenirs. You can find it inside the island's prison, iron bars and all. It's a veritable turducken of useless infrastructure: an information center for no visitors stuffed inside a jail with no prisoners on an island so extremely far-flung, its mere

distance functions as an effective blockade—keeping tourists out
and convicts in—from the rest of civilization. But there's something
even odder about this tourist office/prison: it is, in my estimation,
the nicest building on Pitcairn—far more modern and tidy than
any of the other dwellings I had seen, especially Steve and Olive's
weatherworn house. I began to entertain a very backward fantasy of
sleeping soundly in one of the empty cells.

On the morning after the *Claymore* departed, I decided to get
better oriented with my surroundings. The island was now all mine
to explore, and I figured the welcome center penitentiary was the
most appropriate place to start.

"I've been expecting you." I heard a woman's voice echo from
within as my flip-flops slapped the steps of the long wooden staircase up to the entrance. Of course she had been expecting me; I was
the tourist.

When I poked my head through the doorframe, I found a woman
in her sixties with big Tahitian eyes and a slender European nose sitting behind a long glass display case that had been refashioned into
her desk. Melva was "a descendant"—as locals with *Bounty* blood
like to distinguish themselves—who grew up on the island and, desperate to leave as a young woman, had run off with an American
engineer sent to Pitcairn to help survey a cable-laying project across
the bottom of the Pacific. After marriage, kids, and divorce—and a
long stint in Alaska—she had finally decided to return home.

A large poster—LIVE THE DREAM . . . MAKE THE CHANGE . . .
MOVE TO PITCAIRN ISLAND—hung behind Melva's desk. She
handed me a small dossier of paperwork printed on letterhead: immigration papers, "you know, if you end up really liking it here."
They get several hundred annual requests for information, she elaborated, but no one had yet to take them up on the island's offer of free
land and the subsidized freight to ship all of the building materials
needed to construct one's first home. "Pitcairn's become a bit of an
old-folks community these days," Melva said with a pursed smile.

Next to the immigration ad was a large whiteboard calendar
on which the *Claymore*'s four annual passages had been detailed in

green washable marker. I counted nine additional dates in the entire year that had the names of other vessels scribbled in: cruise ships expected to pass within proximity of the island, whose passengers would not be allowed to disembark but only glimpse Pitcairn from afar, as even a small shore excursion of passengers would completely overwhelm the island.

I turned my attention back to Melva, who had prepared a bulleted list of inhabitants' names on a long sheet of paper, each with a four-digit code scrawled beside—their phone number. "But you can just use the marine radio," she reminded me. It was an informal selection of activities available during my stay, each paired with a different islander: hiking with Kevin 0162, tennis with Darralyn 0150, beekeeping with Vaine 0160. She then handed me two final items: a white hat with *Pitcairn Islands Tourism* embroidered on the front—"A gift"—and a map of the island.

I unfolded the small accordion map, brushing its creases to better flatten it across the glass display case. With the tip of her pen, Melva tapped the island's essential points of interest, from the lonely cliffs of Tedside in the west to the swimmable shallows at Saint Paul's Pool in the east. There was Taro Ground, a verdant plateau well suited to farming, Highest Point, and the Hill of Difficulty, rising up from the Landing Place—names that got right to the point.

The entire map was covered in names—so many landmarked destinations, in fact, that for a moment I forgot just how small Pitcairn was until I noticed the legend at the bottom parsing out distances in quarter miles. Without scale measurements, one would have easily assumed the brochure charted an expansive continent instead of an island the size of New York's Central Park. These were not the names of cities and towns but of curious clefts in the rock or spots where dusty paths converged at odd-looking trees.

Many of the designations were remnants from the mutineers' era. There was Brown's Well, where the *Bounty*'s gardener had found fresh water, McCoy's Valley, and Mills' Harbour, to name a few. But the most common labels were not of geographical features, but of events that had occurred on those sites instead, like my favorite: Side

Dan Cack on Big Jack, where—as Melva explained—long ago, Dan hid in a high tree and took a shit on Big Jack while he was napping underneath. The majority of these commemorative monikers, however, were grim reminders of the island's treacherous terrain: Johnny Fall, Freddie Fall, Robert Fall, Nellie Fall, Down Duggi Fall, and Break Im Hip. It was the punishing verticality that made Pitcairn feel like a continent again.

No one walked on the island, even if they were visiting a neighbor. Instead, everyone tooled around on their quad bikes, which guzzle the same diesel as the generator. Walking was a deliberate choice couched as hiking or exercise, since it always involved an ascent or descent of some kind. Melva warned me that, on foot, I'd only have time to explore "town" before lunch, as everything else was deceptively far.

"Town" meant Adamstown—a cluster of municipal dwellings around which most of the islanders lived—coined in honor of John Adams, the last remaining mutineer after eighteen years of solitude, the "sole survivor" whose name conveniently never appears in any of the *Bounty*'s annals or its aftermath. Adamstown is affectionately known as Pitcairn's capital. There are no other settlements on the island.

Like untied shoelaces, a network of rutty roads loop around a main square, which consists of a church, post office, assembly hall, and a nucleus of government offices. Almost all able-bodied adults have an administrative job on the island, and just as the scales of geographic magnitude have been tapered down to every nook of this tiny place, so, too, have titles of great importance been bestowed upon the smallness of every occupation. There's a director of transportation (guy who sweeps the paths clean of fallen branches), a minister of agriculture (guy who tends to the public farming plots), and a postmaster general (guy who sells Pitcairn stamps to philatelists around the world)—all salaried by a coffer of UK taxpayer money. Interestingly, everyone earned the exact same wage: $10NZ an hour (around $7.25US), whether they're shoveling manure or leading council meetings, an unusual act of social progress acknowledging the cooperation needed to make the tiny society function. The position of mayor, Pitcairn's highest office, was currently being held by Shawn Christian, Steve and Olive's youngest son, whom I had seen in passing but hadn't yet properly met.

Technically, Pitcairn is a British Overseas Territory, think Bermuda without the pastel shorts—a final vestige of the lapsed British Empire, composed of a smattering of autonomous islands from the Caribbean down to Antarctica that still recognize British royalty as their head of state. This means that Pitcairn has the distinct honor of being the smallest self-governing democracy on the planet, with only forty-eight inhabitants.

Forty-eight people. What's forty-eight people? Forty-eight people fit on a standard-size coach bus. My father has more than forty-eight first cousins back in Quebec. The US National Oceanic and Atmospheric Administration estimates that each year about forty-eight people die from lightning strikes around the world. Forty-eight people is exactly double the number of men who've been to the moon.

The novelty of this micro-nation's population dynamics hadn't yet worn off, and as I walked around the island, each encounter stoked my arithmetic amusement: There were four people waiting to send parcels at the post office; I was standing in line with 8 percent of the country. There were nineteen people swimming at the Landing Place to escape the oppressive midday heat; 40 percent of the country was taking a dip. On birthdays, I was told, everyone gathers together for a potluck meal. I relished the thought of telling friends back home that I had eaten dinner with an entire nation.

"You're just in time!" Olive smiled as I walked in the door after my morning exploring Adamstown. "Lunch is ready!"

I sat down beside Steve and once again took in the view of the sea out the window. Olive approached the dining table holding a large plastic mixing bowl brimming with passionfruit, pineapple, and rock melon.

"Here, try this. It's my fruit salad. It's award winning!" She plunked the bowl down right in front of my empty plate.

I served myself a heaping portion and smiled back—"Looks
delicious!"—then debated the merits of a cooking accolade in a
country with only forty-eight people.

————————

OFTEN, PITCAIRN FELT like an island of one. I enjoyed the solitude during the day as I wandered down the different trailheads to
find rugged cliffs and boulder-ridden bays. But there was something
troubling about the island's unusual stillness after nightfall. The heat
never seemed to subside; it baked bricks of humidity that weighed
down my chest as I lay in bed staring up at the ceiling through a
shroud of gauzy netting.

My mind raced each time the broiling warmth wrestled me back
to consciousness, parched. I had begun to relive the nightmares from
my childhood—never about monsters, but of the facets of man's cruelty instead—and wondered when the island's purported bad mana
would reveal itself. So far, after several days on Pitcairn, I had found
only familiarity lurking beneath the island's superficial quirks, and
tonight that strange sameness—a certain ordinariness—had begun
to disturb me even more.

Was Pitcairn indeed a cultural Galapagos born of the mutineers'
malign intentions, or was this little rock merely a microcosm of the
world at large: a diamond, a pressurized fragment, that condensed
the defects of humanity into a magnifying prism and reflected the
onlooker in its brilliance?

I couldn't stop thinking about Simon Young/Yung's outburst on
the pier. What I hadn't known then was that many of the islanders
felt the same way—they didn't want me snooping around; they just
had a much cagier way of showing it.

CHAPTER 14

THE DEVIL'S WORKSHOP

1790–1791

N ight is when a spider makes her progress. Back and forth she moves in the dark, tracing intricate, invisible trails, then waiting patiently until morning when waking critters tangle themselves in her web.

While everyone else slept, Jenny roamed the island. The blackness blurred the borders between the nine tiny provinces—one plot of land for each mutineer and his wife—and the territory to the east where the Polynesians lived. Without her dogs, Jenny had become the mother to less loyal creatures who toiled between dusk and dawn. When the moon was high, Pitcairn was all hers.

By day, the island had started to look like the Eden that Christian had envisioned. It wasn't as grand as his aspirations on Tubuai, but the tiny colony was thriving; a little slice of England, with its country gardens and cottages, that had drifted toward the edge of the world. This was the closest Jenny would get to Great Britain, she now realized. The mutineers remained adamant about never returning, and instead sought to manipulate this wildest outpost of the tropics until it bore comforting similarities to home.

While the others delighted to see the first fruits of their toils, Jenny grew angrier at this great deception; Pitcairn was by no means a paradise. Admittedly, at the outset of their journey she had been the most enthusiastic among the Tahitian tagalongs; tales of Europe had awakened the spirit of her voyager ancestors within. But now, like the stones and timbers that had bent the tropical overgrowth, the mutineers sought to impress their British ideals—and biblical virtues—upon the island too. Jenny was free of Tahiti's rigid castes, but she resented the backward covenant of social servitude that had neatly divided everyone into man-and-wife pairings. She was to temper joy with guilt and shame, lest she be denounced as a whore. Men, however, somehow seemed absolved of this duality of deportment. What was the point of searching for a bright new life only to live in its shadows?

Up the ridge then down the valley and around the bend—Jenny had developed a nightly routine, but something was different. She sensed that she was being followed. At first, it was the distant crunching of fallen leaves, crisped into confetti by the uncompromising sun. Now the stomping grew louder; something was approaching. The steps were heavy. Maybe it was one of the island's goats that had freed itself from the communal pen. Smith had been tasked with mending the animals' fencing; his slothfulness, however, proved just as annoying as his lechery. But there was no clip-clopping of hooves. It was a person who approached. Could it be Faahotu out looking for medicinal flowers that only bloomed by starlight? The gait was too careful, furtive even, as though the nightwalker carried a secret in their stride.

Jenny hid behind the dense sagging limbs of a banana plant as the stalker passed. Through the green hillocks they moved, climbing up into the rocky headland that led to the Polynesians' encampment. It was Teatuahitea, Brown's wife. She hummed a sweet Tahitian tune upon reaching level ground where she found Tetahiti, the hulking Tubuaian. Jenny quietly followed, and watched as they giggled while undressing one another on a soft grassy patch not too far from his hut.

Even the smallest of indiscretions threatened to throw the island's delicate mathematics out of whack. Jenny pondered telling the others about the entanglement but decided she'd keep it a secret, at least for now, if only because she was sure that Brown didn't care. He seemed far more interested in his various gardening projects. And Martin was always eager to help him plow; often he wouldn't return home until morning, which made it all the easier for Jenny to perform her nightly ritual. No, she wouldn't pull at this thread just yet.

———————

THE SEEDS OF the gardens had indeed been sown; after Mauatua's long spell of nausea came a baby boy, almost exactly nine months after they arrived. Christian called him Thursday October for the day and month on which he was born. The name—following neither British nor Tahitian tradition—was the nomenclature of a new generation and race: he was the very first true Pitcairner. And soon there would be more. A couple of the other women were also pregnant, including Tevarua.

The temperature began to swell once more at the end of the year, but most of the islanders' labor was complete. Vegetables grew abundantly from tilled plots, new clothes were fashioned for the mutineers out of the *Bounty*'s sails, and up went more permanent homes made from the ship's floorboards and felled lumber fastened together with the dozens of copper nails the women had acquired back on Tahiti.

Christian had devised a veritable chore wheel, assigning a different sailor and his wife to guard the watch for passing ships, and a lookout shelter was built on a high ridge with sweeping views of the sea. Shifts rotated each week, and a system of flag signals would warn the islanders to snuff out their fires and hide inland should something be spotted on the horizon. Everyone obliged, even Quintal and McCoy, whose tempers had softened now that the last quaffs of alcohol—fuel for their outbursts—had long been consumed.

Christmas had crept up on Christian once again. It would be the fourth time he would fete the holiday with his fellow Englishmen, and he made preparations for a feast bigger than any *heiva* or royal banquet. There was some pushback from Mauatua again, who remained superstitious about dining with the opposite sex, but Christian insisted, choosing the island's fattest hog to be spun on a spit over an open fire.

Christian had a special surprise to celebrate not only the yuletide but a full year at home in their new island country: the last bottle of Madeira wine—the *vinho da roda*—from Bligh's personal collection, once hidden down between the *Bounty*'s ballasts.

"Ugh! It tastes like shit!" McCoy grabbed it out of Christian's hand and took a swig. How many times had the drink crisscrossed the equator? Christian couldn't even remember now; it was sour and unrefined without having cooled in colder climes after its journey around the globe.

"Gimme that!" Quintal didn't care. It was probably the last sip of alcohol he'd ever have.

There was enough liquor for everyone to take a few turns with the bottle, and a raucous fit of singing and dancing soon broke out. The men slurred their lyrics with hearty smiles as the women waved their arms and, in their new bark-cloth dresses, galloped around the roasting pig. Without Byrne's fiddle, their chanteys sounded truly strange. "Coventry Carol" was almost unrecognizable, now a Tahitian tune when accompanied by Teimua's nose flute.

Unworried about passing vessels, Christian let the bonfire burn as the festivities raged on late into the night.

While the others were sleeping off the excesses of Christmas, Faahotu awoke with the first flashes of sunlight and headed up to the taro ground to pluck some produce: fruits and vegetables to sustain her and Williams during their weeklong turn at the lookout. She climbed Pitcairn's staircase of stacked stones and rutty paths, humming a jumble of the celebratory tunes sung the night before—the anthems of her new country. She mimed the flowing *ori* arm movements passed down from her foremothers, faltering only when she needed to catch her balance as she hiked into the bowl of farmland that carved a hollow between the island's two turreted ridges.

From a short distance she could see that the still-untended fencing had allowed several of the goats to jump their pen. They had trampled the communal garden and started unburying most of the crops. Cursing Smith's indolence, she raced over to the potato patch to save whatever food she could from more feral mouths. On both knees, she took the hem of her tapa dress and folded it up toward her waist, creating a small cloth basket, which she hastily filled with one hand—spud after spud—while shooing away an increasingly ornery buck with the other.

It happened in an instant. Faahotu flew onto her back, spilling the vegetables she had gathered on her lap. The goat's horn was dripping red, an insatiable animal guarding its stash of sweet potatoes not yet devoured. Faahotu clutched her neck, but her delicate hands—perfect when ferreting through the island's undergrowth for exotic ferns and follicles—couldn't catch enough of the bleeding. With careful fingers, she felt the nuances of the goring, which had torn through the strings—ligaments and bone—that puppeted the fabric of her head. She tried to stand, desperate to shout for help, but the air escaped from the hole in her throat before reaching her pallid lips, her mouth now a vestigial aperture. Falling back onto her knees, she frantically drank from the atmosphere with big lapping gulps—an attempt to fill her lungs and try again—but she choked on the surging blood, each throbbing heartbeat now the rhythmic pumping of a spring.

A cloud of fatigue rained over her, heavy like the humidity unquenched by the dew of the morning's earliest hours. But the ground was still cool, and Faahotu unfolded herself onto her stomach, soothing her limbs from the hot pain flaming through her body. With her ear pressed against the soil, the little blades of crabgrass seemed like an impenetrable jungle of long-stalked trees, and the mess of half-mashed tubers formed large, unclimbable boulders over which she couldn't see. It was the realm of bugs and beetles; scavengers who would soon complete the mortal cycle. It was too late to wish for serendipity, that a passerby might come to check on the crops and save her. She only hoped to roll herself onto her back and spend one final moment in the human world. But she couldn't. She belonged to the island now.

———

MADE OF BRANCHES and thatch, the hut at Lookout Point was much cruder than the rest of the structures on the island. Christian, however, preferred the airy dwelling to his big house of *Bounty* boards down below and had started spending more time on the perch as the others grew tired of watching for passing ships. A year of isolation confirmed the prevailing sentiment that they were indeed living off the map, but Christian wasn't convinced. He stared out to sea, certain that a vessel's masts would suddenly sprout up along the horizon, ruining the tiny society he had worked so hard to build.

Democracy was on everyone's lips after the American Revolution, and it suited the Pitcairn experiment rather well. Free of the Royal Navy, each mutineer was now the captain of his own soul and an equal shareholder in the island's success. Up went a veritable neighborhood of dwellings and dirt roads, but in putting down their hammers and trowels, the men's idle hands and minds had unwittingly invited the devil to build his workshop next door. Trouble hadn't found their hideaway yet, but it did not mean that trouble could not be found.

Within weeks of Faahotu's death, Williams broached the subject of a new wife. There were, however, no uncoupled women on the island. It was suggested that perhaps he could wait until Baby Sully was of proper age, but then a hideous debate ensued as to when she'd be old enough to become Williams's consort. Fifteen? Twelve? Ten? Baby Sully was still very much a baby, born only a few months before the search for Pitcairn began, and it would be a full decade—regardless of any perverse arithmetic—before she'd be deemed womanly enough to marry.

Christian had hoped Williams would resign himself to life as a widower, but when he threatened to leave the island on a fishing dinghy, Christian hastily asked everyone to gather once again and find a new solution: to take a woman from one of the Polynesian men. Democracy was an easy discipline for the mutineers when decisions were made along bloodlines; there were nine Englishmen and six Polynesians. Only Brown vehemently objected to this sinister game of bride roulette, while the others—not wanting to covet their neighbors' wives outright—pointed to the sharing of women already embedded in Tahitian culture to justify their intentions. The Polynesians made an impassioned plea to consider other options, suggesting that Smith should give up Obuarei since he had let the goats' fencing go un-mended, but they were easily outvoted.

While Christian had dared not repeat his mistakes from Tubuai—ensuring that each of his loyal conspirators had a Tahitian partner—he worried less about the needs of his six Polynesian comrades, who found themselves divided across only three women. The problem wasn't immediately apparent. Oha, Tetahiti's young Tubuaian cousin, was only around seventeen, and Minarii, the boyish Tahitian, was even younger. But as they grew, so did their desires. To strip them of a lover would be the second egregious act committed against them after being politely relegated to the island's rock-ridden east.

Christian was consumed with regret as he studied the patchwork pattern of reefs—dark shadows under a shining sea. He should have spoken up on behalf of the Polynesians, but it was too late. Tararo, the noble Raiatean, was forced to deliver his wife to Williams, who quickly renamed her Nancy. Christian began to entertain a divergent reality in which he hadn't relinquished control over his men; they still called him "Mr. Christian" after all, while the others went by diminutive nicknames like Neddy, Billy, and Jack. Besides a predictably dissident Quintal, would it have been so difficult to convince the others to allow him to continue his captaining on land if he kept their best interests at heart? He knew deep down that this newfangled imitation of democracy wasn't a symbol of social progress but an act of cowardice. Bligh was right; Christian remained overly concerned about others' opinions of him. In a strange way,

Christian had become jealous of Bligh's vainglory, an armor of self-love against the chiding remarks he so often used to denigrate those around him. It was the same self-assuredness that would undoubtedly drive Bligh's little launch to safety. Christian remained certain that an arriving search party was inevitable.

"Tevarua had her baby," Mauatua returned to the lookout with Thursday October in her arms, interrupting Christian's introspection.

"I know." Christian held his gaze forward out into the blue abyss. He had heard her screams of agony down below—without Faahotu's help, it was a difficult delivery.

"It's a boy. Matthew Junior."

Christian clicked his shoulders. "Pah. Of course." He exhaled a half-laughed breath. This was not the taxonomy of a new order but how kings named their princes. Up at the lookout, Christian found himself alone in his ideologies as well.

OFTEN, WHILE JENNY wandered in the darkness, she'd think about Faahotu's lifeless body. It had been four months since she found her in the grass, drained of all color and vigor and frozen in a twisted tableau of desperation as goats grazed, unfazed, nearby. Oh, how Faahotu hadn't wanted to leave this place, Jenny remembered. She had knelt down beside the body to examine her face more closely; both her mouth and eyes were open wide with the indelible knowing of someone who was about to die. In a way, Jenny envied Faahotu. She had found a way off of this wretched rock, which had become even more unbearable after her death.

There was no democracy here. The British psyche allowed its constituents to build their successes on the backs of others. Slavery existed outright in the Caribbean, and the "savages" who made up the rest of the conquerable world were expected to bend to their will. To be free in England meant having the right to rob others of their liberty. And worse than their treatment of women—predicated on religious misogyny—the *Bounty*'s men never truly saw their Polynesian brothers as kin. To perpetuate the illusion of equality was the cruelest form of apartheid.

Jenny tempered her wrath with tramping steps on soil muddied by an afternoon raincloud. With the blindfold of a new moon she roamed alone, back and forth, tracing intricate, invisible trails by rote. She then heard the familiar treading of unsure feet—too delicate and purposeful to be an animal in search of food—and slid behind a tree as the tiptoeing came nearer. Surely it was Brown's wife sneaking away to see Tetahiti again, but something seemed different—there was no humming. No, these steps were more tentative. There was another interloper in her country of night, someone who desperately didn't want to get caught.

Up the shadow went, climbing higher into the stone towers of the island's east end, and although they moved carefully, their steps were noticeably quick. They knew the way; they had trespassed here before. A bolt of a white tapa cloth flashed between the tree trunks like a matador enticing a bull. Jenny followed. Which of the mutineers' wives was betraying her husband this time? Mauatua was too loyal, but Christian's despondence was tiresome. Tevarua was too meek, and Quintal's ire knew no physicals bounds. Was it Susannah? She was insatiable.

Caught up in her curiosity rather than eyeing the path, Jenny accidentally cracked a twig underfoot, causing her visitor to turn around. It was Nancy—she glared through the darkness, then started her route again all the way up to Tararo's hut. The white men would be livid to learn that Nancy was sneaking out of Williams's house and spending the night with her former companion, Jenny thought—a new tangle in her web of secrets.

Jenny watched as Nancy and Tararo had sex, but there was something in her field of vision that distracted her predacious gaze, a twinkling of light too low on the horizon to be a star. She climbed over a series of boulders to reach the island's edge for a better look. Jenny's fervent desire to leave Pitcairn had often ignited delusions of boats at sea—similar to the frequent manifestations of Christian's paranoia—but this time it was real: the flicker of a galley's furnace glowed under three towering masts with draped sails attached. It was a British warship.

Jenny launched into a full sprint down toward the home she shared with Martin. One large fire would get the passing vessel's attention, she hoped. They'd arrest Christian and the others for their crimes, and she'd be back on Tahiti by the end of the month.

CHAPTER 15

PANDORA'S BOX

2018

I woke up in the middle of the night to the unmistakable stench of death.

Despite the sopping heat, I had been sleeping rather soundly over the last few days. Tonight, however, a most wretched smell had crept into my nostrils as I dozed. With fumbling fingers, I reached down and patted the carpeting next to the bed. I located my iPhone and quickly tapped the flashlight function on, but nothing else seemed out of the ordinary besides the noxious odor that had overwhelmed my bedroom in the last breezeless hour before dawn.

Arm extended, I pointed my iPhone toward the doorway and slid out of bed. The hall smelled as it always did: old paper and dirty shoes. I shut my bedroom door behind me so as to not let the awful mortal reeking permeate the rest of the house. As I tiptoed toward the kitchen, I felt like I was exploring a shipwreck at the bottom of the ocean. In the glowing beam from my iPhone shone millions of little particles suspended in the heavy air. The pewter and sterling frames around the Christian family photos flickered and gleamed as their rusted flourishes caught my flashlight's rays.

Before reaching the kitchen I paused in front of Shawn's old bedroom. The door was closed—it was the only door in the entire house that was always closed, unlike the former bedrooms of Steve and Olive's other children. I had politely poked my head into their daughter Tania's room several times to snoop around. The shelves and cabinets were still decorated with My Little Ponies, porcelain ballerinas, and handwoven necklaces made from shells and hardened seeds—all covered in a fine patina of ocher dust that had petrified the trinkets of her childhood like the ashes of Pompeii.

Steve and Olive's house didn't even have a front door anymore—the sea air had long chewed it off at the hinges—but Shawn's old bedroom seemed off-limits.

I had surmised that they had at least partly repurposed his former bedroom into a home office. Steve would sometimes disappear behind the door, emerging fifteen minutes later with an update on the weather he had gleaned from Facebook, which begged a whole other line of questioning: Facebook? For a forecast? For a forecast from an off-island meteorological station? And why did we need data projections when the infiniteness of every vista on Pitcairn afforded an actual preview of the weather ahead?

But I digress. There must have been another reason why visitors weren't welcome in the room. I impulsively swung open the door. Someone was always home—either Steve doing housework or Olive in the kitchen—so this was likely my only opportunity to sneak a look within. I aimed my glowing iPhone deep into its cluttered interior and found exactly what I suspected: bins and binders everywhere, labeled with their contents and purpose. Few traces of Shawn's childhood remained. There was a large black computer monitor near the window that looked more like a cathode-ray tube television, the source of Steve's comically pointless weather forecasts. I wondered how long it took him to reboot the dusty relic each morning after the power surged back on.

A built-in bookshelf flanked the far wall. It was filled from floor to ceiling with a smattering of waterlogged books (mostly *Bounty* related), crusty photo albums, and storage boxes marked "Paperwork" containing reams of what seemed to be government documents. There were another dozen or so boxes on the floor without lids. Each one overflowed with useless miscellany: old manuals and appliance warranties, plastic magnets from a trip to Europe, cowboy boots, and an empty bottle of Château Margaux.

There was one box, however—neatly stacked on the shelf with the others—that caught my attention. "VR6SC" was scribbled on the outside in black Sharpie, and nothing else. I cleared an empty space on the carpet with my foot, then slid the box off of its ledge and lowered it onto the floor. It was heavier than expected.

I waved my iPhone over the open box after removing the cover, trying to ascertain the purpose of the materials inside. There were a handful of dictation notebooks marked with different years in the early 1990s that contained the names and locations of hundreds, maybe thousands, of people, carefully printed along the ruled lines: "Ed Nusko. Henderson County, Texas, USA." "Jim Seybels. Hesperia, California, USA." "Jack N. Hague. Douglasville, Georgia, USA." And after each entry was a sequence of confusing numbers and letters, like a cipher.

The rest of the box was filled with small rectangles of thick blue construction paper about twice the size of a business card. "VR6SC" was professionally printed on each one along with a small clip-art graphic of a beachcomber lying under a palm tree. They were Shawn's QSL cards. VR6SC was his call sign; he was a ham radio enthusiast, and each time Shawn made two-way contact with another amateur, he would dutifully log the exchange with their name and location, plus the date, mode, rig, and frequency.

I ran my index finger down page after page of Shawn's notebooks and wondered what life must have been like as a teenage castaway so eager to engage with the rest of the world before the prevalence of the internet. Then I realized I was no longer reading his ledgers by flashlight; the morning sun had begun to creep in. I quickly closed the lid on the box and placed it back on the high shelf. Nudging the door open only a few inches, I glanced down the hallway to make sure Steve and Olive were still asleep before exiting past their bedroom toward the kitchen.

The generator had yet to whirr back on, so I sat in the silence at the dining room table and thought more about the names in

Shawn's logs, people from all over the planet whose lives had for only a brief moment—ten short minutes across the crackling of a radio transmission—intersected with his; voices whose bodies would never touch down on this place.

Most amateur enthusiasts solicited QSL cards from the stations with which they made contact, and Shawn eagerly obliged. A calling card from faraway Pitcairn was considered a collector's item compared to, say, a receipt from Sheboygan, Wisconsin. Shawn would transmit the details of his postal address

> Shawn Christian
> Pitcairn Island
> South Pacific Ocean

(yes, really, that's it), and the eventual recipient of his little blue slip of construction paper would place a self-addressed envelope in the mail along with a few dollars to cover the cost of the return stamp. Judging by the packets of loose currency at the bottom of his hobby box, it seemed Shawn had devised a clever little side business by embellishing the price of postage and skimming some cash off of each interaction to save for when he'd eventually travel abroad.

"You're up early." Olive startled me. My tired mind had begun to drift. I was staring out through the solarium windows into the void where the *Claymore* used to be.

"Me? Oh yeah. Well, I figured I'd go on a hike before it gets too humid out." It was a half-truth; I had made a daily routine of walking out to Saint Paul's Pool each morning for a refreshing dip before starting the day.

When I returned about an hour later, Olive was serving breakfast to Steve. A breeze had kicked up and the angry whiff of decay was gone from my bedroom.

"Let's take a holiday," Steve announced as I walked past the dining table.

"To where?" Surely we weren't going to leave the island on one of the rickety longboats at the pier.

"Lookout Point." It was another defect of island perception; when you lived within a two-mile-long domain, your measure of distance shrunk accordingly. For Steve, traversing Pitcairn was like visiting the other side of a country. The length of a holiday was commensurately adjusted as well: three hours.

I eagerly obliged. I hadn't yet visited Christian's perch, a turreted ledge soaring over the site where the mutineers had smashed the *Bounty* against the rocks, then turned the ship into cinders.

We waited until the humidity began to dissipate in the latter part of the afternoon before setting off. Olive had prepared a picnic for an early dinner: hard-boiled eggs, frozen shrimp from the bag, macaroni salad, and, of course, her award-winning blend of passion-fruit, pineapple, and melon. She packed the food into taupe and tan Tupperware and instructed me to source enough cutlery and plastic dishes for the three of us.

Olive stowed the various containers on the back of her ATV and I rode with Steve, following behind. Around halfway across the island, we veered off the road to tackle one last chore for the day before our holiday began—feeding the goats.

Steve pointed to a thicket of overgrown fronds farther down the path and asked me to tear the leaves from their stems and bring them over.

"These damn goats. I don't know why we keep them as pets," he offered. "All they do is eat and eat, then when the food is gone they start gnawing on the fences."

There was something Pavlovian about the puttering of our vehicle. As soon as we were within earshot of their pen, the goats came galloping toward us, mouths open. We must have fed them at least two dozen plants, which were voraciously devoured midair before being coated with mud and dust on the island's floor. Jowls again agape, the goats wanted more.

"Tomorrow fellas." Steve motioned me back to his ATV and we trundled off toward the other end of the country.

By the time we reached Lookout Point, Olive had set up an impressive spread along the flatbed rear of her vehicle. She handed both Steve and me a plate and ladled a gloppy portion of macaroni salad onto each, then gestured over to the green Adirondack chairs farther out on the stony ledge. Steve continued to mock the goats as the three of us sat down to enjoy the view over the island and beyond. "Oh they're fine," Olive interjected. "It gives us something to do." Then she changed the topic of conversation, pointing out a particularly angry storm cloud in the distance, maybe three or four days away.

More pleasantries about the weather, and other banalities meant to be exchanged but never considered, soon muffled themselves into chewing as we eagerly shoveled down our portions of macaroni salad. After a few rubbery bites, I turned my attention back to Steve and Olive as they busily speared their scatter of dwindling noodles. My gaze then shifted beyond the ledge of the precipice—I could see their ramshackle home and the rest of Adamstown in the distance down below. Steve looked up after forking a final curl of macaroni and I watched as his dark eyes slowly shifted focus as well, out toward the infiniteness of the sea.

Knowing with complete certainty that we were alone—the chances of spotting a passing vessel beyond improbable—it was hard to imagine that Christian once sat on this very spot, day after day, and obsessed over the possibility that word of the mutineers' crimes had reached England and their hideaway would eventually be found. Few people had heard of Pitcairn even today—two hundred years ago, only he and his compatriots knew the island truly existed. But Christian wasn't wrong—while he was commandeering the *Bounty* back to Tahiti, then onto Tubuai and finally Pitcairn, Bligh was tackling a most ambitious journey of his own.

———

AFTER PENNING *Mutiny on the Bounty*, James Norman Hall and his partner Charles Nordhoff used Bligh's old logs (purchased in that antiquities shop in London after the First World War) as inspiration for their second book in the *Bounty Trilogy*, *Men Against the Sea*, which detailed Bligh's fight for survival after being cast out into the night by Christian and the other mutineers. Set adrift on the open ocean in a twenty-three-foot launch, Bligh—along with eighteen of his loyalists, including Hallett and Hayward—had only a compass and a quadrant for navigation and enough rations to last five short days. The nearest landmass, the smoldering volcanic island of Tofua in present-day Tonga, was over thirty miles away, about a five-day journey from where they had been dumped overboard. But when they slid ashore to restock their supplies, Bligh and his men were met with a volley of hurled weapons, and in a mad dash back to their lifeboat one of the *Bounty*'s sailors was speared through the throat then dragged back to shore and bludgeoned to death with stones.

To spare himself and the others a similar fate, Bligh made the decision to chart an impossible course to the nearest European colony where he could assure their safety: the Dutch-held Timor in present-day Indonesia, over four thousand miles away. So for the next twenty-three days, the members of the launch carefully apportioned their waning rations, eating only around an ounce of bread each daily and lapping up the falling rain during the seemingly ceaseless barrage of storms until they reached the Great Barrier Reef, where they were able to properly restock their foodstuffs. (Not a single fish was caught, despite their best efforts.) Then, after navigating yet another interminable stretch of landless water, Bligh—with all of his men still alive (but only barely)—reached the Coupang settlement (present-day Kupang) on Timor, forty-seven days after Christian and his coconspirators had left him for dead.

Flagging strength did not abate Bligh's pettiness, however. He put two of his men in irons immediately upon their arrival for having accused him of sneaking extra rations of bread along their arduous journey. Bligh then purchased a small schooner to safely transport his crew to Batavia—the capital of the Dutch East Indies, present-day Jakarta—another 1,800 miles away, where they would seek passage back to England.

But pestilence soon swept across the colony and four of Bligh's men—still languishing from their voyage in the launch—quickly

perished of fever. Bligh contracted malaria as well, but he was, unsurprisingly, the first of the *Bounty*'s crew to secure a spot as a passenger aboard a Dutch vessel bound for Europe and escaped the
disease-ridden outpost.

Bligh was met with a hero's welcome when he finally reached England, as word spread about the mutiny and his arduous open-water
escapade, which is still considered to be one of the most incredible
feats of navigation ever recorded. Bligh was acquitted of all wrongdoing involved in the loss of the *Bounty*, and the Admiralty soon
began its preparations to launch an ambitious and costly manhunt
across the far side of the world.

The HMS *Pandora* was tasked with the transcontinental voyage. A towering warship that measured more than twice the size
of the *Bounty*, it could carry almost three times as many crewmen.
And, like the *Bounty*, the configuration of the vessel was expressly
altered for the purpose of its mission, only this time instead of
clearing deck space for a thousand breadfruit seedlings, a large and
sturdy brig was constructed in anticipation of capturing and lugging
home two dozen traitors to be tried and hanged for the utmost
of crimes.

Captain Edward Edwards was selected for the expedition. While
Bligh had earned a reputation for his immature outbursts, Edwards
was notorious throughout the fleet as one of England's cruelest
commanders—the perfect choice to guarantee the return of the
Bounty's missing men. Of Bligh's lackeys, a half-paralyzed Hallett
was still suffering the effects of their open-boat journey, but Hayward eagerly joined Edwards's ranks to help identify and corral his
former shipmates.

The *Pandora* left England in the late fall of 1790 and successfully
rounded the storm-ridden tip of Cape Horn at the bottom of South
America. A flourish of trumpeting conch shells announced its arrival in Tahiti in late March 1791, almost a full two years after the
Bounty's mutiny. Christian, Quintal, and the others had long parted
ways with the rest of the mutineers, all of whom had now grown
very much accustomed to life in Polynesia. Churchill had become

the chief of a prominent clan, and many of the sailors had started families with their tawny-skinned brides. For a moment, it seemed almost possible that they could remain in Tahiti and live out their island fantasies forever. Then the draped sails of the *Pandora* manifested along the turquoise horizon.

Heywood heeded Christian's advice and immediately greeted Captain Edwards upon his arrival in an effort to absolve himself of any complicity in the mutiny. But Edwards didn't care. All former members of the *Bounty* were destined for the purpose-built brig, which was quickly dubbed "Pandora's Box." Over the following two weeks, Edwards and his crew thoroughly scoured the shadows of Mount Orohena until they had captured all but two of the mutineers: Churchill and Thompson. Jealous of Churchill's newfound admiration and power among the Tahitians, Thompson had drowned his former friend in the shallows of the lagoon several months back. Then, in a swift act of retaliation, Churchill's *taio* tribesmen hacked Thompson to death with hatchets.

The imprisoned mutineers explained to Captain Edwards that Christian and eight of their comrades had absconded with the *Bounty* long ago and were never heard from again. So the *Pandora* departed Tahiti and spent three more months combing every isle and atoll in the South Pacific in search of Britain's most wanted criminals, until it was decided that they had likely perished at sea.

But the ordeal wasn't over. On the voyage back to England, the *Pandora* smashed against the outer fringes of the Great Barrier Reef, and over the course of a very short night, the heaving warship broke up along the shoals, sending torrents of waves through the berths and the brig. A ruthless Edwards, afraid his prisoners might attempt an escape in the confusion and flee the foundering vessel, waited until the cell had filled to the brim with seawater before instructing his officers to extract their captives. But it was too late for some. Four of the fourteen mutineers drowned in their chains, including two of Bligh's precious midshipmen, whose families had entrusted the social-climbing lieutenant with their young sons' safe return. Over thirty of Edwards's men perished as well.

Four small lifeboats were pulled from the wreckage, and, in a rather karmic fashion, the survivors began their own grueling misadventure across a long swath of the Arafura Sea to reach the Dutch East Indies. Then, again like Bligh's loyalists, many of them died of mosquito-borne illnesses while waiting in Indonesia for their safe return home.

Finally, back in England, six of the mutineers were found guilty of treason at their widely publicized trial. Hallett and Hayward provided damning testimony against young Heywood, who perjured himself under oath, maintaining that he had been forced to stay aboard the *Bounty* during the skirmish. His conviction was eventually pardoned by the king, but Millward and Burkitt were strung up and hanged for their crimes.

Years later, upon studying Captain Edwards's logs, historians realized that the *Pandora* had in fact sailed so close to Pitcairn it was almost uncanny that none of the warship's crewmen had spotted the island off the bow. Edwards's journal recorded not a single disturbance in the unending blue on the day he crossed the true coordinates of Christian's hideaway.

The Pitcairners may have had the luck of a moonless night on their side, but soon thereafter the machinations of men left to their own devices would trigger a sequence of events more grisly and unhinged than either the taking of the *Bounty* or Bligh's thirst-racked voyage across the ocean. This eventual undoing of Pitcairn's inhabitants—the plot of Nordhoff and Hall's third and final installment (titled *Pitcairn's Island*)—proved a most diabolical end to their saga.

THE STENCH OF death had become unbearable.

After another restless night, I finally alerted Olive to the pungent smell that seemed to only linger—stronger now—in my bedroom.

"Perhaps it's the rats?" Olive was unfazed as she opened a carton of eggs.

"The rats?!"

"Mm-hmm." She didn't look up and broke two large eggshells along the rim of her cooking pan instead. The yolks sputtered when they landed in the boiling oil.

The Polynesian rat likely arrived with the ancients long before Steve and Olive's forefathers. I hadn't seen a single rodent thus far, but Olive reassured me that they were there in droves. "Maybe one died in the floorboards?" She cracked open another egg. "Or the walls?" Then another. "Or under the house?"

Within seconds, the contents of Olive's pan had congealed into wobbling colloids. One by one, she lifted the fried eggs out with a spatula and placed them each on a little raft of toasted white bread. As she approached the table, plates in hand, she spouted off more theories about the origins of the reeking odor, listing a handful of other creature culprits that claimed Pitcairn as their own while the humans slumbered. I had seen hermit crabs as big as catcher's mitts—a definite possibility—but did the island really have spiders with enough meat on their bones to inspire such fetid decay?

After breakfast I was determined to solve the mystery. I swapped my flip-flops for hiking boots before braving a look through the overgrowth beneath their home. While Steve and Olive's front yard was flush against the main street, the back of their bungalow was hoisted up high on stilts over a sloping property that tumbled precipitously back down toward the shoreline.

Out the back door of the solarium was a long staircase leading down to an outside laundry area with a Soviet-era washing machine and wooden gallows from which Olive's Rutgers jersey and other stained T-shirts were dangling in the soupy air like lifeless torsos. I passed the catchment tanks, containing years' worth of rainwater, and tramped through the tall weeds that grew in the perpetual shade. There was no smell under the house.

I returned to my bedroom, where I began to tear through my belongings once again. I grabbed the cover for my scuba-diving mask and through the clear plastic casing I could see the long spiral seashell I had saved from Motu Mapeti, the Hall family's private island.

A small mollusk had in fact been hiding inside, and after weeks without food and water it had perished. The putrid stink intensified as I loosened the clasps on the lid. I chucked the rancid shell through the glassless window and watched as it whizzed through the air and out into the forested brush.

I was glad to have solved the mystery of the stench, but something else was haunting me now.

Seeing the physical limits of Pitcairn during our "holiday" at the top of Lookout Point had instilled within me a sense of mastery, that I had conquered this place and made it mine. But Olive's musings of a hidden dimension—a realm of night creatures—helped me realize that I had fallen prey to the island's greatest deception: its size. Just because one could survey the entirety of Pitcairn in a single glance didn't mean one had glimpsed all there was to see.

The closing of the door to Shawn's former bedroom seemed to be nothing more than a self-conscious reflex—the mess within a point of embarrassment for Steve and Olive. But I was having trouble making sense of the box of Shawn's radio logs. The contents belonged to a bright young man full of ingenuity and promise—a teenager who cared deeply about connecting with the world. The Shawn I had briefly encountered was cold, distant, and paranoid.

I had expected Shawn, as mayor, to at least extend me a cordial greeting, especially since my presence had increased the population of his little nation by two whole percentage points. I, however, had been on the island for almost a week and he still hadn't stopped by to say hello, which was doubly strange considering I was staying with his parents.

There were no threats of warships on the horizon. What trauma had Shawn sustained that had turned him so deeply inward and fearful of the outside world?

CHAPTER 16

DREADFRUIT

1792

M cCoy was out walking, searching, but wasn't quite sure what he was looking for. He'd often stroll around the island in the early morning hours before the sun shone too brightly on his freckled shoulders. Despite the pervasive heat, McCoy had kept his thick, bristly beard—a light brown shag that turned strawberry blond when he strayed too far from the shade. He cured his boredom with a layman's interest in botany, uprooting different shrubs and ferns, which he'd take back to his cottage to examine more closely. There was plenty of time to devote to his burgeoning hobby now that everyone except Christian had stopped searching for ships at Lookout Point. It had been months since the mutineers' last gathering to discuss various island matters. He occasionally stopped by Smith and Mills's houses and would regularly visit Quintal too, but lately he spent most of his time alone wandering around the far side of the island—Tedside, as they called it. His wife, Teio, had just given birth to a baby boy he named Daniel, and for the first time in years McCoy thought of his own childhood.

Growing up, McCoy had always ridiculed the fuss made over one's pedigree in aristocratic circles, the careful attention paid to the titles of great uncles or third cousins that formed the branches of a distinguished family tree. More amusing, however, was the stark divide of such obsessions between the haves and have-nots; if your lineage wasn't worthy of scrutiny, then you weren't given a second look. And McCoy was indeed a nobody. After years of service in the Royal Navy, no one had ever so much as asked him for his father's name.

But that was the appeal of a life at sea, where the named and the anonymous worked in tandem to move their ships across great and treacherous expanses. Middle-class men like Bligh were constantly consumed with thoughts of England as they tried to raise their station. McCoy, instead, saw a different version of himself at each port he visited—he rarely longed for home.

A light Scottish brogue hinted at McCoy's origins; he was a storehouse boy for a distillery near Aberdeen before enlisting in the Royal Navy. On his first assignment he met Quintal and they became fast friends; both motherless children—alone in the world, like the rocky outcrops they passed on their way to the West Indies—trying to grab hold of their own destinies. Quintal had made it clear from the start that he swore no allegiances, but he found an easy ally in McCoy. They were both, most of all, in pursuit of a good time.

The Caribbean was the perfect backdrop on which McCoy and Quintal could pin their dreams; the women were loose, there were slaves to bear the burden of hard labor, and the roaring sugar trade produced seemingly endless barrels of cane molasses rum. And while Quintal made reckless use of all three, McCoy was his ideal foil. A scar on his lower abdomen—clearly a stab wound—was the only hint that perhaps McCoy wasn't always in charge of his emotions, but over the years he had become quite adept at tempering his discord with apathy. Hot-blooded Quintal remained the whip's favorite, while his partner in crime, cool McCoy, always managed to escape recourse.

They'd wind up as rum barons on Barbados one day, they'd figured, with a harem of girls and a legion of slaves. But an impulsive decision at the Spithead dockyards to fill the last two positions aboard Bligh's *Bounty* had changed their fate forever. And, consciously or not, the two men had begun to manifest their colonial dreams on

Pitcairn by taking advantage of the deference of the Tahitian disposition. The mutineers had long called the Polynesians "Blacks," which made it even easier to rationalize their bondage. Minarii and Oha, the two teenagers, were easy targets to dominate—especially Oha, who was still young of mind but had started to bear the broad shoulders of his hulking cousin.

Scrawny Minarii was harder to wrangle. He often scurried away to root around the island, throwing stones at birds and tearing hermit crabs from their shells. Lately, however, he had developed a new interest: Susannah.

Every morning Susannah made her way to the far eastern edge of the island where a curling ring of stone buttressed a natural tide pool, the mouth of a caldera lurking just below the ocean's surface: Saint Paul's Pool. She'd wade in the bathwater, as clear as Tahiti's rivers, and tend to her grooming the way the other women tilled their taro plants.

Floating on her back, Susannah spotted Minarii hiding behind the tree line. It wasn't the first time she had caught him spying, but today she called out to him, inviting him down for a swim. As he fussed with his loincloth—dropping it beside Susannah's tapa dress—she rose to her feet and approached the water's edge. Standing ankle-deep in an eddy of coral and pebbles, she reached for Minarii's arms, drawing him in. He was taller than her now.

Susannah placed Minarii's hands on her bare breasts, then slicked his unkempt mane back into one long tress that rode the dimples of his backbone all the way down his waist. She coiled the last few inches of his hair around her clenched fist; a gentle tug coaxed his gaze skyward. Susannah busied her other hand along Minarii's frontside, and each time he'd try to steal another glance at her body, she'd yank at his thick lock of hair like a huntress breaking her pony. His breath began to hasten, and with eyes widening in the blaring sun, Minarii suddenly lurched forward, clouding the clear pool below with his adolescence.

———————

ALTHOUGH THE MUTINEERS rarely gathered, their wives would convene daily to share in the chores: cooking, weaving, and trying to scrub their clothing free of the island's dirt. There were now many infants that needed caring as well. Mauatua had just given birth to a second son, Charles, named for the long-lost brother who remained a fixture of Christian's wandering thoughts as he scanned the ocean for ships.

Never adept at domestic duties, Susannah often entertained the others with jokes or songs while stirring boiling taro in the *Bounty*'s cast-iron cauldron. On the days when Tevarua bore a new mark of Quintal's anger, Susannah would try to lighten the mood with a verse from "Coventry Carol":

> *Oh sisters too, how may we do*
> *For to preserve this day.*

Darning a braid of frayed pandanus palms, Jenny suddenly chimed in:

> *Why do the Blacks, sharpen their axe,*
> *For the white men to slay?*

Susannah stopped singing, confused by Jenny's ad-lib. Mauatua's face turned instantly pale with panic—she dropped baby Charles on Obuarei's cradled arm and frantically dashed out of sight. Jenny rarely spoke when Mauatua was around. If this was her gambit, then the game was already afoot.

"What the hell is going on?" Susannah and the others were thoroughly confused. Jenny silently smirked as she returned to her stitching.

Consumed by the indignity of losing his wife to Williams, Tararo had fled to live deeper in the wilderness shortly after Nancy moved out of his hut. For weeks, Jenny continued to watch Tararo and Nancy reconvene in the middle of the night, until one day she approached them with a plan: Her hope of returning to Tahiti now dimming, Jenny would instead try to change her circumstances on the island. Without divulging the details of the other tryst she had uncovered—Tetahiti and Brown's wife—Jenny made it clear to Tararo that if he were to stage his own mutiny against the Englishmen, he could rally enough support.

As the seeds of dissent began to germinate, Tararo formed his strategy. After Tetahiti, he also recruited Oha, who had come to endure not only Quintal and McCoy's forced labor, but their cruel beatings as well. As their plot ripened, however, Tetahiti had misgivings. He had once sworn *taio*-like devotion to Christian—a bond more sacred than blood—and could not fathom the dishonor of being responsible for his murder. Months of waffling ensued, and Jenny had become exasperated by their indecision. She would force them into action by announcing their intentions to the others.

Mauatua, making sense of the lyrics, raced toward the lookout to alert Christian.

TONIGHT IT WAS Minarii, not Jenny, who traced Nancy's footsteps through the woods on her nightly dalliance. Armed with a musket, he carefully followed her, ten steps behind, then quietly tucked himself into the overgrowth when she arrived at Tararo's camp. Sliding the barrel through the twigs and branches, Minarii cocked the trigger, targeting Tararo's head. He had never shot a gun before, but he always paid careful attention to how the mutineers took aim.

BANG. The kickback from the hot weapon surprised Minarii as the butt of the handle smashed against his shoulder. He missed. Tararo jumped up and scanned the brambles for an intruder. "Who's there?!" Minarii, full of resolve, angled the musket's bayonet like a spear and came charging out of the jungle with a grunting battle cry. Tararo, a trained warrior, easily rebuffed Minarii's advances, sending the heavy gun flying out of his hands. But Minarii would not relent, and each time Tararo shoved him back, he would attack again with more determination until Tararo finally had to pin the young Tahitian to the ground.

Tararo looked into Minarii's crazed eyes as he squirmed to break free—who was this motherless child becoming without tending or care? With one arm firmly pressed across Minarii's neck, Tararo used the other to feel around for a rock to put a permanent end to the brawl. No, a shell wasn't hard enough to crush Minarii's skull. Tararo kept tapping the soil without taking his gaze off of the riled teenager's face.

SLISH. The bayonet suddenly sprouted out of Tararo's chest, slicing through flesh and bone. Blood spattered down onto Minarii's face. Tararo heaved backward, craning his spine, then collapsed onto his side, releasing Minarii from his grip.

From the ground, Minarii could make out Nancy's shadow hovering over Tararo's slain body. It was the only logical thing to do, Nancy reckoned. As Susannah had corrupted Minarii's body, so, too, had Jenny bent his mind—she always knew how to make loyal dogs out of strays. Jenny had secured a gun for Minarii and sent him on his way: ten paces behind Nancy, she told him, like the way he stalked Susannah, until he found Tararo's hideout. Clearly Nancy's affair was no longer a secret. If she didn't abet Tararo's murder, then she'd be cast out as a traitor too.

At Mauatua's insistence, Christian climbed down from his lookout to put a definitive end to any other mutinous machinations. Gun in hand, he marched eastward to suss out who among the Polynesian men were Tararo's coconspirators.

Beyond the Englishmen's cluster of fences and farms, much of Pitcairn remained a rugged wilderness, where one could easily get lost among the tangle of vines and thorny bushes. Christian could hear the familiar nothingness, the deafening quiet, once more. His pulse quickened. The island seemed deceptively large now, as though he was discovering it for the first time. Memories of his early days on Pitcairn started to resurface, back when they were haunted by those who had long ago lived on this rock—the *marae*, the ruined dwellings, and the whalebone comb. Under cairns of gathered stones,

Christian had later found their remains, shallow graves of skulls and bones flecked with pearl shells like the buttons Mauatua had sewn into his shirt. But the iridescent clamshells were found nowhere else on Pitcairn—perhaps the ancients had traveled here from Tahiti as well.

Christian steadied his grip, slowly swaying the gun barrel as someone approached. "Stop or I'll shoot!" With only powder in his charge, he clacked a warning shot, which echoed through the forest. Oha briefly emerged from between the trees like a skittish deer, then ran off.

When he finally reached the Polynesians' huts, Christian loaded his musket with bullets and handed it to Tetahiti, his trusted *taio* brother, and sternly implored him to tend to the traitors, whoever they may be.

The burly Tubuaian spent hours searching for his cousin until he found him sitting cross-legged on an embankment of large rocks.

"Are you here to kill me?" Oha muttered, resigned. He had taken his eyes off the horizon when he noticed that Tetahiti was carrying Christian's musket.

"No, Oha. I've come to take you home." Tetahiti placed the long gun on the ground and leaned back on the boulder beside him. Oha returned his gaze toward the sea and Tetahiti studied the teen's profile: his nose had gotten bigger, and his cheeks were fuller too. They sat silently for a while before Tetahiti rehearsed a plan to make amends with Christian and the others. Since Tararo was the ringleader, his death would be enough of a mea culpa, he rationalized. For better or for worse, they'd reaffirm their allegiance to the Englishmen.

When the walking path narrowed, Oha took the lead back toward their hut. Tetahiti slowly lifted Christian's gun and fired a single bullet through the back of Oha's head. Lifeless before he hit the ground, Oha toppled forward, and a puff of maroon dust enveloped him as he thudded against the island floor. This was, Tetahiti had decided, the only way to truly prove his loyalty to Christian and free himself of suspicion. The pledge of a *taio* meant more than blood, after all. He also needed to further bury the affair he was having with Brown's wife. It was wimpish to have shot Oha from behind, but he simply couldn't bear the thought of seeing his cousin's face staring up at him, stiffened by betrayal. In truth, however, Tetahiti had long robbed Oha of his life by bringing him to this miserable place.

"TRY THIS," McCoy tilted the *Bounty*'s teapot over a halved coconut husk, and out came a stream of syrupy liquid.

"Christ, McCoy, you're gonna make me go blind!" Quintal puckered his lips, trying to choke down the strange beverage. "What the hell is this?"

McCoy had fermented dozens of leaves and fruits to no avail, but finally, after months of diligent foraging, he pulled up the roots of the ti plant—a suitable replacement for sugar cane. It wasn't quite molasses rum, but with the help of the *Bounty*'s copper kettle, McCoy was able to make a high-proof brandy using the distillation methods he had gleaned long ago in Aberdeen.

Smith, Mills, and Williams had gathered at Quintal's house as well, squinting as the fire brew touched their tongues for the first time. With some tweaking, the liquor had promise—breadfruit was long forgotten now; the flowering ti plant was the *Bounty* men's newest obsession.

Nightfall had arrived unnoticed as the gang eagerly emptied the kettle's contents. By torchlight, they wobbled their way up the mountain to Lookout Point, scaring the night creatures away as they raved incoherently to the tunes of different naval chanteys.

Quintal chucked his torch at the watch hut's halo of dried brown thatch, crisping the tufted fronds. McCoy cheered as the little shack began to fill with soot and ash, raining down from the shriveled roofing. The fire then turned its attention toward the four supporting posts, devouring them instantly. In seconds, the lookout— their temple of fraternity, once built by all hands and manned by all eyes—was gone. There would be no more watching for passing ships. Christian had fully surrendered himself to his obsession with being discovered, and in his absence, Quintal and McCoy had seized control. Pitcairn was now their Caribbean-esque colony of rum, women, and slaves.

CHAPTER 17

PORTRAIT OF A FAMILY

2018

T he majority of Pitcairn's forty-eight inhabitants can be neatly divided into two distinct families—"piles," as they're called on the island. There are the Christians, headed by Steve and Olive, and then there are the Warrens.

Carol and Jay Warren are in their sixties, the same ages as Steve and Olive. And, exactly like the Christians, they also have four grown children, two of whom live on Pitcairn: daughters Charlene and Darralyn. Charlene and her husband Vaine have five children, just like Isabel Christian's parents, Randy and Nadine. And, like Steve, Jay has a sister living on the island too.

The Warren's house, Up Tommy's, is less than a three-minute walk from Big Fence, and yet Jay insisted on picking me up in his ATV.

It had been decided long before my arrival on Pitcairn that I would split my time between the two clans and stay with the Warrens as well. The tourist homestay program I seemed to be trialing had palpable economic gains for the host families in question. Travelers paid $100US for a day's room and board, a windfall by local standards, considering that the hourly wage—be it as mayor or general store cashier—was a trim $10NZ. It seemed only fair to live with members of both piles and spread the wealth.

But surely the Christians and Warrens were related in some capacity, since they both vociferously clung to a shared history of their mutineer forefathers? And, let's face it, on a sparsely populated isle inaccessible by airplane, the size of the gene pool was more Jacuzzi than Olympic. But, nonetheless, the similarities between piles abruptly stopped at the precisely equal number of respective constituents.

Jay was Pitcairn's transportation minister (guy who clears coconuts off the dirt tracks when they fall), and Carol was the manager of the *Bounty* museum. If this were a regular-size country, perhaps one would consider her the head of the national archives or something. Additionally, Carol was in charge of the island's only church, which formed the fourth corner of Adamstown's small municipal square.

The Pitcairners were Seventh-day Adventists, which seemed a bit odd considering that their infamous ancestors were disciples of King Henry VIII's Anglican church. But their conversion—a tale as implausible as the story of the island's settlement—has served them well over the decades. Besides stamp sales and nominal government assistance from the United Kingdom, church donations have played a major part in allowing the Pitcairners to sustain themselves in isolation.

Pitcairn's only place of worship was constructed in the late nineteenth century. Several years earlier, the Adventist movement had lost its momentum in the United States and was in great danger of dissolution. Spellbound by the *Bounty*'s story, two church members living near San Francisco decided to prepare a crate of promotional materials to ship to the mutineers' progeny on the unlikely chance that they may be curious about conversion. And sure enough—in what might be the most passive missionizing effort in the history of Christianity—word eventually got back to California that, after a visit from an Adventist sailor, there was indeed interest in their newfound faith.

An elder was dispatched to Hawaii to better determine the type of transport needed to carry a small legion of ministers across the ocean. He disappeared at sea en route to Tahiti. This did not dissuade the Adventists' efforts, however. After strong-arming their members into donating large sums of cash, the church's leaders were able to build a sizable schooner to sail halfway across the Pacific and indoctrinate their prospective members. They named the vessel *Pitcairn*. The eventual success of their foray led to five more missions across Polynesia, and, ultimately, a resounding resurgence of the sect.

Six Adventist pastors landed on Pitcairn in 1890, and upon their arrival they escorted the eager islanders down to Saint Paul's Pool, where, one by one, they were baptized by submersion, reborn into their new denomination. The pastors then began the proselytization in the ways of the church, which erased the final traces of Tahitian tradition.

Adventists believe in the imminent Second Coming of Christ (two thousand years and counting), and their day of rest and worship is Saturday, not Sunday. Hand-holding and dancing are strictly prohibited—singing, too, unless it's in solemn praise of the Lord.

Next, the Pitcairners were forced to remove the unclean foods from their diets as dictated by the Bible, which explicitly meant no more pork. A swift hunt for all the island's pigs occurred. Once gathered, they were pushed off the rocky cliffs to rid the tempted society of their filth.

Most important, however, was the strict prohibition of alcohol, which was written into Pitcairn's code of law all the way until 2009, when a "license to carry" amendment was voted into existence by the Christians. The Warrens have continued to abstain.

Today, without an ordained minister, the other tenets of Adventism are only loosely followed as well, but it seemed that Carol still liked to make sure that no one was having fun. Steve may have been the undisputed patriarch of the Christians, but it was Carol who ran the other half of the island—her own little fiefdom, ruled with an iron fist.

To enter Carol and Jay's home, I had to walk through a gauntlet of used auto parts, rusted tools, and broken boat motors in the vestibule. There was a chalkboard propped up on a broken chair, too, where the family would leave messages for one another: "Gone

Swim." The front door had long been removed, and inside, bushes and branches had grown through the empty window frames in their desperate search for shade. A long couch covered in a floral bedsheet ran down one side of the living room. A built-in bookcase flanked the other; its contents were neatly arranged on the upper shelves but devolved into a mess of crammed and crumpled papers further below. There were still Christmas ornaments scattered about the room, though it wasn't clear if they were left over from the festivities two months prior or if they had been sitting there for years.

At the back of the house was Carol and Jay's bedroom and a galley-style kitchen next to a small dining table for six, with no space for extra chairs. My bedroom was up a thin but very steep staircase back near the mess of mechanical bits at the entry, lofted high like a child's treehouse. The furniture was rudimentary: a chest of wooden drawers, a chair that looked like it belonged in a dental clinic's waiting room, and a pedestal fan at the end of the flimsy bed—operational during the "power hours" but never when I really needed it.

At Big Fence, the nightly electric outages would catch me off guard, usually in the middle of a conversation with Steve and Olive. Here at Up Tommy's, Carol and Jay retreated to their bedroom long before 10 p.m., leaving me alone in the kitchen, waiting with quiet dread for the puttering sound of a distant quad bike bound for the generator's off switch. After a few days, however, I had begun to develop a very precise routine in those boring, in-between hours before my forced bedtime: chamomile tea, a cold shower, and some light snooping. I'd pull down a book or two from their shelves and flip through the pages. I would also more closely ogle the family photos on display.

There was one particular portrait that had caught my attention: black and white and set within a cracked ebony frame. I had begun a rather strange habit of saying goodnight to each of the people pictured: a youthful Carol and Jay, and four small children with big smiles and restless limbs. I recognized two of the children as daughters Charlene and Darralyn. Carol was smiling too, serene and genuinely happy. It suited her pretty face, which was embellished by large, wavy locks. Nowadays, Carol's hair had been styled in a pragmatically short coif; her mien was freckled and furrowed. I had yet to see her grin.

Like the Christians, the Warrens also had a room with a closed door. It was just down the hall from the black-and-white family portrait. And since Carol and Jay went to bed early, it was quite easy to pry. If curiosity killed the cat, then I was about to lose the second of my nine lives.

Inside, there were two beds tucked under the roof's eaves. Both of the mattresses were bare, but there were hundreds of little items neatly stacked on each, mostly T-shirts and trinkets, all wrapped in plastic to guard them from the elements. It seemed Carol was running an ambitious *Bounty*-themed boutique, and I had stumbled upon her warehouse. The recent arrival of wireless internet meant that she could solicit shoppers with a new online store, but her main customers were the passengers traveling aboard the nine or ten annual cruise ships detailed in felt marker on the whiteboard at the tourism office-jail. Without permission to dock, the vessels would welcome the Pitcairners on board instead for an afternoon of singing and history lessons and—most importantly—an opportunity for Carol to hawk her goods, offering cruisers a chance to take a piece of Pitcairn home. Through the cellophane, I could make out the three masts of the *Bounty* silkscreened on blue and pink jerseys. There were mugs with modern-day photos of the island as well, and dozens of blocks of Pacific rosewood carved into sharks and whales. I gently unraveled a particularly cartoonish looking fish from its wrapping and found *Carol Christian* scrawled on the back in gold ink—a clever way to capitalize on the infamy of the main mutineer. It wasn't necessarily a lie; Carol was born a Christian before marrying into the Warren family.

"Do you like fishing?" Carol asked me in the morning as I took a seat across from her at the kitchen table.

"Sure, definitely!" I was hoping her question was the prelude to an invitation. It had felt like a while since anyone on the island had been available for an outing, let alone a conversation.

"Well then you'll need to catch some bait." Carol stood up, dead-pan, and disappeared toward the front of the house. Her constant matter-of-factness always verged on exasperation; it wasn't clear if that was the end of our conversation or if I was meant to follow her out of the room for more. I took a tentative bite of my mushy cornflakes and waited.

"Here." Carol returned to the kitchen with a flashlight and a large white pail similar to my barf bucket back on the *Claymore*. She plunked them both down on the table beside my cereal. "So, you shine the light in a crab's eyes. It'll confuse them long enough to grab 'em and chuck 'em in the bin." I nodded, still chewing, com-pletely unsure of where exactly I was meant to find this surplus of crustaceans.

"C'mon, I'll take you."

Outside, I hopped on the back of Carol's ATV as we climbed up all of Pitcairn's vertiginous rungs, then back down the ladder of grit and stone on the far western end of the island that the locals still called Tedside.

"This is Miz T's territory," Carol muttered as we got off her quad bike, reminding me that I had yet to track down the island's resident giant tortoise. There was something rather forlorn about Tedside. A paved path led down to an abandoned harbor that had been deemed unusable after its elaborate assembly due to the constant onslaught of waves—an awful waste of resources considering an infrastructural investment like solar panels would have better served a community that uses a rattling diesel generator as its pacemaker.

The slabs of concrete, however, had become the home to a roar-ing colony of crabs—the perfect bait to catch big fish. I watched as Carol confidently shook her torch, paralyzing the pincered creatures with blinding confusion. She'd grab each one by its hard belly and chuck it into her pail with a scoop of mud on top to keep it cool. I was much more hesitant at first, maybe verging on dainty with my attempts, worried I'd be nipped by a rogue claw. Carol smirked.

"So what do you think of this tourist activity?" Apparently Carol had been busy developing another facet of her business of the *Bounty*: beyond her trinkets and the daily $100US payouts garnered when hosting a visitor, she was keen on leveraging an additional guiding fee each time she accompanied an outsider around the island. Suddenly, I was very aware that, to Carol, our little crabbing expedition was nothing more than a gig worth several billable hours. She did, however, seem pleased to be topping off her coffers with a few extra bucks. I didn't really mind because, for the first time since I had moved in with the Warren pile, Carol flashed me a genuine smile—broad and toothy, like the one in the black-and-white family portrait collecting dust on the mantel back home.

CHAPTER 18

HUNTING PIGS

1793

After the arson at Lookout Point, Christian continued to watch for passing ships from the shaded groove in a craggy ledge that the others had dubbed Christian's Cave. Mauatua never visited; the pathway up the rock face was too perilous, especially with two young children and a third on the way. She spent her time with Young instead, listening to stories about God and his disciples while waiting for her husband to return from his extended spells of isolation up on the cliffs.

Still fixated on the imminent arrival of a British warship, Christian had become emotionally withdrawn as well, consumed by thoughts of happier times. Alone in the refuge, he excavated the ruins of his life as though each of his memories were a different room in a derelict fortress. He'd carefully wander the imaginary halls, opening different doors to rescue his favorite souvenirs from the dusty cupboards and shelves of his past: The pulpy touch of a Bible's pages he'd fiddle through, bored, at church. The kind smile of his first love, his cousin Isabella. The scent of lilac as he climbed the hills of heather on the Isle of Man. And out through the castle windows he could faintly see the outlines of recollections unmade, the artifacts of alternate histories that hadn't found their way onto the figurative mantle. What if they had stayed on Tahiti instead of trying to find a hideaway? What if they hadn't burned the *Bounty*? What if the mutiny hadn't happened at all?

Casting Bligh out into the night instead of putting a bullet through his head was not Christian's folly; murder wasn't in his nature. But the uncertainty of Bligh's fate remained just as damaging to Christian's psyche as his captain's vulgar insults. Christian frequently thought of Heywood, his surrogate, too—rescued from the sequence of events that had marooned the others on Pitcairn. These were unavoidable choices that now seemed irrational in retrospect. Heywood was likely back in England, continuing the budding career in the Royal Navy that had once been promised to Christian.

There were alternate futures for Christian to consider as well. What if he left this place?

When they first arrived on Pitcairn, Christian had been overly concerned with whether his fellow mutineers would ever truly grasp the foreverness of their decisions. They weren't thinking men like Christian, schooled in philosophy and the arts. Later, he realized rather ironically that it was the others' inability to self-actualize that saved them from the throes of angst Christian constantly sought to quell. Everyone had pangs of claustrophobia on tiny Pitcairn, but no one felt them as acutely and obsessively as Christian, a man destined for greater things. He was only twenty-eight years old—there were far too many years left in his natural life for him to remain stranded on this rock.

What if Christian returned to England? He cringed at the notion that the details of the mutiny were circulating among the Admiralty with derisive whispers. They had certainly slandered his character: Fletcher Christian, notorious criminal, thief and murderous mastermind. He couldn't bear the notion that his actions had brought such dishonor to his family's name. But he knew, if he showed up on their doorstep, they'd be relieved to learn he wasn't lost at sea. Perhaps he could explain his actions to his brothers—surely Charles would understand—and they'd help him live anonymously. He was sick of the spotlight that shone so brightly on those of noble birth anyway. He could steal a small fishing boat, and—with all of the knowledge

Bligh and Mauatua had taught him—follow the stars home. Orion and Polaris, Ana-mua and Hokulei. He had made himself disappear once. Would it be so hard to do it again?

Christian returned his drifting focus to the waves. Strong winds had turned what was once a sunny afternoon into a sky ominous and stormy. Thick clouds cast strange shadows over the sea, taking on familiar shapes before they coalesced into one large cradle of thunder: a serpent, a tiger, his mother, a scythe.

SMITH WAS BACK on the white sand beach with its cobalt-colored water and a sprawling field of clover just beyond. Down from a cloudless sky shone the warm rays of a midday sun. Smith could feel the honey-tinged light on his eyelids; they drooped like awnings down to his cheeks. With deliberate breaths, he slowly let the tropical wind fill his body. In through the nose the cool breeze flowed, clearing his mind then traveling down through his chest, hips, and legs and exiting through his toes. Gone was the vile spit of humidity that made afternoons on Pitcairn so unbearable. He smiled.

When Smith opened his eyes, he noticed a body in the shallows again—it had gurgled up from lower depths and drifted aimlessly, facedown. With panicked panting, he dashed into the water, his legs trudging like battering rams as they smacked against the incoming tide. Waist-deep in the lagoon, Smith finally reached the lifeless corpse and rolled him over. It wasn't the Tubuaian boy from his last dream—this time it was Churchill, his face contorted and water-logged. Smith was too late. He desperately tried to pull Churchill to shore, but his drowned friend was much heavier than the boy had been. "Please help me!" Smith yelled out when he saw the shape of another man approaching from the clover pasture. "Please!"

When the stranger reached the sand—smooth, like a sash of bleached tapa cloth—Smith could finally decipher his features: it was Thompson. "Thompson! Please help!" The sound of the splashing water masked Smith's pitiful cries, which quickly switched to calls of concern when a faceless man, hatchet in hand, appeared once more in the distance. "Run, Thompson! RUN!" Unbothered by the loose pebbles and powders that normally hamper one's beach walking, the anonymous stalker effortlessly slid across the sand, hoisting his axe high when he reached a cowering Thompson waving pleading hands of surrender.

Smith let go of Churchill's body and watched helplessly, his ankles still in the waves, as the attacker chopped a shrieking Thompson down. His yelps grew fainter with each swing until his various body parts were nothing more than a pile of bloody limbs. Smith wanted to yell out "WHO ARE YOU?" to the faceless man, but the sea air had long left his body. Suddenly he couldn't find the wind to expel the words.

Smith awoke in a violent fit of gasps as though he, too, had been drowning in the shallows. He sprang to his feet and walked out into his garden, where he dunked his hands in a basin of well water then washed away the sleep from his eyes. There was only a half hour until morning, Smith figured. The ghost glow before dawn had already wiped the slate of night clean of its stars. He lumbered back toward his house but stood frozen in the doorframe when he saw the silhouettes of two men standing over his bed. They were careful not to make a sound while examining the folds of Smith's linens to see if he lay somewhere underneath. Each one aimed a gun at his pillow.

"Who's there?" Smith startled the intruders. They quickly raised their musket barrels and fired bullets at the door, but Smith ran back outside, escaping harm. Emerging from the shadows, Teimua and Niau leaped into the daybreak, reloaded their weapons, and tried again. This time, Smith collapsed into the overgrowth before he could reach the safety of denser trees. The Polynesians were exacting their long-awaited revenge.

———

WITH CHRISTIAN SEQUESTERED in his cave, it had been easy for Quintal and McCoy to transform Pitcairn into their version of a

British colonial paradise. They dismantled any remaining semblance of democracy on the island, forcibly recruiting the four remaining Polynesian men—Teimua, Niau, Tetahiti the Tubuaian, and young Minarii—as their personal servants while they drank incessantly under the shade of trees. Smith, Mills, and Williams, and even several of the women, had begun to subscribe to Quintal's irrational despotism, fueled by McCoy's batches of moonshine. For over a year, the welfare of the island had fallen squarely on the shoulders of the Polynesian men, who toiled ceaselessly in the punishing heat. But it wasn't enough. Their suffering had become a new form of entertainment for Quintal and McCoy, who whipped them for the most minor of indiscretions then doused their wounds with seawater for the sadistic pleasure of watching them well up with tears.

A year of such torturous treatment had finally broken the Polynesians' spirit. Vengeance was their only outlet, and for months they planned and plotted until finally the day had arrived when all of the white men had to die.

After Smith—blamed for the untended goat pen that had led to Faahotu's death—Williams was the next target for having demanded that the Polynesians relinquish one of their brides. Everything went smoothly. Tetahiti and Minarii had arrived early enough to shoot the Englishman dead as he lay sleeping in bed. But they would have to work quickly to carry out the rest of their plan. By now, the other islanders had been roused either by the sun or the sound of a firing gun. There were seven more mutineers to execute.

Old man Mills was tilling his sweet potato patch when Tetahiti and Minarii approached with weapons in hand. "What are you doing?" Mills casually leaned his hoe against his garden's fencing.

"Hunting pigs," Tetahiti smiled. Shovels were for dogs; you needed a pistol to kill swine. Minarii's aim was still uneven, so Tetahiti had to finish Mills off with an axe.

Following Williams's murder, Teimua and Niau made their way to McCoy's house, where they hid behind his oversize European furniture. Word had been dispatched that someone was rummaging through his belongings trying to steal his precious ti root brandy, which had sent McCoy homeward in haste. A deafening clatter of gunshots echoed through McCoy's cabin as he walked through the doorway. "It's a MURDER!" the mutineer cried out as bullets tore through his walls made of *Bounty* floorboards. Unscathed, McCoy zigzagged through his garden, arms flailing, screaming out to whoever might hear. He then ran down the rutty path toward Quintal's property to warn his friend.

By the time Teimua and Niau reached Quintal's house, however, neither he nor McCoy were anywhere to be found. They had escaped to the mountains. It could take hours to uncover their hiding spot in the forest, and there wasn't enough time. The Polynesians needed to strike with the element of surprise before the other Englishmen had a chance to arm themselves. Before launching a search for Quintal and McCoy, Teimua and Niau would try the next name on their hit list: Brown the gardener.

Brown was not a constituent of Quintal and McCoy's tyranny, preferring to spend his time with Martin out near the ancient obsidian mine—their own little enclave—rather than chugging the ti root brandy or abetting the mistreatment of the Polynesians. He had been the closest thing to an ally—the only Englishman to explicitly vote against the handing over of Nancy to Williams after Faahotu was gone. For that, Teimua schemed for Brown to be spared, even though his compatriots categorically wanted all of the mutineers dead.

"LIE DOWN!" Teimua yelled at Brown when he and Niau marched onto the gardener's acreage. "Don't move!" They could hear the rustling of other footsteps hurriedly approaching. "Brown, you must play dead!"

Confused, Brown listened to Teimua and dropped to his knees. Teimua fired a single shot into the air. Lying quiet on the upturned soil, Brown squeezed his eyes shut as the sound of someone drew near. It was Martin, who hobbled into the clearing, holding his stomach—his hands were covered in blood. He was calling out to Brown for help between howls of searing agony.

Tetahiti and Minarii were stalking Martin close behind, eager to deliver him his final blow.

Losing balance, Martin crawled his last few steps toward Brown with tears in his eyes. "Please help." His begging whispers were overpowered by the frenzied chatter of the gathering Polynesians.

"Brown's dead," Teimua insisted. "Didn't you hear me shoot him?"

"We need to finish Martin!" Minarii brandished a hammer he had picked up along the way.

With an outstretched palm, Martin reached out for Brown, cupping his hand around his bicep before slumping over in the grass to begin his decay. Brown could feel the thrumming of Martin's pulse as blood raced toward the tips of his fingers—it was fading. Martin desperately tried to hold on, as though he would plummet from a craggy precipice if he were to let go of Brown's arm.

With eyes still closed, Brown could hear the squeaking of rusty hinges as Tetahiti dropped more bullets into a musket. He stopped playing dead and threw himself over Martin's body, trying to save him from a fatal shot. "Don't kill him!"

"Brown, no!" Teimua called out, knowing he could no longer save the gardener. Minarii was ruthless with the hammer. The first bash to the head warped Brown's expression into a look of piteous confusion; the second crack of the mallet emptied his clock of its wheels and cogs. Brown burbled incoherently as Minarii, unrelenting, climbed on top of him to deliver a decisive third.

Martin, flat on the ground, was too weak to even wince at the horror of Brown's violent undoing. He slowly closed his eyes, resigned, and felt a ring of hot metal press against his temple. Pop.

During the evening before the massacre, the women had decided they would venture out to the bird cliffs at dawn to collect fresh eggs. It was the perfect opportunity for the Polynesian men to realize their premeditated plot against the mutineers. In the morning, only Mauatua stayed behind, belly wide, expecting her third child any day. She heard every single gunshot as they rang out around her. Christian had left before sunrise to tend to the taro ground. Mauatua called out to him each time the musket fire shattered the island's quiet. He never responded. She started to imagine the worst.

Minarii interrupted Mauatua's nervous pacing when he arrived unannounced at the Christian household. He held a crinkled clump of bloodstained fabric, which he quickly chucked at Mauatua's face. She unraveled the cloth to find a long line of gray pearl-shell buttons—it was Christian's beloved shirt.

"Where is he?" Mauatua spoke softly as she squeezed her husband's garment tight, her face turning sallow.

"Gone."

"*Where is he?*" Mauatua sternly pressed Minarii for a better answer.

"He squealed 'Oh dear' when I shot him in the back. And said nothing when I shot him again in the head." Minarii sauntered off with a disturbing lack of remorse.

Was it true? It couldn't be. Christian would have easily outmaneuvered the young Tahitian with faulty aim.

Mauatua urgently needed to find her husband, but she was too pregnant to even try to wobble her way up to the taro ground. She called out for Susannah and Tevarua, but they hadn't yet returned from collecting eggs.

Alone, Mauatua fell to her knees when the possibility of Christian's murder began to take shape. Twinges of guilt tangled into little knots in her throat—she felt responsible for her husband's demise. But Mauatua wasn't angry at Minarii—she realized now that she had failed him; he had left Tahiti at too young an age, before the credo of community could be tattooed upon his psyche. Without her guidance, Minarii had grown into a wild man tamed only by the selfishness of others. Pitcairn had taught him that malice was the hallmark of survival.

Mauatua cried out—a guttural moan of despair—clenching the bloody shirt and running her fingers along its pearlescent buttons. She'd never stare into Christian's silvery eyes again.

CHAPTER 19

AN EYE FOR AN EYE

1793

When the other women returned from collecting eggs along the cliffs, they found Mauatua alone and pale, stricken with such immeasurable grief that she spoke not a word. The shock of the morning's bloodbath soon triggered contractions. It was impossible to distinguish between the cries of despair and the labor pains as Mauatua brought her third child, a baby girl, into a world that was now so different than the day before.

After, Susannah stayed with Mauatua as she rested under the extravagant layers of linens and goose-down duvets, reminders of England that had once so delighted her husband. Although Christian had long sequestered himself in his cave, their house had never truly felt empty until now.

The other women had departed to tend to another islander who needed care. Smith, left for dead in the overgrowth, had managed to hobble down to Quintal's cabin, where Tevarua was nursing his wounds and keeping him safe from further harm. He had been shot twice—through the hand and shoulder. Though bloody, his injuries were superficial. Smith was going to survive.

For over a week, McCoy and Quintal remained in the high ridges on the far side of the island, trying to decipher every noise— every yell, every laugh, and every gunshot—down below. They had left in haste to avoid harm, carrying only a small trowel each for self-defense.

The hours were excruciatingly long without a jug of ti root brandy to dull their senses.

On the tenth day, they angled their gardening spades like weapons as the sound of rustling footsteps furtively approached the glade. It seemed the Polynesians had finally tracked them down and were coming to finish what they had started. The metal shaft of a musket swished through the dangling vines and branches, then Minarii appeared, gripping its handle, readying his aim. McCoy and Quintal waited anxiously for the other Polynesians to emerge. Minarii, however, was alone. It seemed foolish for the Polynesians to pit their smallest member against the two most hardened mutineers, but Minarii hadn't come to kill McCoy and Quintal—he wanted to join them in their hideaway.

"By guns and hammers," Minarii broke the anxious silence, detailing the bloody demise of each of their fellow seamen: a bullet for Williams, an axe for Mills, a mallet to Brown's head.

"And Young?" Quintal interrupted. Yes, what about Young? Where had he been this entire time?

Young seemed to possess a special talent for evading conflict. No one could recall the role he had played during the mutiny on the *Bounty*—he had practically vanished off the ship during its seizure, reemerging only after Bligh and his loyalists were cast off into the dawn. On Tubuai he had faded into the background during the colony's spectacular battle and subsequent downfall. And this time, it was even more exceptional that Young could escape harm, as a protracted fit of asthma had left him particularly vulnerable and in the constant care of the women. If Young had survived the massacre, then it was surely by design, which meant at least some of the Tahitian women knew about the murderous plot beforehand and had warned him to stay out of sight. Over the course of the previous year, Young seemed to have been well hidden from the throes of Quintal's despotism too; he had quietly garnered loyalty from Mauatua and the others as he sought to impress his own version of Britain upon Pitcairn.

Quintal flung his trowel with disgust when Minarii confirmed Young's safety, angered not only by the Tahitians' continued preference for his "half-breed" comrade but because none of the women—especially his wife, Tevarua—had tried to warn him of the impending peril. He realized that, like Bligh's reign on the ship, his oppressive authority afforded only the illusion of control but did not inspire obedience, especially among a group of women who still looked to Mauatua for guidance.

But there was more to Minarii's story beyond detailing the various fates of the Englishmen. Like Christian and his followers aboard the *Bounty*, the Polynesians had found that their camaraderie began to disintegrate shortly after their mutinous uprising.

The massacre of the Englishmen had been carried out with a modicum of success, enough to shift the balance of power on the island once more. With Quintal and McCoy cowering in the hills, the four Polynesian men were now in charge. Teimua nominated himself as leader, laying immediate claim to Susannah.

But Minarii, like Quintal, would soon become a man who swore no allegiances. Jealous, he shot Teimua dead while he serenaded his new consort on the nose flute. And when Susannah sought solace in Tetahiti's protective embrace, Minarii tried to murder the Tubuaian warrior too. Mauatua intervened, however, warding him off with a stern warning that he was no longer welcome in the village. Minarii was a fugitive, Quintal now realized. He wanted the boy's weapon in exchange for asylum, but Minarii knew better than to trust a person who—more than anyone else on Pitcairn—was a ruthless advocate of self-preservation above all else. They quarreled as the sun began to set, both certain to be murdered by the other if they remained in the glade, until McCoy suggested they work together. Although neither man was capable of trustworthiness, they now shared a common goal: retake the settlement below.

Minarii kept his musket—he gripped it tightly with both hands as he tried to rest on a grassy tuffet along the forest floor—but McCoy and Quintal stripped their visitor of his bullets as a compromise. Everyone slept with one eye open that night.

In the morning, Quintal had an idea: with a little planning, he, McCoy, and Minarii could easily subdue the four remaining men in the settlement and reclaim control of the island; Smith was hampered by his bullet wounds—as was Tetahiti after Minarii's ambush—and Young had yet to completely recover from his aggravated bouts of asthma. That left only Niau as a potential adversary. They'd gang up on him first, then quickly dispose of the other three before the women had a chance to intervene.

They eagerly plotted their foray throughout the day and emerged only briefly from their refuge in the late afternoon. High on the ridge, with a view of the village below, Minarii fired a single shot into the dusky sky as Quintal and McCoy banged their rusty trowels in solidarity. It was a war cry: long live their band of motherless children.

After sunset, the three men dropped their instruments to devour the bananas and guavas they had nabbed on the short hike back to their encampment. McCoy stared at Minarii—blithely chomping on the overripe fruits—wondering if he remembered this place from before. It was exactly here that Christian had set up his landing party's hideaway when they first arrived on Pitcairn to explore—a shaded glade offering protection from the threat of other inhabitants lurking throughout the island; the spot where McCoy had taunted Minarii and the others with the story of Jonah and the whale. McCoy was curious if Minarii still remembered the tale: how Jonah, after being swallowed by the great sea beast, finally accepted his fate and ventured down to the city of Nineveh, a place whose citizens were consumed with acts that violated God's will.

An early bedtime was imperative—they'd need to start their ambush well before sunrise in order to gather a few more weapons. But as Minarii once again began to recline on his thin mattress of crabgrass, he could no longer locate his musket. His stomach sank as he patted around in the darkness. The glint of the gun's brass fasteners caught his attention, and when he looked up he found himself on the wrong side of its barrel. Quintal's lips slowly furrowed into a sadistic smirk. He had slid the bullets back into their cartridge, then squeaked the musket's hammer back and took aim.

A clap of metallic thunder tore through the stillness of the tropical night. Quintal fired a single bullet into Minarii's stomach. Stunned, Minarii paused while the cottony gun smoke stitched itself back into the night. Then he slowly looked down—an aura of blood and bruising had begun to form, spreading out from the new wound like an expanding ring of wildfire engulfing the skin. He dabbed the warm wetness of the puncture with the tip of his finger—singeing hot at the point of entry—then looked back up at Quintal, confused. What had happened to their cadre of three? And their plans to retake the village? There was a better offer, it seemed: rid the island of this imp, this menace, and they could return down below unscathed. Quintal never swore allegiances, after all.

Minarii lifted his gaze to find Quintal still grinning, satisfied that he wouldn't need to waste a second bullet.

As Minarii began to lose his balance, he swiped his arms outward through the blackness but was unable to find a branch or tree trunk to prevent himself from falling. On his hands and knees, he wanted to crawl away, to scurry into the overgrowth and burrow himself in the weeds. Instead, he flopped onto his side, his expression still racked with disbelief. He tucked his knees into his chest and gently rocked himself back and forth on the ground, cheeping when a surge of searing pain would course through his curled body. Quintal and McCoy sat on their logs and watched. Minarii was cold now—he pulled his folded legs even closer and whimpered in Tahitian as he shivered; perhaps he was calling out for his long-lost mother. His chattered words soon became whispers, then thoughts, until finally the quiet returned to the glade.

For a while, neither Quintal nor McCoy spoke. They both leaned forward to examine Minarii's body. Quintal rested his chin on a closed fist; McCoy strummed the bristles of his beard with pensive fingers. Minarii had grown from a naive boy into a teenager with taut muscles toughened by three long years on the island, but suddenly he was a child again, or smaller—another puppy murdered to perpetuate a version of prosperity on the island.

Quintal reached down to unravel Minarii's crooked body before the rigor set in. Outstretched on his back, Minarii's limbs finally went limp. His face, however, remained clenched, shocked by their treachery.

———————

OUT THE WINDOW of Young's home, Mauatua could see a figure approaching in the distance holding a mace. It was Quintal, and as he got closer Mauatua realized that he was not in fact carrying a weapon. It was Minarii's severed head, gripped by the hair and swung around like a ball and chain.

Quintal had fulfilled Minarii's draconian destiny, but, after returning to the village, he no longer wanted to stay. With Teimua dead, Tetahiti and Niau were now in strict command of the remaining Pitcairners—they had moved into the Christian homestead and taken Susannah as their consort. Young and Smith were now their deferential aides.

Mauatua still deeply detested Quintal, but for the first time since they'd left Tahiti she was willing, even keen, to abet his request: kill the last two Polynesian men. That night, as Quintal climbed back up to the mountain ridges to await the heads of Tetahiti and Niau, Mauatua gathered the women at Young's house to plot yet another round of vengeance. Tetahiti was supposed to have been Christian's protector *taio*, and despite his wicked mistreatment by the other mutineers, he was a traitor in Mauatua's eyes. He needed to die.

Jenny knew exactly how. It was time to reveal the one tidbit still trapped in her web of secrets: the affair between Teatuahitea—Brown's wife—and Tetahiti.

Jenny's complicity seemed as uncharacteristic as Mauatua's scheming, but it allowed her to recapture some of the leverage she once held among the other Tahitians, especially since her dreams of leaving the island or installing new leadership seemed definitively dashed. Most of the women had long written her off as a lonely eccentric, but now they were quickly remembering how she had once been the most outspoken and intrepid member of Mauatua's clan. They eagerly heeded her advice.

The women proceeded to pressure Teatuahitea into resuming her dalliance. She'd call on Tetahiti in the middle of the night, as Jenny had witnessed her do dozens of times before, and after they had sex, she would stab him to death while he slept. A presiding Young then unveiled a dagger and with a crazed expression—an unsettling streak of his personality the women had yet to see—he mime-jabbed the knife against his jugular to show Teatuahitea exactly where she'd need to land the killing tool.

The following evening, a hesitant Teatuahitea roused Tetahiti out from under the goose-down covers of Christian's old bed. She led him by the hand through the night, back to the eastern part of the island where the Polynesians' dwellings now stood empty and bare—in only a few weeks' time, the jungle had already begun its savage reclamation of the untended huts. They had sex under the stars. Afterward, when Tetahiti had fallen asleep, Teatuahitea propped herself up on one elbow and, for a while, stared at the slumbering Tubuaian as he snored softly, content. He was a gentle giant, with bulbous muscles the size of ripened gourds, but he possessed a tenderness within, rarely found in other men.

She couldn't do it. Nancy may have been able to drive a bayonet through Tararo, but that was an act of self-preservation. Teatuahitea couldn't murder a man she had grown to love, even if the other women were aggrieved by his righteous revenge against the Englishmen. Instead, she nuzzled up against his trunk-like torso and wrapped a protective arm around his waist. Perhaps in the morning she could ask Mauatua to reason with Quintal. He had already disposed of Minarii, who had been bewitched by European bloodlust. They needed Tetahiti's brute strength to till the soil and mend their cabins; they needed Tetahiti to ensure Pitcairn's eventual prosperity.

As her thoughts began to drift, a loud *shunk* of metal startled her awake. A long throaty groan quickly followed. Teatuahitea let out a piercing shriek when she opened her eyes: a battle axe was protruding from Tetahiti's bleeding chest. He began to thrash around on the ground in a shock-stricken fit. At the other end of the gleaming weapon were Susannah's little hands, clenching its long wooden handle. Without hesitation, Susannah lifted the heavy blade above her head and plunged it down once more. This time it fell directly along on the bridge of Tetahiti's nose, splitting his face in two.

Susannah had quietly followed the couple up onto the rocky mounds of the east—like Jenny's ritual night stalking—certain that Teatuahitea would not go through with the murder. At Young's insistence, Susannah had volunteered on behalf of Mauatua, who was too weak after giving birth. Now she wondered how many bathing sessions it would take to wash away the memory of such an ugly act. She knelt down to muzzle Teatuahitea's screaming, then trilled a few notes of birdsong into the quieting midnight air. A response from the other side of the island was almost immediate: a crackle of gunfire, then a resounding hoot of victory—Young had rid the island of its final Polynesian man, Niau.

In the morning, Young hacked off the heads and arms of the two dead Polynesians and had Smith march them up to Quintal and McCoy's hideaway as proof of their demise. By the end of the day, the women had redistributed themselves among the four remaining Englishmen: Mauatua and Nancy moved in with Young, and Susannah joined Tevarua at Quintal's house. Only Jenny remained alone, in the cabin she had nominally shared with Martin before his death. On an open windowsill she displayed the collected skulls of the deceased like little dolls with mouths agape—she had removed their jawbones and fashioned them into jewelry.

A dozen lives had now been lost in less than four years' time, and like some cruel Darwinian joke, the least fit people had survived. While the next four years would pass rather uneventfully, Pitcairn was only biding its time, preparing to push its residents to the brink of extinction.

CHAPTER 20

A SPIDER'S PROGRESS

2018

Despite an enviable amount of fresh fruit and fish at their disposal, the Warrens had a serious penchant for canned food. It seemed that half the pallets of Spam from the *Claymore* had wound up in their pantry. And there was corn and chicken, too, often mixed together in a giant bowl with a dollop of salad dressing—a main course, with a ripe banana served on the side the way the French ate baguette.

I had begun to dread dinnertime at the Warrens. While everyone on the island would occasionally break into Pitkernese, a pidgin amalgam of English and Tahitian spoken with piratical inflections, Carol and Jay would frequently have long conversations in the local language at the kitchen table fully knowing that I couldn't parse out a single word from their jargon. Linguists classify Pitkernese as a cant—a dialect purposefully constructed to be arcane so as to exclude outsiders from grasping it. "Hello," for example, was "watawieh."

Worse, however, were the long stretches of quiet when no one spoke—so hushed I could hear the distant clinks of the generator between chews. Carol seemed perfectly comfortable with the silence, as though she was willing me out of existence each time she dropped her gaze to aggregate another bite of preserved peas.

One evening, the voice of Carol and Jay's daughter Darralyn crackled on the marine radio inviting herself over for dinner, rescuing us from our nightly tedium. She regaled me with a story of a Michelin-starred chef from Italy so enamored by the legend of the *Bounty* that he insisted on cooking an elaborate meal for the Warren family when they were visiting Europe: antipasti, risotto, and osso buco. When the final course came out of the kitchen—handcrafted pasta with a luscious tomato sauce—Darralyn pulled a ripe banana out of her purse, peeled it, and plopped it right on top of her noodles.

"Have you ever seen a chef cry?" She burst out laughing. Carol and Jay chuckled as well.

The other nights at Up Tommy's were dull. We had already gone around the kitchen discussing the various paintings and pictures that enlivened the walls. The only thing that was left was the magazine feature that had been defanged of its staples and pasted page by page on the refrigerator with yellowed tape. Its edges were frayed and words faded, but I couldn't decipher how long the article had been there, since the rate of decay—the speed at which the climate subsumed paper, or any organic material, in its aggressive return to a primordial state—was ten times faster on Pitcairn. Maybe Carol had put it up right before I arrived; maybe it had been hanging there for thirty years.

"I didn't realize that another journalist had come to the island," I said, motioning to the matte photos of jungle ferns. I had certainly been given the impression that I was the only one to visit in recent years.

"That's not Pitcairn." Carol scooped another forkful of Spam and corn salad into her mouth without looking up. She was right, of course. As I looked more closely, I realized that the ecology was slightly different—more temperate, with a preponderance of tall, thin-trunked pines. "It's Norfolk Island," Carol continued. "It's where the others live."

"The others?"

"Yeah, the other descendants."

I was stunned. I had read Nordhoff and Hall's *Bounty Trilogy* before my trip. Although it was a fictional twist on fact—it ends with the brutal massacre of most of the mutineers—there was no mention of another impossible rock lost in the South Pacific that completed the *Bounty* puzzle.

"So, there's a second island, with more Christians and Warrens?"

"Yeah," Carol responded as though it were perfectly normal—obvious, even—for lightning to strike twice.

Some fifty years after Mayhew Folger—the American captain aboard the *Topaz*—had met the mysterious John Adams and accidentally uncovered the secret of the mutineers' hideaway, news had finally spread across the entire world of Pitcairn's existence. By then—the second half of the nineteenth century—there were, of course, no more fugitives to try for treason. Instead the little society had become a darling of the Christian world, lauded by all for its naive prosperity. Two generations after the barbaric undoing of the original settlers, the Pitcairners were indeed thriving—perhaps even a little too much; there were now almost two hundred inhabitants clinging to the two-mile rock, and resources were beginning to thin.

A request was sent to England that perhaps there was another, larger enclave the Pitcairners could inhabit somewhere within the span of the British Empire. Queen Victoria eagerly obliged, charmed by the notion that a real-life Utopia existed within her domain. She had the perfect solution.

Norfolk is a lonely freckle on the surface of the sea, halfway between Australia and New Zealand. First found by Captain Cook, the island was praised in the explorer's diary for its abundance of "New Zealand flax," sturdy conifers that made excellent sailing masts. Around thirteen square miles in size (roughly seven times larger than Pitcairn), Norfolk seemed too small to support England's ambitious colonial plans, so it was selected instead as the site of one of the first penal settlements when Britain began exporting its convicts Down Under. Initially, its isolation was a huge financial burden on the Crown, but later, far-flung Norfolk was the perfect repository for the most hardened and fearsome criminals of the empire.

Conveniently, the Pitcairners were petitioning the queen at around the same time that Australia's convict ships were reaching the end of their service. Norfolk's criminals had all been removed

and consolidated on Van Diemen's Land (which later rebranded itself as Tasmania when it sought to attract free settlers). The island
now sat bare, ready for the descendants of the *Bounty* to inhabit its
ruins. On June 8, 1856, 194 weary travelers—every last person on
Pitcairn—arrived on the *Morayshire* after five miserable weeks at sea
and moved into the derelict officers' barracks.

There was a snag, however. The Pitcairners hadn't properly fath-
omed that not all the world shared their native tropical weather. Although Norfolk was warm, its lower latitude meant that coconuts and
a few other staples of the Pitcairn diet wouldn't grow. Nevertheless,
they began to settle in and were pleased to discover that their new
home—with plenty of fresh water and timber—was a strategic pro-
visioning station for the still-booming whaling industry. Hundreds
of American whalers passed through, many staying on Norfolk in-
definitely. The Warren name was American in origin; a particularly
virile sea captain shacked up with the great-granddaughter of one of
the mutineers and had over a dozen children of his own.

After two years, a contingent of Norfolk Islanders were still
grumpy about their resettlement and decided to brave the hideous
voyage back to Pitcairn, returning to pry their abandoned cabins out
of the jaws of the jungle and live in a state of half reclamation—
slaves to nature's relentless ambition, much like Carol and Jay. The
rest—the majority—remained on Norfolk, and today the island,
now a part of Australia, has around 1,700 inhabitants, most with
last names like Christian, Quintal, and McCoy.

With Pitcairn's population back down to a manageable sixty people, the island had once again achieved homeostasis, just in time
for the Adventist ministers to target the colony of world-wary and
impressionable loners. And there were others, too, who were keen on
taking advantage of the community—including an eccentric British
conman who briefly installed himself as leader, forging a land deed
from the Crown. After years of predatory intruders, maybe it had
become second nature to shut outsiders out.

So why, then, were the Pitcairners even interested in tourism
when a latent—or blatant—xenophobia was so deeply embedded in
their psyche? Why not, say, ramp up production and exportation of

the island's premium honey, which the Warrens were already successfully farming as a pastime? Perhaps they hadn't realized that the cornerstone of the hospitality industry was having to actually be hospitable. Carol certainly hadn't gotten the memo, but it wasn't just her.

Steve and Olive were welcoming and gracious hosts, but after leaving Big Fence, it was as though I was dead to them while I stayed with the Warrens. Rather than resolving whatever petty, small-town disputes the two families had, they simply pretended the other pile didn't exist. Their son Shawn, the supposedly affable mayor, was still nowhere to be found, and their other son Randy had reneged on an offer to take me fishing. I could hear the crabs I had trapped with Carol still clicking their claws in the buckets we had left by the mess of mechanical parts at the front entry.

It wasn't as obvious as Simon Young/Yung's unprovoked outburst at the pier when I first arrived on the island, but apparently, without my knowing, a court of local jurors had sentenced me to spend the rest of my time on Pitcairn in solitary confinement. It now felt very fitting that the tourism office was in a jail. I had been enjoying my solo time, hiking up to the various viewpoints and swimming in Saint Paul's Pool—being comfortable with protracted amounts of aloneness is a basic prerequisite for field reporters specializing in remote travel—but there was something unsettling, something poignant and lonely, about feeling completely isolated while surrounded by other people. The houses on Pitcairn didn't have front doors, but it had been made clear to me that I was most definitely not welcome inside any of them.

"YOU MISSED CHURCH today." We were back at the dinner table—Carol, Jay, and me—forking through another mishmash of nonperishables loosed from their cans. Carol was talking to me again without lifting her focus from her plate. "Everyone else was there."

"There were some beautiful clouds above Saint Paul's Pool that I wanted to photograph." I was lying. I had, in fact, taken great interest in the kind of off-brand Adventism that was being peddled on Pitcairn by an unordained pastor with a fondness for Spam. It seemed like an awful waste to have hunted all those pigs long ago.

I had stopped by the church when it was empty—the thick walls smothered the pews in humidity as though its architect believed that sweating was the ultimate form of penance. I had swiped a couple of pamphlets—conversion literature—printed in the United States on shiny paper stock and shipped across the Pacific aboard the freighter. But something seemed disingenuous about going to mass for reasons other than prayer. I felt like I'd be an anthropologist from the Captain Cook era if I were to attend, studying the "noble savage" and their unenlightened ways.

"What time will the *Bounty* museum be open tomorrow?" I tried to change the subject.

"It won't be open tomorrow," Carol snapped back, quick.

"Oh, but I have a flyer from the tourist office that says—"

"It will not be open tomorrow," she cut me off.

I paused, trying to decide if this was an act of spite—retaliation for not attending services—or if Carol simply enjoyed lording whatever power she had over others. Either way, I think I had started to hate Carol. Yes, hate was the prevailing emotion, which troubled me doubly because the ferocity seemed like a ridiculous overreaction to someone I'd never see again after I left Pitcairn. And yet I wanted her to like me.

Maybe my feelings were amplified because I couldn't leave. When I'd hit an obstacle on other research trips I'd simply rearrange my itinerary. "Change your place, change your luck" was a credo that had served me well over the years, but I had nowhere to go. I was trapped, with thousands of miles of ocean all around, on an island whose perimeter was guarded by impenetrable rock formations with ominous names like McCoy's Drop. The only place to go was down.

Carol and Jay had started jabbering in Pitkernese again. I pushed my food around my plate; it was too humid to eat. But then, looking up, I felt my body drain itself of all color and vigor: on the doorframe was one of the wicked Pitcairn spiders I had heard of but not yet seen, like some kind of mega-arachnid that had evolved without predators over thousands of years of isolation. Its body was easily the size of a human hand, with eight spindly legs erect like full-length fingers. And it was fearlessly approaching, not scuttling away like other bugs.

I held my breath, transfixed by the spider's plotting, exacting motions. Carol had noticed it too. She looked up at the doorframe, then turned back in my direction and stared me straight in the eye. "It's pregnant. Very pregnant."

My stomach churned. I began to ascribe a vindictive quality to the spider's persona, that she would leap down onto my face and claw my eyes out with her hairy digits if I were to threaten the well-being of her babies hidden in the fat, translucent sac on her abdomen. "Wha—what do we do?"

The unflappable Carol didn't respond. She was frightened too.

If I tried to swat the spider, I might burst her belly open. I had to nudge her, coax her, in the other direction, as though it were her idea to crawl back out the door. It was better to deal with one adversary than a raining torrent of her scurrying progeny. Slowly, the spider retreated into the alcove that led to Carol and Jay's bedroom. I was pleased. Carol had turned away, pretending the spider no longer existed, as she was wont to do.

"Carol, I was wondering, who will take over your *Bounty* boutique when you decide to retire?" I gave up my secret, that I had rummaged through her private storeroom behind the closed door. But I had a thought, a way to cajole Carol into giving me what I wanted while making it seem like her idea.

"My grandchildren, I suppose," Carol was skeptical of my intentions. "They're going to continue the traditions of our people and island."

"That's really nice to hear. And so I'm sure you've been busy training them as guides like yourself?"

I could almost hear the words "billable hours" manifest in her brain. Clearly the only way I was going to extricate myself from this isolation was to hire the islanders as my friends, and maybe, soon enough, they'd want to spend time with me of their own accord when they realized I wasn't a missionary or a conman.

Carol buzzed the marine radio, signaling for her daughter Charlene to send her kids over for breakfast. And the following morning, three of the Warren grandchildren appeared at the entry to Up Tommy's: two swaggering teens just back from high school in New Zealand and one eagerly smiling, not yet old enough to go. "We're taking you out in our boat," the oldest explained, and within an hour we were circumnavigating the island, stopping at the best spots to fish for *faafaia* and *nanue* and spear-dive for lobsters.

That evening, the entire Warren pile gathered for a barbecue, loading up their plates with our fresh catch and taking a seat in front of the television just in time to watch the latest episode of the Australian soap opera *Home and Away*, airing on the only channel Pitcairn received by antenna. Everyone was rapt. A nuclear bomb could have detonated on the nearby Mururoa atoll and no one would have noticed—hypnotized by the drama unfolding in the fictitious town of Summer Bay: alcoholism, teenage pregnancy, and suicide.

CHAPTER 21

THE BOOK OF FEAR

1797–1798

N o. It was so early, too early. Tevarua's tapa dress was damp. She held herself like a child needing to urinate. There was still another month left—probably two. It wasn't time. She alerted Susannah, who immediately ran off to gather the other women, and when she returned Tevarua was already on her knees with her arms propped up against a nearby tree. Something had gone wrong after that time Quintal had shoved her. She could feel it. She had fallen on her stomach, and everything changed.

Susannah crouched down beside Tevarua and rubbed her back as she pushed. Her syncopated breaths became louder—panting—as the contractions intensified. It was so easy, too easy. Tevarua cranked her body into a squat, and, with a bellowing groan, pulled the baby out as it crowned. Susannah readied a clean bolt of bark cloth and wrapped the writhing newborn, dabbing the blood and afterbirth off of his face. He was so small, too small. And he didn't wail like the other children when they had been taken from the womb and cast out into the coldness of the world. He was a little lamb, bleating. So weak, too weak.

They named him John. He died seven days later.

For seven more days Mauatua, Susannah, and Jenny remained at Tevarua's side as she rocked the lifeless baby in her arms, breaking the quiet only once to sing a single verse from her favorite song:

> *Herod the king, in his raging,*
> *Chargèd he hath this day*
> *His men of might in his own sight*
> *All young children to slay.*

———————

SMITH WOKE UP screaming. He had been back on the white sand beach, only this time no one was drowning in the shallows. Neither Churchill nor the Tubuaian boy were lying lifeless in the waves like hunks of flotsam scavenged from a wrecked vessel. And beyond the dunes, the sprawling field of clover was empty as well—Thompson was gone, as was the Tubuaian warrior, both saved from the faceless stalker and his searing weapon. This time he was coming for Smith. Down into the water? Up toward the pasture? He couldn't decide on the best path to evade the stranger that had always lurked so menacingly in his dreams. Smith remained on the crest of shells and stones, but his legs were getting heavier as he ran. His feet began to disappear under the sand—deeper and deeper—with each labored step until he was finally stuck, unable to scoop himself out of the muddy paste. He fell onto his back, and with palms pressed tightly together he pleaded desperately to be spared a fate similar to the others'. Now hovering over a trembling Smith, the hunter untied the large blue robe that had long concealed his identity: it was the archangel Michael, banisher of heaven's evil, who had cast Satan out of the sky. Wings akimbo, he lifted his dart high—it glittered in the tropical sun—and in one elegant gesture he plunged it straight through Smith's chest, piercing his heart.

Obuarei shook Smith as he convulsed in bed. She had tried to rouse him several times as he rolled around in a sweaty fit until finally he sprang up, eyes wide, and patted his chest with frantic fingers. He breathed an exhausted sigh of relief. The flourish of cosmic steel hadn't left a mark, only a warning: to expel the evil within.

When morning came, Smith walked over to Young's house and announced that he needed to learn the Word of God.

At the same time, Obuarei wandered over to Quintal's to fetch Tevarua and check if the long stalks of their plucked *poepoe* grass were properly dried; the leaves had browned and their grains marbled. As they gathered the sun-bleached stems that were lying across warm stones, Obuarei told Tevarua of Smith's repeated dreams and how he was eager to seek Young's religious guidance.

Tevarua seemed just as keen, even though Quintal never allowed her to spend time with the other men. She had always been a little envious of Susannah, and now Mauatua, when Young would regale them with fantastical stories of his Christian god. She gathered her drying stems—they would preen their *poepoe* reeds on the grassy lawn near Young's house. No one could stop them from simply lounging within earshot of Smith and Young's conversation.

Rather than starting with the genesis of man, Young immediately thumbed through the *Bounty's* Bible to find the book of Proverbs. It held the advice, he explained, that God gave to King Solomon, the wisdom required to live well.

Young laid out the landscape for his new believer: God is just and has organized the world so that it's fair. The righteous are rewarded and the wicked damned, but in order to access God's infinite wisdom, you must first learn to revere him, to respect his delineation of what is good and never cross into the bad.

"The fear of the Lord is the beginning of wisdom: and the knowledge of the holy is understanding," Young completed the book's preamble of verses, then began spouting off short adages to which he hoped Smith would now abide.

Obuarei shucked her plant stems of their little bluish nodules, then gently pushed the point of her awl through each bulb, clearing out a hole for string. Tevarua had dried and stretched several sinuous roots, which now resembled thin strands of brown fishing line. As Obuarei passed Tevarua each bead, she would polish them on her tapa dress, then carefully string them along the wire, one by one.

Although Tevarua, as well as the other Tahitian women, had been exposed to the Christian mythos for many years now, she had never witnessed its proselytizing outright. And the first lesson, a tutorial on fear, seemed unfathomable. To her, fear wasn't an emotion, it was an instinct: a back-of-brain shock that curdled the spleen and shot tremors through the body down to one's quaking shins. It was the visceral, animal dread when confronted with an apex predator. There was a second type of fear in Tahiti, too, with its own special name: *mehameha*, an inexplicable, unquantifiable feeling of angst as though you're being haunted by a ghost. Neither definition bore any resemblance to this learned terror that Young described.

There must be a counter-emotion as well, true to the dual nature of all good-and-evil Christian traits: if reverence was fear, then God—its receiver—possessed power, and if you taught a man fear then you also ingrained within him a desire to control it. The men of the *Bounty* were so confused as to why Tahiti had remained a delicate realm of many chiefdoms; even teeny Tubuai was parsed out into three separate clans. Without the construct of fear, the want for authority hadn't been given its lease of the Polynesian imagination. Sure, there were factions who warred over unreconciled issues, but the bloodlust for absolute rule of the realm—to crave the fear of others—was a distinctly European obsession.

Young swiped through the pages of the Bible to another section. There was more to learn than Proverbs; the scales of justice had to be weighed in a human experiment.

"There was a man in the land of Uz, whose name was Job; and that man was perfect and upright, and one that feared God, and eschewed evil," he started, reading from the next issue of the books of wisdom.

Uz was a far land, uncountable miles from where the rest of the Bible's action unfurled. And at the suggestion of Satan—a most adversarial voice among the choir of angels—God puts Job's devotion to the test by stripping him of all he was grateful for: his children perish, his health declines, he loses his home, and his spouse shuns him. Shortly thereafter, three friends learn of his misfortune and for a full week they grieve at his side until finally he breaks the silence, sobbing, and curses the day he was born: "Why died I not from the womb? Why did I not give up the ghost when I came out of the belly? . . . For now should I have lain still and been quiet . . . with kings and counsellors of the earth, which built desolate places for themselves . . . or as a hidden untimely birth I had not been; as infants which never saw light."

The three friends then try to rationalize Job's undoing—perhaps he has acted in a way to warrant God's punishment—but they come up short as their ailing friend maintains his righteousness. Finally, Job demands the attention of God, who manifests as a storm cloud. Instead of explaining his actions, God takes Job on a grand tour of the planet, showing both its vastness and the intricacies within: the winds and ice of the poles, the stars of Orion above, even the ways in which wild goats carefully negotiate the crags of a mountain, lest they plummet. The journey culminates with the discovery of the Leviathan—"Behold, the hope of him is in vain: shall not one be cast down even at the sight of him?"—a most complex creature of which God is infinitely proud, an untamable monster, beautiful but dangerous, that rises from the deepest of seas.

Job is finally humbled by the complexities of God's work in the world he has created, but the man does not learn exactly why he— and others worthy of mercy—has suffered.

"So why do bad things happen to good people?" Tevarua interrupted, slinking the pliable root through one final bead. Young, surprised that Tevarua had been paying attention, let the Bible clap shut before he could finish its final passages. He didn't respond; there wasn't a clear answer.

Tevarua tied her long string of earthen pearls in a loop—her necklace of Job's tears—as Young's parables wound their way through her mind. If God was so busy carrying out justice all across the globe, then perhaps he had forgotten about Pitcairn.

THE LARGE BANYAN on Smith's property was an ideal drinking spot, with a thick trunk perfect for reclining and a generous canopy of shade-bearing branches overhead. Now that Smith had "felt the fear of god"—as McCoy and Quintal mocked him—the two friends could idle under the tree uninterrupted while Smith spent his days over at Young's house, their noses buried in the *Bounty*'s Bible. Although McCoy had refined his recipe for ti root brandy, his prolonged bouts of drunkenness had made him careless with the quality of the latest batches—the proof was too high, sending the faithful imbibers into incoherent rants on most afternoons.

Conversations under the great banyan always started out the same way. McCoy and Quintal relived all of the funniest moments they had shared over the last few years: the look on Heywood's face as the medic burned him free of venereal sores, that weird sound Thompson made when he'd bring a woman back to his berth, the time they tricked Hallett and Hayward into eating biscuits full of squiggly maggots, and then there was that whore back at the shipyards who gave "Spithead" a whole new meaning. They'd chuckle deliriously, but tensions would begin to flare when neither friend could concede that their habit of reminiscing was a battle of willful ignorance against their current condition. They may have been on an island, but it no longer bore any resemblance to their Caribbean dream. They had lost all of their drinking buddies, there were no more "slaves" to do the hard labor, and Pitcairn was now home to fifteen young children—the same number as the adult inhabitants (four mutineers and eleven women)—who needed constant care.

Quintal sprang up when the aroma of fire-broiled fish wafted past his nostrils. He left McCoy sprawled against the tree, lost in a monologue of drunken mumbles. Quintal's first few steps were tentative: four paces to undo the effects of the moonshine, then a dozen more to push his way through the tangle of vines that blocked the untended path. With flapping jowls numbed by too much alcohol and a mouth outstretched with growing hunger, Quintal started to drool from his smile of fangs; his gait was lupine too. He emerged, haunches high and arms forward, into the clearing around his garden, where he found Tevarua searing her catch over the glow of crackling embers.

"What the fuck is this, woman?" Quintal barked, wafting away a cloud of hanging smoke to examine his wife's cooking; the *faafaia* were disappointingly small and he hated choking down the *nanue*'s little needle-bones. There would hardly be enough for him to eat once all the feckless children had been fed their portions. He toppled over the hearth with a ravenous howl and, in one exaggerated leap, trounced a screaming Tevarua, pulling her down by her hair and slamming her face against the ground. It wasn't just the fish. Quintal had suddenly—and soberingly—confronted his own pathetic state, reflected back at him in the eyes of his frightened wife. His fit of frustration intensified, sending Tevarua's cries into a high-pitched shriek as he yawned his jaw wide against her trembling cheek and chomped down on the cartilage of her ear, tearing it off in one clenching bite.

Meanwhile, McCoy hadn't moved. He was still sitting under the tree as its shadow grew longer in the last hour of the day. The grog jug was empty. He jammed his finger down its narrow neck and swished it around in a sloppy effort to sop up the droplets of liquor-tinged condensation stuck inside. He rescued his thirsty digit with a loud thunk of suction and went to lick it like a lollipop, but quickly spat it out when it tasted earthy and bitter like the dirt that encrusted his fingernails. Half forgetting that he was alone, McCoy turned to express his disgust to a long-gone Quintal. His seat was warm and wet—had he been sitting in mud and not noticed? It took McCoy a few blinks to realize he had pissed himself. He sprang to his feet and, with one hand gripping the tree bark, he used the other to wag the fabric of his trousers dry. But there was a distinct sound from deeper in the woods that interrupted his cursing: echoing giggles.

"Who's there?" With blurry eyes McCoy scanned the overgrowth as the laughter crescendoed into a rolling fit of ridicule. *"Who's there?*" He took his hand off the tree trunk to wave an angry fist in the direction of the noise but stumbled to the ground instead. "Show yourself!" He popped back up to his feet. "Jenny, is that you?" Finding better balance, McCoy plodded toward the taunting laughter, his legs striding wide to avoid the swishing of soggy canvas between his thighs. "Come back here!" She was getting away. "Stop!" McCoy untied the cord around his waist and climbed out of his dropped pants. He quickened his speed. The white flash of a tapa skirt haunted the greens and browns of the brush. "Jenny I know it's you!" He breathed fire, hurling himself into the valley and up toward the cliffs, his feet unbothered by the shells and fallen thistles that threatened to puncture his toes. When the cackling grew even louder, McCoy paused to lift a giant stone—"I'LL FUCKING KILL YOU, JENNY!"—and heaved the rock onto his shoulder as he picked up his pace again. Faster he sprinted. "I'M GONNA GET YOU, YOU BITCH!" Faster, still. Then, suddenly, the rug of red rock and soil was no longer beneath his feet. Boulder in his arms, he tore through fifty feet of air and smashed into the waves. And down McCoy went, entering into the springs of the sea in search of its depths until he found the gates of death.

Sometimes bad things happen to bad people too.

CHAPTER 22

DOWN ROPE

2018

There are no restaurants on Pitcairn, but on Friday afternoons there's a bar—the Whale's Tooth Inn—with a much-touted trivia challenge hosted by the heavily pierced and tatted Pawl Warren. His wife, Sue, a hardy New Zealander, had originally come to the island as the prison warden, which prompted far more questions than the one at hand: How many people were actually going to show up to their pub challenge?

That answer, it turned out, was just two: me and the professor from the freighter, still in the midst of his astronomical evaluations.

For two hours a week, Pawl and Sue charged visitors a premium to sip drinks in their living room, which to me seemed like a sneaky ploy that further leveraged their unhealthy appreciation of alcohol. Each time I took a swig of my beer, they matched me with a shot of vodka.

Sue handed us each a sheet of paper with a long list of ditloids, word puzzles deduced from numbers and letters: 18 H in a G C, or eighteen holes in a golf course; 7 D S, or seven deadly sins; and so forth. We had ten minutes to jot down as many answers as we could decipher while she poured herself another round.

It felt like homework. The professor, unsurprisingly, was very much enthused.

The second part was more interactive. Sue simply called out questions—each with a numerical answer—and we could chime in as we pleased.

"In 'The Twelve Days of Christmas,' there are how many pipers piping?"

I knew that one: "Eleven."

"What is the atomic number of cadmium?"

The professor answered with certainty: "Forty-eight."

"Until what age can a giant Galapagos tortoise live?"

Neither of us had any idea.

"One hundred?"

"120?"

"According to *National Geographic*," Sue piped up, flaunting her answer sheet, "the giant tortoise is the longest-lived vertebrate on the planet. The oldest on record died at 152."

There was no clear winner. It seemed the game really served to satisfy Sue's need to show others that she knew things they didn't. Afterward, she began to quiz us on what we had seen around the island. The professor, however, was prone to long siestas during the day to escape the oppressive heat before venturing out in the evenings to watch the stars.

"Have you been to Lookout Point?" Sue aimed her machine-gun questioning at me instead.

"Yes."

"And Christian's Cave?"

"Yup."

"Tedside?"

"Mm-hmm."

"And Down Rope?"

"Not yet."

On the eastern part of the island near Saint Paul's Pool, there was a trailhead marked "Down Rope" because hikers needed the assistance of an old nautical cable strung through iron ringlets to climb down what was essentially the sheer side of a cliff. At the bottom was Pitcairn's only beach, but that wasn't the main draw—on the boulders below was a collection of rock carvings: geometric and anthropomorphic designs etched into the primordial stone.

"You've gotta go Down Rope to see the hieroglyphs," Sue insisted.

"I believe the term you're looking for is petroglyphs," corrected the professor.

"No. They're hieroglyphics, put there by the ancient Egyptians."

The Pyramids of Giza were over eleven thousand miles away and yet Sue, trivia mistress, was sure that the pharaohs had gotten in the little canoes they used to float down the Nile and sailed all the way down to Pitcairn to leave a few squiggly shapes on some volcanic stones.

I remained silent, but the professor couldn't resist. "Surely they were left by the proto-Polynesians who visited the island before the arrival of the mutineers." There was a pamphlet at the tourism office that posited as much: the carvings were made by the seafarers who quarried Pitcairn's obsidian. But Sue stood her ground, insisting that not only she, but all of the islanders, were wise to a great global conspiracy that sought to cover up the ancient Egyptians' navigational prowess.

With such a hotly debated and most fantastical origin story, the glyphs (whichever they were) of Down Rope were high on my to-do list, but I hadn't yet visited, as a descent on one's own was strictly forbidden. Three years earlier, a visitor had tried going down without assistance and fell a full seven hundred feet, tearing both of his arms out of their sockets as he struck every snaggy branch and ledge on the interminable drop. I had heard the story of the "Great Mangling" numerous times, repeated like an admonition. On an island with practically no new news, it was regularly divulged as though it had happened only days before.

———

"I CAN STILL hear his cries of agony." Steve's sister Brenda had offered to take the professor and me Down Rope the next day. "That poor man screamed for days—and all night—as we waited for a vessel to take pity on his situation and pick him up."

I immediately thought back to Steve and his crooked gait, and what it must have been like to suffer for such a protracted amount of time without the possibility of care. Olive had a story too, even more tragic than fractured bones. Her ailing aunt had perished en route to the hospital in Tahiti when her appendix ruptured at sea. Afterward, in what seemed like a bit of an overreaction, Pitcairn's entire population was ferried off the island to have their appendixes preventatively removed. I had seen all of their belly scars when everyone had gathered down at the docks in their bathing trunks for a communal swim.

Before being issued my paperwork to board the freighter, I had been mandated to purchase travel insurance that covered a full million dollars' worth of evacuation and medical care. It had even been suggested that I get my affairs in order and draft a formal will. The number one rule on Pitcairn, it seemed, was don't get hurt on Pitcairn.

The professor peered over the cliffside—the narrow path shrouded in vines and brambles—and faced the very-real possibility that he may be the next mangled visitor spoken of in cautionary tales. "You two enjoy yourselves. I'm staying behind." We couldn't convince him to change his mind.

Brenda was tiny in stature, with flowing strands of salt-and-pepper hair tucked under a grimy baseball cap. She seemed particularly adept at negotiating the scatter of little toeholds required to make the descent. We barely spoke on the trek down, stopping only halfway to both admire our progress and evaluate the rest of the path ahead. I followed her footing, step for step, until we finally reached the bottom, where a small spit of sand fanned out under the cliffs. There was garbage everywhere—plastic moorings, logs, and fishing nets—that had washed up from distant shores after spending months, or even years, languidly looking for a place to make landfall. Brenda led me to the stone etchings nearby. They were larger and more pronounced than I had thought—bigger than my hand and head—and only looked slightly weathered despite the centuries of salt air: a wheel, a cross, and many representations of the human figure. I ran my fingers through the chalky grooves chiseled into the dark, damp stone, wondering exactly how long they had been there.

———————

THAT AFTERNOON I visited Jay's sister Meralda. Their mother, Mavis, was sitting in a rocking chair on the front porch, nose dipped in a tattered magazine trying to complete the word search at the back. She squinted her eyes—a lazy smile—which granted me entry through the doorless passage into the house she shared with her daughter.

Inside I found Meralda in the dungeon of a kitchen—a traditional Pitcairn hearth, she explained, dug into earthen walls and reinforced with wood and iron. She was a wide woman, her stride accidentally overbearing as she approached me to say hello. Her beady black eyes beamed behind wire-framed spectacles. There was a softness to Meralda—a kindness, even, despite her lumbering demeanor—easily apparent when she grinned.

I had seen Meralda around the island before. She didn't smile often, but her face lit up when she guided me deeper into her house to show me some shelves stacked high with mason jars, each filled with pickled pineapples. "A delicacy, you know. I ship these all over the world for a very handsome price." The entirety of her pantry was filled with passion projects: homemade honey, hand-milled soaps, a little machine with Japanese characters that turned fruit into ice cream, and dozens of notebooks documenting her favorite recipes.

Locals joked that Meralda was the witch of Pitcairn. The island's men had a less humorous nickname: the spinster. Perhaps she would have found a suitable husband had she left long ago, but Meralda was the caretaker of Pitcairn's traditions now, a responsibility she claimed with utmost seriousness. She knew how to weave the intricate lattices of the pandanus palm; she could even bleach tapa cloth from native bark. A skilled painter, Meralda proudly showed me a portrait of Mauatua she had made that hung in the guest bedroom.

We passed Mavis—eyes squinting again—as we exited back out the porch. Meralda wanted to show me her latest endeavor, but we needed a quad bike to get there. I climbed onto the back just as the motor coughed up more dust than usual.

"Ugh. I've been praying to Oro for some goddamn rain," Meralda laughed, the two of us now covered in chunks of dried mud. We had all grown a tad desperate for a storm cloud to soar by and lower the temperature, or at least pack down the sooty gravel with some moisture. What I wouldn't give for a little of the Tahitian weather that had practically drowned me a few weeks earlier.

We drove deep into the island's interior, parking in a narrow rift between two hills, where rows of shady trees bore fruit the shape of cherries but growing in clusters like grapes.

"If you look at the *Bounty*'s history," Meralda explained, "there were no coffee beans on board." These arabica plants, she believed, predated the arrival of the mutineers. "They were brought here by Muslim traders, or the Ethiopians themselves many centuries ago."

I nodded.

Up the hill, where the sun leased a sprawling expanse of parched earth, Meralda had crafted a series of rudimentary racks so her ripe coffee berries could rid themselves of their moisture. Nearby, a second drying rack was already full of the *poepoe* plant's nodules. Meralda swished them around as they grayed, and only then did I realize that it was she who had strung a lei of these seeds—Job's tears—around my neck when I first set foot on the island.

Of all of Pitcairn's cautionary tales—stern warnings against the perils of harm—it was Meralda who guarded the most tragic secret. Pregnant some thirty years prior, she had been advised to deliver the child in New Zealand as a precautionary measure, but insisted on staying home instead. The birth, however, was long and difficult. The baby died without the proper care of an obstetrician on hand.

Yet, still to this day, Meralda remained dedicated to Pitcairn, even after the island had taken from her the most precious of things.

———————

AFTER THE GREAT Egyptian hieroglyphs found Down Rope and the wild arabica beans growing in the shaded valley, there was one more rabbit hole of apocrypha I needed to venture down before leaving the island. It was time to visit the grave of John Adams.

Of the twenty-eight people who arrived on Pitcairn in 1790, John Adams is the only one whose life is commemorated with a gravestone. Ironically, in all of the documented history of the island's settlement—in the *Bounty*'s manifest, in Bligh's logs, and in the records kept thereafter—he is also the only one who seems never to have existed. Well, yes, there was indeed a John Adams, but it was the alias used by the sole surviving mutineer who greeted Mayhew Folger in the early nineteenth century.

Most deceased Pitcairners, including Olive's aunt and Meralda's stillborn infant, are buried in the cemetery near the tourism office-jail. The grave of John Adams, however, occupies a lonely plot on the far side of town along the rutty path up to Taro Ground. And although constant reverence is paid to Adams and his mutineer comrades, his burial is untended and overgrown with wild ferns, flowers, and weeds. If it weren't for the white picket fencing, passersby may never know it's there.

The original lead-covered headstone was forcibly removed and hauled back to England (the British really do love putting things in museums). However, the current memorial seems just as old, with blooms of lichen covering much of the faded inscription:

> *Sacred*
> *To the memory of*
> *John Adams*
> *Died March 5th 1829*
> *Aged 65 Years*
> *In Hope*

Like the petroglyphs, I ran my finger along all of the grooves ground into the mossy stone. Then I knelt in the overgrowth surrounding the plot, wondering just how big of a lacuna existed between fact and fiction—how many times do we repeat a lie before it becomes the truth? Tales of Pitcairn's marvels told today—of rogue Egyptians and Africans—seemed too outlandish to be real. But were there other stories, equally as improbable, rehearsed since the island's founding over two hundred years ago, that had been smoothed of their jagged, fictive edges by successive recitations?

A red shroud of earth, still un-tamped by any whisper of rain, hung above me in the dusky air. I had lost track of time, and I left immediately back toward Adamstown before the island's cape of darkness enrobed me as well. In my haste, however, I took the wrong shortcut and found myself wandering deeper into the haze. There was someone following me too; I could sense it.

"Is anyone there?"

I tried to dismiss the horrible notion as an echo of my dread, but I had begun to hear a furtive rustling in the brush as I traipsed down to the water's edge. Was this the bad mana Kate Hall had spoken of back on Tahiti, or an ancient Polynesian who had haunted Fletcher Christian long ago? Or maybe it was John Adams himself, back from the grave.

"Hello?"

Still no answer.

Along the shoreline, a mess of boulders formed quaking tide pools in between; the waves hissed on their approach. The only route to safety was back the way I had come, back toward the sound of approaching steps crunching dead leaves. But then a shadow crept out from the overgrowth, low to the ground, sending a cold pang of shivers down my neck and shoulders. I tripped backward, drenching my right foot in one of the tidal eddies. It was Miz T, the giant Galapagos tortoise, hoping for a morsel of banana. I wanted to laugh, or sigh with relief, but the reef had sliced into the marrow of my ankle, deep like a razor blade. The seawater breathed searing, screaming fire into the wound.

I had broken the cardinal rule of Pitcairn: I was hurt. It wasn't yet clear just how badly I was injured, but the one thing I knew for certain was that I was very far from help.

CHAPTER 23

TIME, CHANCE,
AND DEATH
1798–1799

J enny yelled each time she tore a plank of wood off the side of her house.

"What in God's name are you doing?" The shouts and screams had caught Young's attention.

"I'm leaving!" Jenny yanked more timber slatting down with a satisfied grunt—she was sick of the drunkenness and tired of the evangelizing. These walls had once belonged to the *Bounty*; she was going to cobble them back together into a ship and finally sail home.

To her surprise, Young reached up and ripped another board from its beam. He was certain her project would fail, but perhaps if he let her try she would finally stop scheming and accept that she, like Young, was bound to this island forever.

For weeks Jenny toiled—often through the night—tying old timbers together with ropes and cords and darning bits of the dead mutineers' clothing into sails. As word spread of her intentions, several other women lent a hand, ready to return to Tahiti as well. Susannah stitched a trellis of pandanus palms they could use for shade. Tevarua and Obuarei began amassing a pile of taro and coconuts down by the shore.

They waited for an auspicious omen—the flattening of the sea, or birds migrating overhead, leading the way—but quickly grew impatient. A fortnight of uninterrupted sunshine was deemed favorable enough, and everyone gathered at the Landing Place to say their goodbyes. Mauatua stood firmly planted where the lapping tide met the parched soil. A couple of women remained at her side, but the others—the majority—were following Jenny onto the raft. Any children belonging to the departing mothers were to remain behind. It was too dangerous—and too many mouths to feed—on the open water. Maybe one day they'd return with a larger vessel to ferry their kids to Tahiti too.

Mauatua leaned forward to touch the stern of the barge where Jenny helmed the rudder, nudging it further into the shallows. She could have defended her unspoken wifely promises to Christian and now to Young to help Pitcairn flourish at all costs. And Jenny could have rebuked her for never properly dismantling the Tahitian hierarchy of castes that had long secured her influence over the other women. But nothing needed to be said. Jenny the outsider had siphoned away the women's loyalty from Mauatua's control.

With readied oars, they steered through the labyrinth of boulders into a wide clearing of thundering waves, but each stroke of progress was met by a huge surge of seawater that slammed the little vessel back, as though Pitcairn didn't want them to leave. The riptide then began to spin the helpless craft toward the backside of the island where there were no spits of sand or tiny coves to slow the blue crush before it slapped fissures into the turreted crags. The women knew how to swim, but the current was turbid and fierce. The undertow loosened sand and coral from the ocean floor and eddied the mixture around their little vessel. The raft soon became drenched—it was disintegrating; its cords and tethers began their furious unspooling from around the fastened logs. Jenny urged the others to reach for the cliff face as the tide smashed their craft into splinters against the rocks. The only way to safety was up, through the bird colonies that lined the island's walls. But the lack of rain had kilned the earthen ledges into shelves of fragile pottery, delicate knobs and handles that crumbled at the touch. With each ascending grip, Jenny sent shards of brittle clay down on everyone below; they'd each need to find their own way up to the small mantel that lay almost out of reach. One by one the women began to climb, turning their grips to dust. Susannah was next, then Tevarua, and the rest. Only Obuarei remained, unable to find a path. With a strained leap, she reached for their perch, but her tentative fingers couldn't curl themselves into a steady hold.

"Obuarei!" Susannah shrieked, watching her slip backward into a chasm of black sea that swallowed her whole. Jenny creased her elbow over her eyes, shaking her head in disbelief. Tevarua was transfixed, mesmerized by the speed with which gravity's clawing, possessive power had ripped her friend from the precipice and dragged her down into the surf. In an instant, Obuarei was gone.

A ship's wooden hull makes the strangest sounds in the deep; long, protracted creaks and moans—like whale song—as it pitches and yaws through the mountains of ocean. It took Young a moment to recognize the very noise that had once lulled him to sleep every night on the *Bounty*, but hearing it again after all this time immediately filled him with dread. He carefully peered out to sea through the trees, where he spotted a massive vessel parked so close to the island he could watch each crewman attend to his duties on board. They were readying a small cutter to sail ashore. How had he not seen them approach?

"Gather the others. Now!" Young called out to Mauatua with as much fervor as a raspy whisper would allow. "Dig up the guns!" he ordered Smith. It had been a year since the women's failed attempt to leave Pitcairn, and it was clear to the three remaining men that Jenny would still not resign herself to this fate—they were never quite sure if McCoy had plunged to his death in a fit of delirium, or if he had been lured off the edge. Planning and plotting continued with sly looks and Tahitian murmurs, which prompted Young to hide all of the weapons for fear of a reprisal similar to the murder of his British comrades.

Quickly, Mauatua had assembled the women and children on the lawn in front of Young's house. Everyone was there except Jenny, who soon emerged from the forest with her arms in the air. Young was marching close behind with a loaded musket, its bayonet poking Jenny's nape. With one loud yell she could alert the passing boat that there were fugitives hiding here.

"The first female who misbehaves will be put to death and this punishment will be repeated on each further offense," Young furiously shook his gun and forced the group to sit in a small circle. Smith and Quintal patrolled the perimeter as Young repositioned his weapon back against Jenny's head. She stared blankly at Mauatua, her hope of ever leaving Pitcairn now evaporating. But there were crying babies to worry about as well; the twenty children outnumbered the adults two-to-one. He'd smother an infant if need be—this was not going to be Young's last day on the island.

Everyone huddled in silence as the sound of groaning timbers echoed in the void. The hours had become elastic as they waited and wondered if the little tender had made landfall to collect some coconuts. Would the sailors try to climb higher in search of fresh water?

But then the waves began to churn—they crashed and fizzed like the white currents that had dragged the women back to land and battered their raft against the rocks. Only this time, in an act of providence, the undertow repelled the large craft farther out to sea until it vanished as fast as it had appeared.

"SING ME A song?" Tevarua rolled onto her side and squinted at Susannah. The two women had spent most of the afternoon napping on a tussock of pillowy grass, enjoying the unusually cool breeze. Susannah obliged without hesitation, rising to her feet then briefly disappearing inside the house to fetch Teimua's old nose flute. She had taught herself how to play it after his death. With one finger,

Susannah gently pressed the bridge of her nose, blocking a nostril. She slid the long bamboo tube under the other and, with forceful exhalations, out came a soft, owl-like hoot as she tapped the different holes that punctured the length of the hollowed-out cylinder. It was a song to cheer up her former maid, now dearest friend, and, after all these years, it had remained the same tune. Her progress was tentative—she often paused to adjust her fingering—but "Coventry Carol" was there, floating on the wind toward the cliffs, then out to sea. She put the instrument down and sang the fourth and final verse:

> *That woe is me, poor child, for thee*
> *And ever mourn and may*
> *For thy parting neither say nor sing,*
> *"Bye bye, lully, lu . . . lay . . ."*

Susannah stared down at Tevarua lying on her back, arms extended over her head. It was always the same glance—something between pity and care. But today Tevarua didn't seem sad; in fact a small smile curled the corners of her lips. She had closed her eyes as the melody showered down on her cheeks, each note a cold droplet of rain that soothed her bruising. Long tresses of jet-black hair flanked Tevarua's face. She had let it grow to her waist over the years to better hide the shape of Quintal's anger, and now she nestled herself in her lustrous mane like a hawk safe in its aerie—you couldn't tell she was missing an ear.

When the island was quiet again, Tevarua opened her eyes and looked up at a kneeling Susannah to find something she hadn't noticed before: her voice was the last vestige of her beauty. Despite Susannah's daily visits to the blue pool, she had relinquished her looks the day they had left Tahiti: the three decorative feathers Christian took from her to barter for land on Tubuai; the diet of cured meat she choked down as they desperately crossed the South Seas; the stitching of tapa cloth and plant fronds that had cracked and calloused her hands; the taking of Tetahiti's life with an axe, which had creased her brow with worry. Now, ten years later, her mien was yellow, her hips wide, and a bump began to protrude. The child in her belly had stolen any remaining luster that had endured. Tevarua beamed a mirrored look—something between pity and care—back at Susannah. She was weatherworn now, a husk like the sun-dried sheaths of *poepoe* grass.

Tevarua had continued to make more necklaces with the jewels shorn from the *poepoe* reeds, always crafted within earshot of Young's religious tutelage. Smith was more than halfway through the Bible now and Tevarua had made a string of Job's tears for every woman on the island. Susannah clutched hers faithfully, as though they were real pearls.

Awakened by Susannah's singing, Quintal emerged from the house, cupping his hand over his brow to shade his eyes as they scoured the garden and adjusted to the blaring daylight. He joined the two women on the grass and patted Susannah's stomach with a satisfied smirk, like he had conquered her body and planted a flag in her womb. Susannah laughed.

Tevarua sat up. She removed her necklace and gently looped it over Quintal's turfy patch of unkempt hair, letting it dangle from his neck down to his belly button. Another version of Quintal would have ripped it off and thrown it in the grass, perhaps with a derisive laugh or cutting line about how he didn't need her anymore because Susannah was bearing his progeny now. But instead he lifted the strand to examine each bead with a smile then drew Tevarua closer and stroked her hair as she rested her tentative head on his chest. Quintal had become noticeably sedate, even docile, after McCoy's death. Could he, like Smith, be capable of such radical and permanent change?

"I'm going." Tevarua backed away from Quintal, interrupting the quiet moment. "Flame ginger." She had offered to fetch some for Susannah's nausea, and there was only one more hour before twilight.

On her walk, Tevarua spotted Jenny alone in her garden but didn't stop to say hello. Further on, she saw Mauatua trying to corral all of the children as Young sat under a tree helping Smith with his reading.

"For in the multitude of dreams and many words there are also diverse vanities: but fear thou God."

Ecclesiastes. After Job, it was the installment of so-called wisdom literature that had consumed Tevarua's thoughts, enumerating the three forces in the universe that cared not if a person was kindly or vile. The first was the ineluctable and unceasing passage of time—not simply the inevitability of growing old or that hours sometimes hastened and slowed, but the notion that the progress of time was unfathomably vast. No matter what you did—right or wrong—your actions would one day be forgotten. And even if one chose to live a life of piety, chance, the second force, was blind in its rationing of serendipity and turmoil.

Although the Bible implored its readers to resign themselves to the march of time and the wheel of chance, it seemed the mutineers were resolved to manipulate both. After the massacre of most of the island's men, Young had begun a journal, documenting the banalities of everyday life as though he were defeating the forgetfulness forged through the generations with his quill. The ancients had left writing on surfaces much more permanent than parchment, and yet neither Tevarua nor the other islanders knew anything about who they were. The seizure of the *Bounty* seemed a noble affront against chance, but were they really that lucky living on this rock? The Englishmen likely believed so, continuing to evade capture, but Tevarua had never wanted to come to this place. It was only by sisterly obligation to Susannah that she didn't jump overboard on that very first morning when the women realized their vessel had drifted into darker water.

She walked between the steep stones of the east, passing the ruins of the Polynesians' huts, now nothing more than piles of toppled trunks overtaken by weeds and moss. In only a few years, these poor victims of chance had all but been erased from memory. Tevarua paused when she neared the top of a high ledge overlooking the shallows far below where Susannah took her daily bath.

Death was the third and ultimate equalizer that knew not the difference between good and bad. But for Tevarua, there was something more pliable about death. The mutineers may have written logs to slow the hands of a clock and stolen ships to stoke their own flames of fortune, but with mortal blows they were able to truly harness this final facet of chaos. Death may have been arcane, but it could be controlled. It could be used to stop the havoc wreaked on one's soul by chance and time. Death, it seemed, was the solution to the injustices perpetuated by God's negligence.

And like a song, Tevarua floated on the wind toward the cliffs then out to sea, turning the blue pool red.

CHAPTER 24

FAR FROM HELP

2018

There was, in fact, one building on Pitcairn with a proper front door: the island's clinic. I hobbled along the dusty track—my right foot throbbing, its plastic sandal drenched in maroon blood—until I arrived at the entrance and pushed it open. Inside, I was greeted by an old man whom I had yet to see around the island. He led me to the hospital bed at the back. I climbed onto the prim white linens, leg outstretched, ready for care.

As the old man poured Betadine on my foot and dislodged several fragments of jagged coral with tweezers, I learned that he was a doctor from Australia with a knack for frontier medicine. Now retired, he thought it a fun late-in-life adventure to run Pitcairn's clinic for a couple of years—a job he found on an online bulletin for medical workers seeking international postings. Here on the island, he handled everything from minor surgeries to obstetrics through the second trimester. For dentistry, one had to visit Big Fence; Steve was apparently quite adept at tooth extraction with his wrench in the shed.

Thankfully cavity free, I waited—still seated—as the doctor rummaged through his supply closet after dressing my wounds.

"Here. For the freighter ride back to Mangareva. I heard the journey here didn't go so well for you." He handed me a fuzzy little sticker, roughly the size of a coat button, meant to curb seasickness when placed under one's ear.

"Thanks. Ha. Yeah. Word sure gets around, doesn't it?"

"Oh, you don't even know . . ."

BESIDES THE DOCTOR, there were four other residents who weren't quite a part of the community, and whom the descendants spoke of—or spoke to—very little. A Commonwealth school teacher had been regularly posted to the island for decades, funded in part by the Adventist church as well as British taxpayer money. The other three positions—an administrator, a police officer, and a social worker, all permanently installed on yearlong rotations—were newer additions following what was known as Operation Unique: the dark page in Pitcairn's modern history, with frightening echoes of its founding past.

Following the opening of the Panama Canal in 1914, vessels began to call at Pitcairn with some regularity. The island was known as "halfway rock" along the shipping route to New Zealand and Australia. Weary sailors were warmly welcomed during their layovers, but the Pitcairners had a favorite verb in the local dialect for the brand of hospitality they provided: to "hypocrite" the stranger— to show, essentially, a veneer of virtue and nothing deeper. Guests would enjoy a pleasant stay, then continue on.

In 1996, British authorities got a peek at what was lurking beneath the sheen of piety when the island's Adventist minister lodged a complaint that his eleven-year-old daughter had been raped by a nineteen-year-old Shawn Christian, Steve and Olive's son. Police were dispatched to investigate, and Shawn readily cooperated, handing over letters written to him by the young girl in question. They were "in love."

It took two similar complaints in 1999—this time made by fifteen-year-old girls against their abusers, other islanders—to properly expose exactly what was going on behind (un)closed doors. A criminal inquiry then began in 2000 with the code name Operation Unique—a broad-reaching investigation that sought to track down every single woman who had spent her adolescence on Pitcairn and assess the true extent of what police feared was a widespread legacy of sexual misconduct.

Dozens of women living in Australia, New Zealand, Great Britain, and Norfolk Island gave statements to authorities about their upbringing: sex at twelve or thirteen—sometimes as early as ten—often with boys around the same age, sometimes with adult men, several of them married. And it had been this way for generations. Pitcairn's official ledger of births and deaths reflected a society in which teenage pregnancy was the norm. Particularly tragic was the death of a young girl named Vanda during childbirth at the age of fifteen. She was Steve's older sister.

Under British law, the behaviors described were child abuse, sexual harassment, molestation, and rape. Named in the women's statements were no less than thirteen Pitcairn men—seven of whom still resided on the island, a third of the adult male population at the time—including Steve, who was not only mayor but the captain of the longboat, driver of the bulldozer, and, of course, the local dentist.

Due to the systemic nature of Pitcairn's sexual culture, the idea was entertained that perhaps a form of radical amnesty was the best path forward. The island was a nation—albeit a tiny one—and a program of widespread forgiveness like in postapartheid South Africa or post-genocide Rwanda could begin reparations without destabilizing the entire population.

The notion was quickly abandoned in favor of a protracted series of trials that sought to remove the accused from the island, like some grand karmic boomerang coming to sweep the descendants of the mutineers away under British authority—much like their forefathers would have been had the Royal Navy discovered their hideaway two hundred years ago.

The problem, however, was that the Pitcairners didn't see themselves as British. Fletcher Christian's mutiny was an act of treason against the Crown, a micro-revolution à la the United States of

America a decade prior. Pitcairn was a free territory with its own set of laws, including a six-month statute of limitations—meaning none of the sexual misconduct was apt for prosecution. The British didn't buy the argument, considering they regularly sent government aid and subsidies to help keep the island afloat. But removing the men from their homeland was deemed unethical, as Pitcairn was, in a way, a nation older than Canada, Australia, and the other Commonwealth countries. To haul a Canadian to England for a crime committed on Canadian soil sounded preposterous, so an agreement was made to move forward with the trials, but they had to take place on "halfway rock."

First, before the hearings began, the construction of a brand-new jail was ordered by British authorities, and, rather ironically, it was the men destined to fill the cells—the most able bodies on Pitcairn—who jumped at the opportunity to build it, as government work always came with that coveted $10NZ hourly fee. Erecting a correctional facility before the issuance of a verdict, however, seemed like a tacit judgment of guilt before the men in question had even stood trial, which made many of the descendants wonder if Pitcairn was merely a boil on the sagging face of the British Empire that needed lancing. Perhaps this was an effort, in part, to rid the island of its inhabitants forever.

The trials finally began in 2004—eight years after the first investigation of sexual misconduct—and the lurid testimonies provided by both the female victims and the accused males regularly made the newspapers in Australia, New Zealand, and the UK, with headlines like "Paradise Lost." But who said Pitcairn was a paradise in the first place? It was, after all, a graveyard of ancients long before Christian and his fellow mutineers set foot on the island.

Six of the seven Pitcairn men were ultimately found guilty of a total of thirty-three counts of sexual offense, including Steve—who was deposed as mayor—and another of his sons, Randy. In early 2007, two additional off-islanders, including Shawn, also received a guilty verdict during their extradited trials in Auckland, New Zealand. Five men—of whom Steve, Randy, and Shawn were three—ended up behind Pitcairn's brand-new bars, with sentences ranging from several months to six and a half years. The others were given community service as punishment. In the end, Britain spent a total of £15 million on the investigations and trials. Within a year, the jail was closed down, its convicts remanded to police-monitored house arrest, where they served the remainder of their abridged terms.

With the court hearings over, and the empty prison now converted into a tourism office, Pitcairn's second unspoken rule—after avoiding harm at all costs—was to never speak of the rape cases again. But people still did, of course. Just as scrapes and nicks occur despite our best intentions never to fall down, derisive whispers escaped on the breeze from the houses with no doors, cursing not the sexual predators who walked among them but the trial's gross injustice that had forever branded them as such.

The litany of confessions secured from the defendants may have seemed like damning testimony, but a rallying cry of support from their wives and sisters—bolstered by other outspoken descendants around the world—begged to differ. The men claimed that these statements were not admissions of guilt but an innocent recounting of their bedroom histories when questioned by authorities. Generational disparities among sexual partners were part of the status quo on Pitcairn; the age of consent—or "carnal knowledge," as it was called—had long been dubiously set at around twelve years old.

While the embrace of Christianity had all but wiped the island clean of its Tahitian touchstones, the lax, hobby-like attitude toward copulation was distinctly Polynesian in style and was little different from the early accounts of promiscuity that once delighted the British and French explorers when they made landfall in the region in the eighteenth century. Most historians believe that the women of the *Bounty* were only around sixteen when the mutineers arrived on Pitcairn; Susannah was even younger.

For those who didn't subscribe to the cultural rationale, there was a wagging finger pointed at the United Kingdom instead. If the Crown was claiming Pitcairn as a dependency, then it was guilty of committing gross negligence—"ineffective long-range benevolence," as it was coined during the trials.

When the first foreign teacher arrived on Pitcairn in 1949, he wrote an impassioned letter to the British government about the "sexual barbarity" that permeated the island. There was no response. This wasn't surprising, however, considering the empire was on the verge of collapse as India vied to become an independent democracy and a red wave of communism threatened to flood colonial Malaya (modern-day Malaysia). An isolated rock with a hundred ragtag inhabitants was the least of Britain's worries.

Almost five full decades would pass without much of a peep thereafter, save a few token visits made by different administrators, while other holdings like Tristan da Cunha (a similarly far-flung island in the South Atlantic with around 250 inhabitants) had a full-time representative from the UK. Many argued that any lot of humans marooned at the edge of the world would eventually succumb to savagery when left to their own devices; Pitcairn's first twenty-eight settlers had certainly proven the *Lord of the Flies* theory.

The third, and perhaps most sobering argument in defense of Pitcairn's men was the notion that there was absolutely nothing unique about Operation Unique. My grandmother back in Quebec, for example, got married at sixteen to a man closer in age to her mother. Nancy Hall Rutgers, the last grande dame of Tahiti, began a relationship with an American naval officer—her future husband—at only fourteen. We look back on the previous generations and cringe (which is how we know we're making progress), but perhaps present-day Pitcairn—where lanterns were the only means of communication with the outside world for over 130 years, and where there was no running water until the twenty-first century—is simply still stuck a generation or two behind.

The corruption of adolescents found its way onto Pitcairn from the outside as well; visiting schoolteachers and pastors were also condemned in the testimonies of the interviewed women. Most appalling was a middle-aged policeman for the British Ministry of Defense, sent to protect the victims before the trials began, who was caught, instead, sending inappropriate letters to a fifteen-year-old. They were spotted together on several occasions, often at dawn.

A million wrongdoings do not, of course, condone or excuse the millionth-and-first indecent act, but should the men of Pitcairn have been villainized as exceptional abusers? The diamond had lost its luster, but the island certainly seemed like a pressurized version—a microcosmic cesspool—of the world at large.

The defense's argument, however, falters with the outright complaints of rape and the documented incidents that resulted in physical injury—aggravated and calculated behavior that is impossible to qualify as anything but sexual predation. Even if there were some kind of anthropological or psychosocial way to excuse these actions, the "breaking in" of young girls had turned aggressive on Pitcairn. The island's culture had spun off into a dark aberration of its Tahitian past, which seemed particularly glaring in light of Pitcairn's purported Christian and Adventist values. So where did things go so terribly wrong?

In my research before traveling to Pitcairn, I had come across an overview of Operation Unique online; the information is readily available. Even before my introductory phone call with Ally, taken way back in my New York high-rise apartment on an icy winter's day, I knew that some kind of sexual criminality had played out on the island, but the details were hazy, overshadowed by the constant barrage of other human tragedies splashed across the headlines every day. On Pitcairn, however, these trials are the island's only piece of international news in the last twenty years, and the memory lingers like a storm cloud, raining down shame on the men who are deeply repentant, anger on those who maintain that they did nothing wrong, and hurt on everyone caught in between.

Pitcairn's second implicit mandate—to never speak of the sex crimes—was another rule I needed to break; I needed to dig deeper. But rather than poring over the trial transcripts for a playback of the carnal mayhem, I became obsessed with combing through the earlier chapters of the island's history in an attempt to isolate the pivotal moment that inspired such depravity. Had the rules of the wilderness been etched in proverbial stone when Fletcher Christian cut the *Bounty*'s cable at Matavai Bay, duping the Tahitian women into joining their search for safety and robbing them of their free will? Or was it Faahotu's death at Taro Ground, a year after arriving on Pitcairn, that set into motion the sharing of women as property rather than treating them as equal shareholders in the business of Pitcairn's prosperity?

After the trials, the British started to pay much more attention to Pitcairn, perhaps as some kind of overcorrection, quashing the rumors that the hearings were a ruse to dismantle the island society. Or, more likely, it was to ensure that such violations wouldn't occur again. The coffer of government aid was increased almost eightfold. Fiscally, the Pitcairners are today the best-cared-for members of the United Kingdom and its dependencies. Plumbing was duly installed, the Hill of Difficulty became not so difficult after it was paved at a cost of roughly $4 million US, the *Claymore* began its seasonal service, a newly appointed social worker allowed families to begin processing their trauma, and a permanently stationed police officer ensured that history was to never be repeated.

THE NEXT NIGHT, after the power cut, no one was in bed sleeping. Instead, the islanders were gently making their way up to Taro Ground, guided by the prevailing moonlight. I rode on the back of Carol's ATV, then laid beach towels over the crabgrass to avoid the itch of their tufted blades when we lay down.

The professor was there. He had invited everyone up to the clearing for a stargazing session before putting the finishing touches on his astronomical survey. While waiting for the moon to dip below the cliffs, I learned that Pitcairn was seeking a "dark-sky sanctuary" certification—the most coveted of designations awarded to the places with the lowest amounts of light pollution in the world—in its ramped-up efforts to attract new and diversified tourism interest, replacing the proverbial darkness of its sordid past with the literal darkness of its starlit future. It seemed that finally Pitcairn's great distance from the rest of the world—usually a hindrance and often a danger—would now, once again, become its greatest boon.

In the quickening blackness, the professor unveiled his battery-operated light meter, which flashed different numbers in red as it absorbed the rays of distant suns. "These are some of the best readings captured anywhere on Earth," he explained, still bemused by the clarity of the cloudless night. I could easily make out the distant galaxies and nebular punctures in the fabric of space that were usually impossible to spot with the naked eye—astrological anomalies I never even dreamed existed when, growing up, I'd stare skyward with my father while standing at the edge of our driveway.

With sweeping hand gestures, the professor guided our eyes across the banner of the Milky Way, pointing out its brightest beacons, which once helped the ancient Polynesian mariners across a sea far emptier than the star field overhead. There was Antares burning scarlet, Spica glowing violet, and unwavering Polaris, which I recognized from my childhood. The professor traced a swooping line toward Capella, then on to Orion—low in the sky, his shield looking more like a bow, with an arrow pointing northeastward, my way home.

They were the same winking lights that Christian had wished upon when seeking refuge from the threat of punishment for his crimes, the same ones that had shown him the way to this place long ago. And as I stared up and beyond, much as Christian once did, it occurred to me that maybe the pivotal moment in question during the rape trials—the one that defined the darkness cast over the descendants—occurred on the last night that Christian stared out at these very stars. For in the early morning of the new day, after he was gone, he was no longer his children's keeper. And that would ultimately set the precedent for the generations to come: that no father would protect his daughters and sons.

CHAPTER 25

BURY THE HATCHET
1799

Young feverishly flipped through the pages of the Bible, searching for a specific verse. He creased the book of Psalms open
with his wrist, then skimmed the remaining parchment more carefully until he found the right chapter: Psalm 82.

"Defend the poor and fatherless: do justice . . . rid them out of
the hand of the wicked."

Smith was confused. Then Young clarified his intentions: they
must kill Quintal.

Quintal had snapped after Tevarua's suicide. His fits of unhinged,
unassuageable anger were fiercer than ever. When an attempt to
make Mauatua his consort had failed, he threatened to murder her
children—beginning with Thursday October—and start a new line
of heirs to Pitcairn with a virgin bride. The women promptly hid
their young daughters away from his predacious gaze; Baby Sully,
the oldest, was still only ten years old.

It was the only way to finally rid the island of its longstanding
troubles, Young concluded. Quintal had earned the very first lashes
under Bligh's command, and since then virtually all of the reasons
for their undoing could be traced back to his insubordination—
namely, the burning of the *Bounty*, which had made leaving their

hideaway an impossibility, as Jenny and the other women had been recently reminded.

There had to be a godlier solution than lethal blows, Smith wondered. Perhaps they could split the island into two equal parts and coexist as neighbors. But Young had already made up his mind and continued to underscore the selected passage with a pointed finger. If the Bible condoned murder—a most grievous sin—then it must hide within its pages the justification for any action or intent.

For a man so intimately acquainted with the Word of God, Young had become awfully adept at rationalizing behavior that wasn't particularly pious or chaste. After the slaughter of his fellow mutineers, Young took both Mauatua and Nancy as his wives; they had each borne him children since. But it was the hazy circumstances surrounding the execution of his comrades that seemed even more un-Christian to Smith than polygamy. Young had played the timid survivor that day, sheltered from the attack by the women as he convalesced from his respiratory infection, a pacifist undeserving of punishment. But Young was clearly capable of brute force, as demonstrated by both the retaliative murders of the Polynesian men and his wrangling of the island's residents when faced with the threat of intruders. He would have easily shot any of the women or children without remorse had they aroused the interest of the passing ship. Smith could recall the determination in Young's eyes and the rage on his breath. And there was another disturbing memory lodged within Smith's subconscious that further affirmed the dissonance between Young's personalities, an exchange he had long written off as another dream, until now: On Massacre Day, as it had become known, while bleeding in the grass from his gunshot wounds, Smith heard his assassins discussing which of the Englishmen they were meant to spare according to Young's wishes. If the recollection were true, then was it Young who had masterminded the killing spree all along, spurring the Polynesians to retaliate after years of mistreatment? It would explain how the "Blacks" were able to secure the *Bounty*'s muskets—perhaps Young had sourced a similar Bible passage to legitimize the murder of his shipmates. He was a font of classical knowledge, always citing myths with flowery detail; clearly Young had also gleaned the art of persuasion from the ancient Greek orators. He had certainly led an eager Smith down a long, thorny path, deep into the brambles of Christianity.

Young remained undeterred in his intentions to kill Quintal, and Smith finally relented. If he was being forced to choose between the two men, he'd rather spend eternity with Young—both on Pitcairn and in hell, although he was no longer sure if there was a difference.

The plan was simple enough: They would lure Quintal into Young's house under the guise of offering him half the island, as Smith had earnestly suggested. The guns had to remain buried, otherwise Quintal would be suspicious, so Young readied a large hatchet, which he'd plunge into Quintal's neck with the advantage of surprise.

It was easy to entice Quintal over, especially after Young had used McCoy's copper kettle to brew another batch of ti root brandy. On mismatched chairs—one from Bligh's desk, another from the old surgeon's cabin—the three men sat around the wooden table and drank until Quintal's accusations had devolved into slurring stutters. He was, however, still alert enough to notice Smith's eyes darting nervously when Young excused himself to fetch more brandy from the still. As Young returned, approaching Quintal from behind with the readied hatchet, Quintal pushed himself away from the table, sliding his chair back into Young and pinning him against the wall. Rising to his feet, Quintal grabbed the back of his chair by the stiles and swung its legs at Young's face, causing him to drop the hatchet when he raised his arms to defend himself from the blow. Then, in one thrashing motion, Quintal brought Young down to the ground and climbed on top of him, cupping his hands around Young's delicate neck and resolving not to let go until he had squeezed the life out of him.

Young shook furiously under Quintal's bulging muscles, trying to free himself from his deadly clutch. Unable to conjure a sound, he mouthed "the hatchet" at Smith, who stood frozen, helpless, on the other side of the room watching Young's final moments elapse in the shadows of his cabin.

"The hatchet!" Young mouthed again, desperate. But Smith hesitated—it was Young who had promised to commit the brutal act against Quintal. He was not supposed to be the hero of this story.

Smith lifted the hatchet with both hands, heaving it high above the brawling men. He trembled as his arms swelled with purpose. There was no half-hearted way to wield an axe; only with the totality of one's intention could a blade bear down with enough force to cause mortal harm. Even then, despots and the disloyal were rarely beheaded by a single stroke, and they knelt still on block at their executioner's mercy. Quintal was writhing on top of Young, tightening his murderous hold. Smith wished desperately that he were brandishing a musket instead—it was easy to disassociate oneself from a bullet's purpose; the mindless flick of a trigger spurred the wrecking ball out from its chamber, tearing through whatever it found at the far end of the barrel. The knife was an extension of the hand; a bullet was separated from man by chance and time—no wonder the Tahitians believed that guns were magic.

With unwavering focus, Quintal rang the last pulses from Young's throat, slamming the back of his head against the floor with each constricting squeeze. Young angled his fading focus up toward Smith. His eyes began to bulge and curl back into their brows, and for a brief moment Smith saw not his shipmate's pleading glances but the face of the hapless boy Churchill had so callously drowned many years ago, the young Tubuaian who had triggered Smith's long-lingering nightmares. His repeated dreams weren't a religious reckoning after all—they were prophetic: Smith had become the faceless man on the sand, the archangel Michael, moving effortlessly through the lea of clover to restore order to the realm with a final act of destruction.

Down came the hatchet, tearing through Quintal's leathery back, a deep slice along the bony nodules of his spine that leaked blood when Smith unstuck the rusting metal from the layers of muscle and skin. He swung the weapon high for another try. Quintal cocked his head back when he felt the warm wound open, and with a snickering snarl he continued to narrow his grip around Young's throat, pressing forcefully against the hinges of his jaw. Again, Smith buried the hatchet—and again—and with each hacking slash came a more menacing growl from Quintal that roared into a wailing exclamation of laughter and rage: "HA! Hahahaha. HA! Hahahaha." Currents of blood came rushing out from the various gashes along his body, but Quintal's resolve only intensified as his fingers remained coiled around Young's windpipe like little serpents cinching their hold— tighter and tighter—around their prey, ready to unhinge their tiny jaws. Smith heaved his battle axe up once more and, with a decisive swing, landed the blade in the back of Quintal's head, splitting it open like a ripe melon. Blood, pulp, and dark flecks of brain matter spurted out across the walls and rafters. Quintal immediately fell silent and collapsed on top of Young.

"Get him off of me!" Young gasped. He pried Quintal's cold, clawing digits off of his neck, and, on his elbows, wiggled backward out from under Quintal's slumping corpse. Neither Young nor Smith could catch their breath. Young, on the ground, massaged his throat, coaxing the air back into his lungs. Smith was panting as he stood motionless over the carnage. He let the hatchet's wooden handle slide through his creased grip and jumped—startling himself out of a trance—when the heavy weapon clunked against the floor, as though Quintal had jolted back to life for a final fit of terror.

Smith stumbled backward, clutching the rounded grooves of the timber wall. He then lowered himself down to the floor and propped his back up against the bloody beams. Across the room, Young was beginning to regain his strength. He sat up and stared back at Smith. A strange and overdue silence permeated the entirety of the cabin, disrupted only by Young's faint wheezing. Smith's heartbeat was still ringing in his ears. The two men locked eyes, and neither one spoke as they turned their collective gaze back toward the murder: a half-dozen boreholes had dredged up gallons of blood from Quintal's lifeless form, encrusting his skin and hair and coating the old bulwarks like a demonic mural.

The patter of timid footsteps approached. It was Thursday October along with a few of the other children, cautiously curious about the frantic howls that had escaped through the windows. The young boy stood frozen when he reached the doorframe, aghast and confused at the grotesque scene that lay ahead. The other children angled their cheeks and necks, trying to glimpse whatever had stopped him from entering. He turned pale, daring not another inch into the abattoir.

"GET OUT!" Smith screamed the loudest, most menacing threat he could muster—no eight-year-old child should witness such horrors. This was the kindling for darker thoughts that could set fire to a placid mind for years to come: nightmares. Smith, still on the floor, turned to Young after the children had run away crying. "I've done a most terrible thing."

Young began to rationalize the murder, reminding Smith of his fatherly duty to protect the weak as enumerated in the Bible, but Smith wasn't talking about the taking of Quintal's life. Nor was he expressing remorse that it had been his indolence that was responsible for the untended goat pen and ultimately Faahotu's demise, the catalyst of Pitcairn's murderous downward spiral. There were other deeds done—long ago, before the *Bounty* had set sail—that he still couldn't extinguish from his memory. Smith went silent again, withdrawn, considering the protracted measures he had taken to refashion his life: journeying aboard the navy's farthest-flung mission, and, when faced with the threat of returning to England, collaborating in his ship's seizure. Yet, after sailing all the world's latitudes and spending almost a decade marooned on a lonely rock, he was still unable to distance himself from his past. Surely the seven other mutineers who followed Christian to Pitcairn had also done so with motives less pure than mere loyalty, but it had always been Smith's plan to start anew, for he had used an alias when enlisting on the *Bounty*'s register. His real name was John Adams.

CHAPTER 26

CHILDREN OF CASTAWAYS

1800–1808

As Smith quietly confronted the inextricability of his past, Young contemplated his future. Although he had narrowly escaped Quintal's mortal clutch, he had not survived unscathed. The fight had worsened his long-lingering respiratory condition; Young did not have much longer to live. A few months later—on Christmas Day 1800—dirges were sung instead of carols.

Smith had delved deeper into his studies after murdering Quintal in a desperate attempt to absolve himself of his actions. But the shock of Young's death now cast him adrift in a vast and confusing sea of God's parables. The funeral was bare; Smith fumbled as he officiated a brief gathering, then left the women to deal with the body. In truth, Smith had never quite grasped how to read; he clung to the *Bounty*'s Bible with sweaty palms and turned the pages indiscriminately when he paused to collect his thoughts. Smith had, however, distilled enough of Young's missionizing to harness the fear of God, and—after smashing McCoy's brandy kettle on the rocks—he resolved to rid his island of vice and sin for good.

Shortly after Young's death, Smith insisted that all of the islanders call him Father—God's proxy—and through makeshift prayer he sought to draw his community closer to heaven, or at least bring paradise down to Pitcairn. Consciously or not, Smith was forcing the burden of penance on the next generation of castaways—they were going to atone for the sins of their fathers.

Several years earlier, after Smith's wife Obuarei fell from the cliffs, he had taken Vahineatua, Mills's widow, as his new consort. She bore him three daughters. When an accident claimed her life as well, Smith then coupled up with Teio, McCoy's former bride, and they had one more child, a son. Like Young's memorial, neither Vahineatua's funeral nor the baptisms of Smith's children were heralded with any pomp. Smith still shied away from the prescribed speeches of the Christian canon, preferring his own sermonizing extempore. Three times a week he gathered everyone under the shade of his giant banyan, where he warned his disciples about the perils of wrath, drunkenness, jealousy, and lust.

But even the most rigid piety couldn't curb the animal instinct within. In 1805, Susannah found herself pregnant again, this time by a fifteen-year-old Thursday October. Using Young's signet ring, Smith married the couple in haste. They had a second child in January 1808.

Then, in early February, a tiny brown speck was spotted along the horizon that slowly began to grow and take form: a boat. But something was peculiar about its provenance. It approached from a southerly direction, rising up from the frigid recesses that flanked the bottom of the world. There were only waves between Pitcairn and the barren ice sheets of the Antarctic—no Terra Australis Incognita, the vast, undiscovered continent that the British Admiralty had once hoped and predicted to find. The ship excited further curiosity as it sailed into better view: with only two masts, it was a small vessel to be navigating the deepest of seas on its own—merchants, likely, definitely not the navy. And it wasn't British either—there was no Red Ensign with its trademark Union Jack, but a flag bearing stars and stripes instead.

Everyone gathered to watch the lonely craft as it steadily trundled through the waves. The sails were drooping like pleated curtains, but with a sudden swing of the boom, the canvas began to billow and flutter. The spar now pointed directly at the island like a drawn arrow waiting for its archer to release his bowstring.

They had been spotted.

"Let the fires burn," Smith decided. Whoever helmed that little ship likely wasn't a threat. And besides, it had been a full eighteen years since they had settled on Pitcairn. Of the twenty-seven adults who had arrived back in January 1790, only five of them remained—four women and a single man, plus two-dozen offspring. They hardly looked like a ragtag band of fugitive mutineers anymore.

In the final minutes of daylight, Smith and the others could hear the vessel's iron anchor splash through the surface, its chains rattling as it searched for the ocean floor only a few hundred feet from shore. No one slept that evening—despite Smith's explicit instructions for everyone to get a good night's rest—especially the children, whose imaginations dreamed up elaborate backstories for the wading savages and the wildernesses from whence they came. Perhaps they harbored mythical creatures on board, like horses and cows. Most of the Pitcairners were excited to meet their very first guests—the adults, however, remained cautious, the terror of the mutiny, Tubuai, and their first few years on this island permanently scarring their memories. Smith instructed Thursday October to deploy his outrigger at sunrise and suss out just who exactly these visitors were and what they wanted with their precious rock.

In the gravelly light before dawn, Thursday October eagerly dashed over to his mother's house and shook his younger brother Charles awake. They then fetched Daniel McCoy nearby. But before the three teens began their march down the island's staircase of boulders and stones, Thursday October quickly returned home. He had forgotten something: his large straw hat with a wide brim and big black feather flourishing out from the stitching like an ethereal flower. It was a pompous embellishment, considering the only other thing he—or any of the other Pitcairners—wore was a small flap of tapa fabric between his legs that dangled from the looping cord around his waist.

With oars in hand, they dragged their slim canoe down the sloping embankment and into the shallows, which roared and churned as they slid in. Thursday October called orders from the rear—"Stroke!"—as they swished across the ocean's swollen surface in perfect unison, negotiating the crush of each conquering wave with ease.

With the outrigger deployed, Smith waited impatiently in his garden, pacing in the shade of the banyan. He had rummaged through his belongings to find his old sailor's uniform, and—with a hasty gulp—he sucked in his protruding gut to push his shirt's buttons through the slits on the other side. He was only forty-four years old, but he suddenly felt ancient. Mauatua, Susannah, and Jenny joined him under the tree, waiting with similar anticipation, uneasy but curious nonetheless.

Thursday October interrupted the quiet when he reemerged from the overgrowth and rushed across the grassy lawn in front of Smith's home with Charles and Daniel at his side. "Master Mayhew Folger is the captain's name. His ship is called the *Topaz!*" He beamed a big smile, assuring everyone that the outsiders seemed very friendly, but Charles chimed in with some concern: the sailors looked like dreadful apparitions, thin and wan. He had watched, transfixed, as Folger obsessively fidgeted with his teeth, chomping on his tongue to extract any last droplets of moisture; all of the sailors were racked with thirst and battered by the unkind elements that lurked beyond. For Daniel, however, the most disturbing part of the encounter was that Folger seemed unfamiliar with their Father. Smith loved to recount stories of the greatness of the British Empire, but until now he hadn't fully appreciated that his naive parishioners could not fathom a world in which it was possible to be perfect strangers.

"He invites you aboard the *Topaz* as their esteemed guest," Thursday October added.

Smith paused. No, he would not step even one foot off of his island home. Perhaps they were bounty—*Bounty*—hunters and would drag him back to England in chains. "Tell Master Folger that Father John Adams invites him ashore for a feast."

Thursday October nodded compliantly, summoning Charles and Daniel once more.

"Wait." There was one more thing.

"Yes, Father?" The three teens turned back around.

"Did Master Folger tell you where he was from?"

Thursday October took a second to recall the unfamiliar name: "He's from a far land called America."

CHAPTER 27

THE STRANGEST BONJOUR

2018

The crackling of the marine radio caught me off guard. It had been days since any of the islanders had exchanged dinner plans or gossip over Channel 16. But the incoming voice sounded different—it wasn't a Pitcairner. There was someone out at sea.

"Bonjour, this is the captain of the *Arago*, patrol ship for the French Navy."

I ran to the window. The vessel was far enough away that it hadn't yet emerged on the horizon.

"Hello, *Arago*, you've reached Pitcairn Island." It was Charlene, Carol and Jay's daughter, who responded after a long, staticky pause to finalize the details of the envoy's arrival.

Every few years, the *patrouilleur* would sail beyond its French Polynesian domain, out into the unclaimed expanses of the Pacific—international waters too deep and remote for fishing or drilling—to make a dedicated diplomatic check-in at Pitcairn. They were due to drop anchor later that night.

At dawn, I made my way down to the Landing Place, where I found a small group of islanders already gathered. One of the longboats had been dispatched to collect the members of the *Arago* and bring them across the threshold of forbidding waves.

With extended arms, we lifted our guests out of the wooden tender and up onto the concrete docks. There were twenty-five sailors in total, all wearing board shorts and tank tops instead of their uniforms. Meralda approached them one by one to drape strands of Job's tears around their necks.

The captain of the *Arago* presented himself to Olive and Carol. He was tall and thin, with a buzzed haircut that culminated in a deep widow's peak at the front. He couldn't have been older than thirty-four or thirty-five—the same age as William Bligh (Mayhew Folger too)—and his baby-faced crew was mostly in their early twenties, just out of the naval academy.

Both Olive and Carol quickly conceded to the captain that perhaps I would be the best person to show the sailors around, since it turned out I was the only one among them who knew how to speak French. A dozen officers soon followed me up the Hill of Difficulty, shaking off their sea legs with the occasional stumble. First we would venture out to Saint Paul's Pool for a refreshing swim, then trek up to Lookout Point for the views. I plucked bananas from the trees as we walked and pointed out strange plants and animals, including an overgrown hermit crab that had refashioned an empty diesel canister into its home.

IN THE LATE afternoon, we gathered in Adamstown's square under the tin roofing that hemmed the gap between the Adventist church and the great banyan tree by the post office. A train of folding tables was set up, each with a floral-printed cloth on top, ready for an assortment of potluck dishes served in mismatched Tupperware: cold noodles, canned beets, black bean chili, homemade breadfruit chips, and, of course, a big bowl of Olive's award-winning fruit salad. From the *Arago*'s galley came steaming flanks of chateaubriand and baskets of fresh baguettes that bookended the long buffet.

Everyone was there: all forty-eight Pitcairners—even cranky Simon Young/Yung from the pier—carrying stacks of plastic dishware from home and doling out extra utensils to our guests as they arrived. Carol was in the corner, manning a small card table piled high with T-shirts and wooden trinkets, all sealed in weatherproof plastic—her *Bounty* boutique open should any of the French sailors want to do some shopping.

Shawn, the elusive mayor, had finally come out of hiding, and he solicited everyone's attention for a short speech to officially welcome the crew of the *Arago* on Pitcairn. Then, before we stormed the entrées with forks and spoons gripped like battling spears, Isabel stood up—the youngest member of the community, as per tradition—to say grace:

> *Suffer me not, oh Lord to waste this*
> *Day in Sin or Folly but let me*
> *Worship Thee with much Delight.*
> *Teach me to know more of Thee and to*
> *Serve Thee better than I have ever done before.*
> *That I may be fitter to dwell in Heaven*
> *Where Thy Worship and Service are Everlasting.*

Excited conversation soon quieted into muffled chews. The sailors had dispersed themselves amongst the Pitcairners, waving me over every so often to help broker conversations between French and English. Steve was cracking jokes near the post office steps while Carol held court across the square, ensconced in souvenirs. The Christians and Warrens had mastered a false facade of unity; only I could discern the great schism between piles.

Banjos and ukuleles then emerged from their leather cases as we angled for second helpings. Meralda handed out hymnals from the Adventist church with the help of her nephews—weathered tomes with soggy parchment, pages dogeared—and flashed me an encouraging look to translate her instructions: "Everyone turn to page 428!" If she was the mini-country's minister of culture, then perhaps I had become some kind of secretary of state, an ambassadorial intermediary.

I flipped past "Coventry Carol" on my way to something decidedly cheerier: "Sweet By and By," a Pitcairn favorite.

"There's a land that is fairer than day / And by faith we can see it afar," Meralda began, strumming a G major chord on her guitar. The other Pitcairners joined in—"for the Father waits over the way / To prepare us a dwelling place there"—with voices so ardent and unabashed that it stunned me and the visiting sailors into silence. "In the sweet by and by / We shall meet on that beautiful shore."

"So what will you say about this place after you get home?" one of the *Arago*'s officers asked me as we walked back down the Hill of Difficulty in the gloaming. I wasn't yet sure. The island, seven generations after the arrival of the mutineers, was most certainly not free of its original vice and sin, but I chose a more diplomatic answer instead. "Perhaps that I—and now you, too—am one of the few people on the planet who can claim to have had dinner with an entire country."

By the time we reached the docks at the Landing Place, the wooden longboat had already descended from its garage and was bobbing next to the pier, ready to ferry the French sailors back to their ship.

I waved goodbye to the members of the *Arago* alongside the other islanders, watching as the tender slid through the harbor's still water—ink black under the graying sky—then out past the jetty, negotiating the high crests of the pelting waves until it disappeared in the brume. With faded smiles, everyone immediately returned to their quad bikes to make the short journey back to Adamstown before dark. My grin softened as well, realizing then that my role as translator and tour guide had been an easy way for the Christians and Warrens to maintain their distance from the visitors and keep the shine on their welcoming veneer. I was not, in fact, some kind of backwater emissary, and was most certainly not a Father John Adams. No, instead I had inadvertently abetted the Pitcairners as they "hypocrited" the stranger once more.

CHAPTER 28

AUSTERITY

2018

Very little is left of the *Bounty* where it was laid to rest by the mutineers over two hundred years ago. The wooden masts and hull are, of course, long gone—their charred remains chewed through by the briny water and carried away by the tides. The ship's cannons were later excavated and removed; they now sit on display in various museums around the world. All that remains of the wreck today are two iron ballasts wedged between several boulders at the bottom of the sea.

On my last day on the island, I grabbed my snorkel mask and ventured out beyond the breakers to find the watery grave. It was guarded by sharks and rays, all vigorously wagging their cartilage. For a while, I hovered near the water's surface and stared down at the unremarkable slabs of metal, tracing their journey in my mind: from England to South America, South Africa, and Australia—a score of worlds—then on to Polynesia, where the *Bounty* would become an ark, ferrying a new society of escapees to their Ararat before the ship's utility was deemed a liability and it was cast down below the waves.

Lifting my gaze up toward the horizon, I could see the *Claymore* in the distance, wading in the safety of the deep. It had returned in the night to take me home.

In the midafternoon I was instructed to bring my belongings down to the Landing Place so they could be tendered to the freighter alongside several crates of mail. There was a second passenger getting her suitcases in order as well: a woman in her seventies, wearing a starched white blouse decorated in silkscreened butterflies. I had noticed her at the French Navy potluck. She had been the only person wearing any semblance of finery for the occasion; she was also the only person whose clothes weren't lacquered in the island's signature filth. Shawn was at the docks, too, and walked directly toward me when I arrived—it seemed he was far better at goodbyes than he was with hellos.

"This is my mother-in-law, Mary. She'll be joining you aboard the *Claymore*." Shawn brokered the introduction, and I learned that Mary had come to the island a year ago to stay with her daughter, Shawn's wife, following the death of her husband. She was bound for her native Scotland now—her brogue tempered, but not twangy, after years of living in Australia—and I was politely asked to keep a casual eye on her during the long journey back to civilization.

Everyone else began to gather at the Landing Place to say their farewells. First Carol and Jay, then Jay's sister Meralda, and Steve and Olive, who, still in her Rutgers jersey, tightly wrapped her arms around me and squeezed. And finally there was young Isabel, back in her braids, who broke away from her parents Randy and Nadine and walked over to present me with a single juicy guava held out in the palm of her hand. I thanked her with a smile, remembering my first day when we drove up to Highest Point and gorged on ripe fruits right off the vine.

———————

EVEN BEFORE THE *Claymore* had lifted its anchor, I heard a tapping at the door to my cabin. It was Mary, coming to share the stash of chocolate and candy her daughter had packed for the journey. I gladly invited Mary inside instead of heading upstairs to the dining mess—memories of the cook's taco lasagna repeating . . . and repeating. I unearthed my precious guava and, with a Swiss Army knife, sliced it into two, offering her half. She was eager to share something else as well. "You know, nothing on Pitcairn is really as it seems." She had been squirreling away island gossip, with no one else to tell until now.

"Carol was a wild child back in the day, I'm told," Mary continued. The perfectly framed, black-and-white Warren family portrait came to mind: pious, Adventist Carol with her brimming smile, wrangling four children. The two boys, it turned out, were not fathered by Jay, but by two other men. One of those boys grew up to be the father of one of Isabel's siblings. Nadine, the self-proclaimed "luxury import," had originally arrived from New Zealand as a newly minted member of the Warren pile, until she met Randy Christian.

The Christians and the Warrens were in fact much more intertwined than it had previously appeared, and Mary was dialed directly into the source of friction.

One freighter ride, two puddle-jumper flights, and three long days later, Mary and I finally arrived in Tahiti. A white van picked us up at the airport in the late afternoon and shuttled us across the island to a small hotel booked by the *Claymore*'s operations manager, where we'd wait for our respective departures back home.

Le Royal Tahitien looked like it had been built in the 1970s, with tiki-tacky finishes and tired furniture in the motel-style rooms. I was, however, glad to feel a few sluggish puffs of air-conditioning coming from the small unit affixed to the wall.

"So, what time is dinner?" Mary wasn't ready to part ways after I carried her luggage up to her room on the second floor. Her flight was early the following morning; mine was still a few days away.

The outdoor restaurant at Le Royal Tahitien was nuzzled right along the beach on a concreted patio that leaned over the sand and waves. The season of storms had finally passed, and the shadow of Moorea brooded across the lagoon in the final fiery moments of twilight.

Guided by our waiter, Mary and I were seated between two young couples on their respective honeymoons.

"You know, my husband and I liked spending time together so much that we never felt the need to have children," Mary remarked, looking at our neighbors holding hands with their new spouses across the table. "But then, of course, we had a very Catholic accident," she laughed. "That was okay, though. Our daughter has always been so wonderful."

As we sipped our Hinano beers, Mary chronicled the major plot points of her forty-year marriage, which included buying a foreclosed home by mistake while drunk at an auction. In their thirties, she and her husband had moved from dreary Scotland to Australia and settled in Newcastle on the coast of New South Wales, which sounded an awful lot like home, but the beach town bore no other resemblances beyond its name.

After our waiter brought our main dishes—a *poisson cru* for me (which wasn't half as good as the one Kate Hall had made on Motu Mapeti) and a chicken breast and fries for Mary—our conversation veered sharply toward Scotland, her destination in only a few short hours.

"I am rather excited to return," Mary continued. "You know the train service is quite good, and they give excellent discounts to elderly folks like me." It had been years—maybe even decades—since she was last in Scotland. And while she seemed somewhat keen to go back now, the most indelible memories of her youth were the difficulties sustained during the Second World War.

"I was young then, and my parents did a good job of sheltering me and my sisters, but we knew. We knew what was going on." The rationing of food—tea, sugar, and flour; the young men sent away never to return; the dirty factories tirelessly cranking out munitions; the barricades flung up along the sea; and the nights—oh, the nights—the unbearably quiet nights when not a sound was to be made or even a candle lit so as to evade bombardment from the Axis air raids.

"What I remember most about the war," Mary continued, "was the austerity. No one understands austerity today like we did back then. Especially the Pitcairners."

Our waiter broke the weighty silence with the check.

"Oh would you look at that. Six whole euros for a bloody bottle of water!" The Tahitian prices were twice as fearsome for someone who hadn't taken a single piece of currency out of her purse in an entire year. "He's paying for the water. I barely had any," Mary informed our waiter (and me, apparently). "I'm a pensioner on a fixed income," she croaked with disdain. "Also I'm Scottish, and we're a bunch of cheap bastards!"

It was only after dinner, as we walked back to our low-slung housing block, that it truly dawned on Mary: after a year on Pitcairn with her daughter—and decades with her now-deceased husband—she was about to be alone for what may have felt like the very first time. I had been a surrogate of sorts, easing the transition between worlds for the last three days, but I would be leaving her now too.

"What if I miss my flight in the morning?" Mary's anxiety about the vastness of her uncertain future began to manifest as an obsession with the little things she sought to control right now. "What if I don't wake up with my alarm? What if the airport taxi doesn't come? What do I do then?"

I walked her up to her room and slid the dials of the Radio Shack clock sitting on the nightstand: "Here, 4 a.m., as a back-up."

"Can you call down to the front desk for a wake-up call as well?"

"Of course. No problem." I wrote out the phone number for a taxi company too—just in case. We then rehearsed how to request a ride to the airport in French should the one she booked not arrive.

"Be well, Brandon." Mary took a step back and extended her arm. It's a strange effect of the goodbye handshake: to add physical distance when the intent is to offer closeness, albeit more formally.

"Be well, Mary." I ignored her outstretched palm and reached mine around her frail shoulder for a gentle air-hug tap on her back.

Mary lowered her head and began to fuss with the linens, preparing the bed for a short night's rest. She sighed quietly as I walked out the door.

In the morning, I climbed the stairs back up to Mary's room and found the housekeeper inside changing the sheets for the imminent arrival of the next guest. Mary was gone. She had begun her journey out into the world, out into the wilderness.

THE DOORS OF the international terminal swished open. I scanned the eager audience, all waiting for their loved ones to arrive, until I found my good friend Elizabeth waving both of her hands to catch my attention. I was stopping in Los Angeles on my way back to New York to review a new luxury hotel in Malibu for one of my regular magazine gigs and had asked her to tag along.

She smiled big as I approached with my suitcase slowly rolling behind.

"What? What is it?" I could tell that she was scanning me from top to toe, evaluating the damage Pitcairn had done.

"I dunno," she laughed. "You look like you just got back from Burning Man or something."

Maybe it was all of the ocher dust still baked into the fabric of my clothing (which, to this day, despite many washings, remains stained), or perhaps it was the look of bewilderment painted across my sunburned face, mesmerized—intimidated, even—by the lights and robots of the connected world.

Elizabeth swung her car keys around her finger and pointed at the correct exit. "This way, *dawww*-ling." She was prone to tossing in a jokey word or two at the end of a sentence, usually sung with a near-perfect British inflection. I'd always respond in kind, my attempts much more Shrek-ish.

With my luggage now in the trunk, we settled into our seats for the drive out to the beach.

"So." Elizabeth clicked her seatbelt and continued, "What was it like?" She fully knew just how loaded a question she was posing.

"It was like . . . a trailer park at the end of the world." That wasn't the answer she wanted to hear—she was expecting something much more *Robinson Crusoe*—and I didn't want to disappoint her further by detailing any strange moments of sameness that reminded me of home.

Still between two worlds—unsure to which I belonged—I began to fill the awkward silence with a torrent of details: the small-town gossip; the penchant for canned meat; the spiders and vermin; the blistering afternoon sun from which there was no solace; the houses without doors, torn apart by nature's tenacity; and the island's red breath that whispered injurious threats in my ear.

I think I was glad to be back.

"But how did these people even come to live on this island anyway?"

I took a moment to organize my thoughts before chronicling the mutineers' calamities, like an elegy sung in memoriam to the world's last uncorrupted realm: the miserable, maggoty existence aboard an eighteenth-century vessel; the strangling grip of colonialism; the taking of young, innocent women from their island home; the charming leader felled by his own paranoia; the madman brewing poison in the jungle; the ardent proselytizing and fear of God; the trauma of bearing witness to the drownings, hatchetings, and suicide; and the nights—oh, the nights—the unbearably quiet nights when they were all left to ponder their wicked misdeeds and inevitable undoing.

"Man. White people and humidity really don't mix."

"You're telling me."

When we reached the highway, Elizabeth typed the address of the Malibu hotel into her smartphone; it was strange to see an iPhone being used as something other than a flashlight. "Aw *feeeck*." There was an accident further down on the 405. It was going to take us about an hour and a half to get there, twice as long as it normally should.

LA traffic. Feck indeed.

"I'm gonna need another coffee or something." Elizabeth was already exasperated by the drive ahead, compounded by my harrowing account of Pitcairn thus far. "Sound good?"

"Sounds great," I had been running on Nescafé fumes for well over a month—a real-deal espresso seemed like the perfect jolt to restart my engine.

The closest Starbucks was situated in a sprawling shopping plaza just off the interstate. Inside, the aesthetic was decidedly industrial— purposefully austere—with exposed black beams hanging over the smattering of faux bistro chairs and booth seating. I counted exactly forty-eight people in the café, most sitting alone, likely working on screenplays that would never see the light of day.

"Two grande lattes please," Elizabeth ordered as I eavesdropped on a nearby conversation, an insipid debate about the artistic merits of the Natalie Imbruglia song playing from the speakers overhead.

"Here. It's on me." Elizabeth whipped out her credit card and slapped it on the counter in front of the barista. "Want anything else? A muffin? Carrot cake? A ba-*nawww*-na?"

"A what?" I was lost in thought, distracted.

"A banana." Elizabeth dropped the British affect.

"Sure."

In the wicker basket next to the cash register were a handful of superstore bananas. They had the right look, yellow and ripe, but likely tasted bland and waxy.

"No, wait!" I had changed my mind. "Only chumps pay for fruit."

TURN OFF THE QUIET

2019

The wide bed had a crease down the middle—a divot where two smaller mattresses were joined together under the parachute of a fitted sheet. It was cooler than the night before. My legs were safely tucked under the goose-down duvet, hands clasped atop my rising chest as the air filled my lungs. I could hear myself breathing.

A harem of spiders had inhabited the bathroom across the hall—a web of limbs in congress, perpetuating the species that had laid claim to this faraway place. I could sense their little legs plinking across the tiled floor like anxious fingers as they furtively searched for a newer, damper place to hide in the shadows and bear their young.

I was at it again.

Almost immediately after returning from Pitcairn, I began planning a second trip, this time to Norfolk Island, home to "the others" as Carol Warren had called them—the other descendants of the *Bounty*'s mutineers. From New York City, Norfolk was over three thousand miles farther than Pitcairn, but a runway built during World War II for the Allied air forces made the journey significantly easier—there was a twice-weekly flight from Sydney.

Norfolk didn't rely on a freighter to move goods and people around the Pacific, and they didn't need to power off a generator to conserve diesel fuel, but there was something familiar about the quiet here—something strangely unnerving. Although nature had more readily yielded to the advancements of humankind, the night creatures were just as prevalent. Norfolk's stamps—once as coveted as Pitcairn's postage—even featured the resident arachnids: golden orbed and red horned. There was no GSM (Global System for Mobile communication) cell tower either—my iPhone was, once again, nothing more than a flashlight.

Norfolk's map did not feature place names like McCoy's Drop or Break Im Hip; the coastline curled more gently toward the sea, creating a smattering of scenic coves. At the island's center was Burnt Pine, the largest settlement, next to the crisscrossing airstrips. Down at the bottom was Kingston, the capital; the ruins of the former British convict settlement were now refashioned into administrative buildings—the tourism bureau may not have been in a former prison, but it turned out that the other government offices were.

While Pitcairn was only slightly larger than New York's Central Park, Norfolk was considerably bigger, about half the size of Manhattan. I rented a tiny red Fiat to putter around, stopping for a swim at Emily Bay, dotted with a single pine tree famously drawn by Captain Cook in his logbook. At Bumbora Beach I collected a handful of black *hihi* shells, double-checking to make sure there weren't, in fact, any snails or mollusks living inside. Back near the bowling club I found Trent Christian—Steve and Olive Christian's eldest son—playing guitar and hawking CDs of traditional Pitcairner music. I purchased his album with one proviso: that he play me a rendition of Meralda's favorite tune, "Sweet By and By."

––––––––––––

BOLSTERED BY MY unrelenting jet lag, I woke up at dawn on Bounty Day and drove down to the pier in Kingston. I had purposefully timed my visit to coincide with the early June anniversary of the arrival of the *Morayshire*, the ship that landed all 194 Pitcairners at the abandoned penal colony in 1856 after a year of petitioning Queen Victoria for a new island home plus five hellish weeks negotiating almost four thousand miles of sea.

The weekend of festivities included a reenactment of the *Morayshire*'s arrival using a wide-hulled canoe, similar to the longboat on Pitcairn that braved the final mile of the freighter's journey. And the water around Norfolk seemed equally as treacherous—the waves violently crashed against the docks, spraying me and the other on-lookers as the little vessel rode to shore.

"Are you Brandon?" A woman in her thirties approached, smiling with her big saucer eyes; "I'm Michelle." It was easy to pick me out of the crowd, and not just because I was one of only a few tour-ists. The descendants were all dressed for the occasion in traditional nineteenth-century attire: white linens, straw hats, and wreaths of *hihi* shells—instead of Job's tears—slung around their necks.

Word had spread before my arrival that I had visited Pitcairn a year earlier. These bona fides earned me a chair at Bounty Day's private events, like the great generational picnic held in the remains of the old penal compound. Michelle—one of the staffers at the tourism office—invited me to join her table under a big yellow ban-ner that bore her family's name: Adams.

After Folger's visit, Smith retained his alias, which he contin-ued to claim as his true identity. His heirs have all been Adamses ever since.

"I'm a Quintal too, you know," she explained. Such were the quirks of the children of a band of people who, for a couple of gen-erations, had a limited assortment of DNA. "But don't worry. I don't have the mad Quintal streak or anything."

Outstretched along a row of plastic tables was an assortment of traditional dishes, like *mudda* (green banana dumplings) and *hihi* pie. The questions began as soon as I sat down, paper plate fully loaded with an assortment of fresh fish and coconut bread.

"So what's Pitcairn like?" one of the cousins shouted while reach-ing for a beer. The island was revered as their Mecca, yet none of them had ever been or even seemed interested in making the pil-grimage. "I heard the place is rather dark—bad mana. Do you know what mana is?"

I did.

"Did you find the ducats?" another cousin wondered.

I didn't.

According to legend, when the *Bounty* was docked in Tenerife on its way to Tahiti, Fletcher Christian pocketed a few extra gold coins while purchasing those coveted casks of *vinho da roda* for William Bligh. Upon arriving on Pitcairn, he buried the ducats, but dug some of them up as a Spanish vessel approached, escaping death at the hands of the Polynesians by bribing his way on board and journeying back to England via South America.

The story may sound outlandish, but in 1809—sixteen years after his recorded murder by guns and hammers—Christian was spotted in Devonshire by someone who knew him well, his protégé Peter Heywood.

Heywood had dodged the gallows by lying at his court-martialing, claiming he was below deck during the mutiny. He had gone on to have the distinguished naval career that Christian had so wished for him when they had parted ways two decades prior on Matavai Bay. With his triskelion tattoo—the Three Legs of Man—still emblazoned on his leg, Heywood was forever haunted by the events aboard the *Bounty*, until he saw a man across a small English common bearing similar markings on his skin. It was Christian. He yelled out, but the man quickened his stride and vanished before Heywood could approach him further.

"It's true you know! He lives!" A slurred voice chimed in from across the table, only to be chastised by another relative. "No he ain't. You're drunk like a McCoy."

To me, Christian's secret survival reeked of a conspiracy theory similar to, say, Anastasia being saved from the Bolshevik firing squad or the whereabouts of Elvis Presley and Tupac Shakur—a fantastical tale that further lifted Christian's notoriety to mythic proportions. My questions about what *really* happened on Pitcairn during the eighteen years of isolation were focused on Adams—he, too, was an unreliable witness—but I felt uneasy broaching the subject with his direct lineage gathered around the table.

After Folger and the *Topaz*, several other ships called at Pitcairn in the decade that followed, and much of what we know about the island's years of solitude comes from the logs of those captains, all of whom interviewed Adams during their brief shoreside stay. Father John tweaked his testimony during each visit, but the narrative remained largely the same: He absolved himself of all wrongdoing aboard the *Bounty* and was only a witness, not an active participant, to the calamities that had befallen his fellow islanders since. He was petrified of being dragged back to England and tried for high treason like the mutineers who had remained behind on Tahiti.

"Only Jenny knows the truth," one of the elder cousins spoke up between bites of *hihi* pie.

Beyond the collection of accounts logged by passing ships, the annals documenting Pitcairn's beginnings do contain a rare comment by the ever-disaffected Jenny. Without the fear of capital punishment that cast a shadow of doubt over Adams's renditions, we can more readily trust that Jenny spoke candidly about her experience. She expressed disdain for her "A.S." tattoo—the erstwhile Alexander Smith—and even assured her audience that, long ago, before the island had ravaged its residents, she was just as beautiful as Susannah. The majority of her recollections describe the fates of her peers: how Tevarua and Obuarei left this world by way of the cliffs, and how many of the others died when the Polynesians "studied revenge." Almost all of her testimony matches Adams's account, except for one small detail mentioned in passing: it had been Young who brewed the ti root brandy, and not McCoy.

For years, the descendants have pulled at that thread, spinning entire yarns about the possibility of an untold history. Perhaps Young and Adams were not the God-fearing men they had purported to be—"sole survivors" not of happenstance but rather because they had best played the game, offing their enemies one by one. Could Young and Adams—instead of Quintal and McCoy—have been the biggest threats to the island's well-being? Or, worse, was it Adams who killed Christian?

"Bring up the bones, I say!" another elder added, wondering who lay beneath John Adams's gravestone on Pitcairn. There was one final theory about the eighteen years of quiet, which married the mysteries surrounding both Adams and Christian: maybe they were the same person.

Perhaps Christian had indeed survived the Polynesians' revenge, but instead of absconding in the night, it was he—and not Smith—who assumed the identity of Adams when Folger later discovered the island. They could dig up the body buried on the outskirts of Adamstown (or should it have been called Christiantown?) to better ascertain its identity, but much in the way that Michelle was part Adams and part Quintal, the gene pool had probably become too muddled with the various bloodlines of the original mutineers to properly discern who came from whom. I stared across the table at all of John Adams's descendants and tried to discern if any of them had flecks of metal gray in their eyes.

———

WITH ONLY FOUR hours left until my flight's departure, I raced halfway across the island, swerving my red Fiat into the dusty driveway of a dilapidated bungalow. Norfolk's archives had proved disappointingly lean when searching for further insight into the downfall of Pitcairn's original settlers. But Michelle had an idea: a hobbyist had transformed his home into an unofficial *Bounty* museum, and perhaps it was worth stopping by to examine his exhibits and artifacts on display.

An old woman answered the door. Concentric wrinkles ringed around her lips, accentuating her mirthful grin like an ancient tortoise. Moira could sense my excitement when I laid eyes on the dusty reliquary within, bolstered by my urgency to gather as much information as I could in such a short amount of time.

"It's so lovely to have a visitor here, and one without gray hair!" She swatted away my hand when I tried to offer her a wad of pleated bills for the $10AU admission. The generation of *Bounty* obsessives—fans of Nordhoff and Hall's trilogy, like her late husband—were all gone now, and without a steady flow of tourists she had let the museum fall into disrepair. "I don't suppose you wanna buy this place, do ya?" she added. "Ever consider moving to the land of the mutineers?"

I smiled warmly, and for a brief moment entertained the idea of staying in this world.

At the back of the house was a small room in which a reenactment of the infamous mutiny had been fully realized with mannequins—Christian's papier-mâché face furrowed with anguish as he roused Bligh from bed. On the walls all around were placards detailing Bligh's fate after surviving his harrowing open-water journey and finally returning to Britain: another breadfruit mission. Yes, a year after being acquitted of all wrongdoing involving the *Bounty*'s seizure, Bligh was given a new ship and sent back to Tahiti by the Royal Navy to harvest a fresh crop of plant cuttings. The mission was a success; he was even able to pass through the squalls at Cape Horn. But when the ship arrived in the Caribbean, the African slaves refused to eat the foreign fruit, and plans to propagate more trees were duly scrapped.

Although Bligh had been welcomed home as a hero, Christian's siblings launched an ambitious campaign both to drum up sympathy for their long-lost brother and to tarnish Bligh's reputation. The stunt worked, and the specter of mutiny would follow the *Bounty*'s former commander for the rest of his career. In 1797, his seamen rioted against unfair wages during the fleet-wide Nore mutiny, and, later, when he was governor of New South Wales, the free colonists temporarily imprisoned him during the Rum Rebellion of 1808. He died in 1817 of high blood pressure.

I made my way back to the main room of the museum, which had a nook in the corner stocked with all of the reading essentials belonging to the *Bounty* canon. There were homemade binders as well: around forty or fifty scrapbooks that had compiled every relevant magazine and newspaper article over the last two hundred years, with annotations made by Moira's late husband who, like me, was trying to make sense of the fallout on Pitcairn.

There were far more documents than I could read in the two hours that remained before my flight, so I furiously snapped my iPhone's camera at page after page, scanning everything from notes on the machinations of Massacre Day—when the Polynesians rose up against the mutineers—to an old *National Geographic* clipping that documented "modern life" on Pitcairn in the 1950s.

Then, at the back of one of the binders, I found it: a page entitled "Jenny the stirrer," with a glued-in photocopy of an old journal clipping. It was the full account of Jenny's time on Pitcairn that one of the Adams elders had mentioned at the descendants' picnic, an interview taken on Tahiti and published in the *Sydney Gazette* in 1819.

After twenty-seven years of desperation, a stranded Jenny finally got her wish. She left Pitcairn aboard the *Sultan*, another American merchant vessel that had passed by the lonely rock in 1817, nine years after Folger's discovery. But when she landed back on Matavai Bay—Mount Orohena towering above—everything had changed. Missionaries had toppled the stone *marae*, forcing everyone to adopt Christianity and wear European clothes. Smallpox had spread, devastating the population. And those who survived had been infected by the fear of God; powerful men now craved complete control of the realm.

I heard a sudden rumbling from high above—a landing aircraft, extinguishing the blaze of quiet with its gusting jets. I had to make my way to the runway. It was time for me to leave, to go back where I belonged. Jenny, however, could never go home.

ACKNOWLEDGMENTS

First, my sincere gratitude to two brilliant individuals who have been so gracious and generous with their time and support over the last three years: thank you to Kevin Fallon—prolific journalist—for offering fresh eyes and invaluable feedback on every single chapter (mostly out of order!), and to E. A. Hanks, who picked me up at Los Angeles International Airport (still covered in Pitcairn's mud and dust) and immediately proclaimed, "This is a book!" Thank you for accompanying me every step of the way since.

To the supercool Ally LaBriola, a Pacific-size thank-you for passing this most excellent expedition my way—I am indebted to you forever. Big thanks to the clever Heather Menzies for setting this adventure into motion, and a nod to Richard Hankin as well. Thanks also to Chris Maggio at Tourism Australia for being a constant advocate for my off-the-beaten-path ideas.

To the inimitable Karolin and Nick Troubetzkoy, patrons of the arts, when Tahiti's emerald waters were out of reach, you gave me a jade mountain—I am truly grateful. An impossibly large thank-you to my dear friends Hayley Barna and Fredrik Marø for offering me yet another cherished sanctuary. Half of this book was written at your dining room table.

On Pitcairn, I'd like to thank Steve and Olive Christian, and Carol and Jay Warren, for having me at their respective homes. And to Meralda Warren for further impressing upon me the importance of the Tahitian women in the founding of the settlement. On Tahiti, *mauruuru roa* to Kate Hall Feist for adding yet another tier to the *Bounty* cake. *Merci aussi* to Emily Boitteau Colas and the late Nancy Hall Rutgers. My time on Norfolk Island would not have been fruitful without the help of Tania Anderson, Michelle Dowling, and the handful of kind islanders who invited me into their homes to show me treasured heirlooms and artifacts from Pitcairn's past. In Sydney, thank you to the staff at the Mitchell Library, the State Library of New South Wales, for helping me scour their repository. And, finally, a big thanks to the scholars, historians, and guides all over the world—from French Polynesia to England, and California to New York—who offered me their sincere expertise on a diverse array of subject matter as I pieced together the myriad facets of this multigenerational saga.

To my manager Dan Bodansky and agent Anthony Mattero, thank you for the endless encouragement as the idea took shape, and for finding this story a place to live. To my editor Colleen Lawrie—and to the entire PublicAffairs team at Hachette Book Group—for being this book's cherished home, and for always engaging with me and empowering me as I tore these characters off the pages of crusty old logbooks, gave them intentions and curiosity, and let them wrestle with their own demons.

To my family and dear friends, thank you for always checking in as this project progressed—writing a book is as lonely an affair as being stuck on an ultra-remote island in the middle of the Pacific. Additional gratitude is owed to Misa Matsuda, Shireen Shafai, Adam Zacharius, Theo Barbagianis, Jennye Garibaldi, Nestor Lara Baeza, Cailin Goldberg-Meehan, Raia Margo, Kate Martin, and Ryu Teramoto. And to Theodore: I'm sorry there are no dump trucks or dinosaurs in this book.

NOTES ON REFERENCES

An exhaustive list of published works mentioning the fallout aboard the HMAV *Bounty* would number in the thousands. And for the last two hundred years, scholars and obsessives alike have attempted to piece together the sequence of events leading up to Fletcher Christian's seizure of the expedition vessel, abetted by his trusted cadre of mutinous comrades. There are, today, enough primary sources gathered (namely the log entries of commander William Bligh and his loyal subordinates) to provide a full account of the *Bounty*'s journey and takeover, but historians have traditionally shied away from detailing the events that occurred thereafter, as far less printed material is available on the topic. Timeline guideposts exist—like the successive deaths of eight of the nine Englishmen who first arrived on Pitcairn—but very little has been dutifully retained about the fates of the Polynesian men and women who accompanied them. In order to properly flesh out a more robust version of the island's settlement and the eighteen years of solitude that followed, I have incorporated non-Western methods of research and sourcing, like tapping into the rich oral traditions of Polynesian culture passed down by the island's foremothers to their progeny. Furthermore, I have interviewed psychologists and religious scholars to better elucidate the intentions of the primary characters in order to more properly recast this history as a cogent sequence of rational (and sometimes irrational) actions, rather than an oversimplified laundry list of casualties.

Bounty buffs may notice that the events portrayed in the preliminary chapters do not call out every sailor registered to the ship; a great effort has been made to streamline the events before the mutiny. I've cherry-picked the most pertinent moments both on board and during the vessel's sojourn in Tahiti to best set up the actions that befell the leading characters later on. Every effort has been made to avoid overcrowding the narrative, but the *Bounty* saga is indeed a chronicle with many key players. As such, each character is referred to by only one name throughout the entirety of the book, but it should be noted that the annals of history list all of the Polynesian characters by two, three, or even four different monikers. Additionally, the mutineers' surnames have variable spelling. Place names herein are depicted in their most current iteration ("Tahiti" instead of "Otaheite," for example) to avoid further confusion.

The following notes are organized by chapter, and the bibliography that follows is a selection of the most salient and useful sources that helped me faithfully reconstruct the *Bounty*'s adventure, the first two decades of life on Pitcairn, and subsequent milestones in the island's history. All facts and details enumerated in the 2018 timeline are true as I remember them and true as they were told to me.

For additional information, please visit www.brandonpresser.com.

Chapter 2: The Strangest Hello

Starting the mutineers' timeline with the island's discovery is an homage to Nordhoff and Hall; the third installment of their trilogy places Adams as the narrator of the quasi-fictive events that befall the early Pitcairners beforehand. Much of the introductory chapter here is an amalgamation of details from the first three vessels to reach the island in the early 1800s, including the reactions and observations of their respective captains. Today, the true identity of John Adams is not couched as a mystery, but for the early ships that passed Pitcairn, there was some uncertainty regarding which of the nine mutineers had changed his name. In 1808, Adams was still working out his backstory when Folger arrived. Folger did in fact puzzle together Adams's true identity (Folger 1809; Delano 1817; Hayes 1996), but—as mentioned in the narrative—his findings were relegated to obscurity for many years.

Unlike the depictions of the *Topaz* on Pitcairn's limited-edition postage stamps, it's likely that the vessel was smaller in size, based on information gathered on the history of Nantucket's whaling and sealing industry, of which Folger was a prominent part (Philbrick 2000).

The conversations had between Folger and Thursday October are pulled directly from Folger's log. The prayer spoken at mealtime and the madrigal sung during Folger's departure were sourced from the Norfolk Island Museum. Adams's speeches are a patchwork of logged quotes sourced by Folger and the other early arrivers (Pipon 1834; Raine 1821; Scott 1982; Shillibeer 1817; Staines 1815; "T. W." 1818).

Chapter 3: *Artocarpus Incisa*

A debt is owed to Caroline Alexander (2003), who, in her hulking tome, has elegantly synthesized hundreds of primary sources involving the *Bounty*'s departure from England, arrival in Tahiti, and eventual mutiny. The book was an invaluable resource when cross-referencing the various nautical logs essential in faithfully plotting out the pre-Pitcairn narrative.

Glynn Christian (1982) deserves full credit for uncovering the conversation had between Christian and his brother Charles after the *Bounty*'s aborted departure from England. The quotes are pulled from Charles's written account of their interaction and his time aboard a merchant vessel. Clearly, the seeds of Christian's mutinous discourse are planted here.

All physical descriptions of the British characters throughout this book were depicted using Bligh's log notes (Bligh 1937), first as they mustered aboard his vessel (a detailed list of the order in which each sailor joined the expedition exists as well), and later when he was asked by the Crown to provide details on the missing mutineers (scars, missing teeth, tattoos, etc.) to track them down during the subsequent manhunt. The descriptions of Bligh—his looks, demeanor, plebeian upbringing, and upper-class marriage—are gleaned from insight garnered by Alexander (2003). The weather—storms that plagued the *Bounty*'s journey and the rain that continued on Tahiti—is also derived from the daily notes Bligh penned in his journal.

Details of Banks's biography, his voyage with Captain Cook, and his epistolary exchange with Bligh were pulled from several reliable sources (Banks 1773; Beaglehole 1962; Chambers 2000; O'Brian 1997). Bligh's thoughts on Cook come from David (1981).

Records of the *Bounty*'s refitting and cargo holdings were kept by Bligh and the Admiralty and feature in several sources (Alexander 2003; G. Christian 1982; Ball 1973; Shapiro 1936; McKee 1961).

Hallett and Hayward's laziness is well-documented by Bligh through-out their journey. Their encounter with Churchill and Thompson—the two most hardened seamen—is meant to introduce the concept of "rum and bum" in the navy, but also mirrors the circumstances by which Bligh is later removed from his cabin during the ship's seizure. Heywood's desire to preserve his integrity and the honor of his family is taken from his perjured testimony during his court-martialing several years later. No firsthand account of Christian's journey remains—his actions and words are borrowed from officers' journals and, eventually, from inter-views with Adams.

Chapter 5: *A Score of Worlds*

As Bligh was the *Bounty*'s purser in addition to its commander, he pur-chased several casks of wine during the ship's refit at Tenerife, which he planned on selling for additional wages upon returning to England. This was common practice among pursers at the time, especially those serving double duty.

The changing of the watch rotations and Christian's promotion is clearly detailed in Bligh's diary and echoed in all secondary sourcing thereafter (Bligh 1937; Alexander 2003; G. Christian 1982), as it would seem doubly treacherous—or confusing—for a man who had seemingly garnered so much of his commander's favor to turn around and rebel later on.

Quintal is used as a surrogate for a prevailing notion in the seafaring world that animals like goats and dogs could sense land before humans. The albatross—made famous in Coleridge's poem about Christian—was not a widely regarded metaphor at this time.

All events detailed during the *Bounty*'s journey, including the "cross-ing of the line," the inability of the ship to pass through the gales of Cape Horn, the stops in Cape Town and Tasmania, and Valentine's death, come directly from Bligh's logs. He meticulously documented all in-stances of official punishment as well, starting with Quintal. Commands uttered to his lieutenants—even derisive comments about the drunken surgeon—originate from Bligh's journals and court-martialing too.

Chapter 6: The Three Legs of Man

The Tahitian women introduced in this chapter were given Western titles by the arriving Englishmen, who found their Polynesian names too
difficult to pronounce. Most historical accounts of the sailors' time on
Tahiti use these English monikers. I have reverted almost all of their
names back to Polynesian in order for them to reclaim their identities.
There are a couple of exceptions for clarity: Susannah's preferred Tahitian title was Teraura (she was also known as Mataohu), which is very
similar in spelling to her maid, Tevarua. And, as stated in the narrative,
Jenny's name was Teehuteatuaonoa. It should be noted that, later on,
both women left Tahiti of their own accord and were more eager than
the others to embrace Western tradition; it is more fitting, then, that
they adopted their European designations.

The logs of arriving British and French captains documented the
way in which nudity and sex were readily embraced in Tahitian culture
(Beaglehole 1962; Chambers 2000; Oliver 1974). Today, much of the
discourse from Polynesian experts posits that the Tahitians were equally
befuddled—and perhaps disturbed—by the hypersexual behaviors of the
British men, who engaged in predatory acts, including public masturba-
tion. Any of the able seamen were candidates for spying. Millward and
Burkitt were selected here because their ultimate fates mirrored their
biblical voyeur counterparts; they were later hanged for their (mutinous)
crimes. The name Susannah was indeed chosen by Young because of
her appeal. The most religiously inclined of the sailors did not have any
familiar connections or relations back home with the same name, which
was largely how the other women earned their Western titles. Mauatua
was known as Isabella, a cousin of Christian's with whom he may have
had a romantic entanglement (Mountain 2014). She was also known
as Maimiti and Mainmast. Susannah, here, embodies the trope of the
bather, fetishized by Gauguin and other Europeans who would later visit
Polynesia. As part of the retelling of the *Bounty* story—and in an effort
to move away from the Christian-centric narrative—the descendants
collectively believe it was Young and Susannah who forged the first relationship bond among the future Pitcairners. Their initial encounter is
also meant to demonstrate the agency the Polynesian women had over
their own sexual exploits.

Bligh kept a log of the men in his crew who had to be treated for venereal diseases; discourse surrounding Christian's and Heywood's initial escapades—and Bligh's reprimands—are taken from his journals. Bligh, however, did not partake, and speculation about his interactions with Teina's wife is borrowed from an earlier account of an unwilling commander featured in Banks's logs (Banks 1773; Chambers 2000; O'Brian 1997). The ceremony at the *marae* is also detailed by Bligh, including descriptions of his men's tattoos and his feeling faint at the end of the festivities. Banks made several colorful references to the cult of the *arioi* in his journals.

In addition to scholarly works on the intricate ecosystem of castes and, specifically, the ways in which chieftains were practically deified (Oliver 1974; G. Christian 1982), information regarding abortion and other practices to curb the population are present in Banks's diary and those of other visiting Europeans. Experts believe that the future women of Pitcairn readily engaged in such methods, as none of them had children with their British partners while on Tahiti. Mauatua would bear a child almost exactly nine months to the day after arriving on Pitcairn. Susannah likely used birth control; she would have a handful of children later on, but none with Young. Of their sisterhood, it was Faahotu (also known as Fasto) who was best equipped to care for the women in such a manner, as abortions and other medical care would cease after her departure from the story.

Mauatua is used as a surrogate character to convey certain crucial elements of the Tahitian story and lifestyle, like explaining mana, establishing certain points of view regarding the British guests, and bolstering the relevance of celestial navigation through Polynesian constellations and lore. Most importantly, many of the Tahitians did in fact know that Captain Cook had been murdered in Hawaii. Glynn Christian (1982; also Alexander 2003) cites these instances, including the manipulation of a naval chemise to include pearl-shell buttons.

Chapter 7: *The Last Grande Dame of Tahiti*

The elements of James Norman Hall's biography were recounted to me by his granddaughter, Kate Hall Feist, and are bolstered by additional texts (Briand 1966; Hall 1934; Hall 1952). Information about Marlon Brando's backstory and the modern evolution of Tahiti as the paradigm of paradise was also provided firsthand by Hall Feist, and supplemented by a visit to The Brando in 2016.

Chapter 8: *Mutiny on the* Bounty

No part of the *Bounty* saga has been given more scrutiny than Christian's seizure of the ship with the help of his friends. Dozens of scholars have pored over Bligh's logs (and logs of some of the other senior officers too), not to mention the notes pertaining to the court proceedings that followed a few years later. The breaking point—the exact reason Christian snapped—remains unknown, as the lieutenant's diary no longer exists, but the disarray at Nomuka was a crucial psychological catalyst, as it occurred only a few days before the infamous event. Bligh's biographers unanimously cite his ability to cut crewmen down with derisive verbiage (he had a penchant for using animal analogy, as seen in Chapter 6); this would not be the only mutiny Bligh would suffer in his lifetime. The scene set here is composed of notes and observations collected from the following sources: Alexander (2003), Glynn Christian (1982), Silverman (1967), McKee (1961), Bligh (1790), Brunton (1989), Danielsson (1962), Wahlroos (1989), and Morrison (1935). Christian made an attempt to use a smaller tender to ship Bligh off into the night, but a larger craft was needed in order to banish the majority of Bligh's loyalists along with their commander. There was no room in the vessel for James Morrison, the *Bounty*'s boatswain's mate; he would follow the mutineers onward to Tubuai before being allowed to stay behind on Tahiti when Christian set off for Pitcairn. Much of what we know about Tahiti, the mutiny, and Tubuai comes from his logs. Heywood's eyewitness account, penned back in England, provides invaluable detail as well, especially during the sailors' time on Tahiti and Tubuai. His account of the mutiny, however, has been disregarded as false. The seaman's testimony was an attempt to distance himself from his crimes rather than to provide a balanced account of the incident.

Chapter 9: *The Backwater Emissary*

The various interviews with Jenny (Teehuteatuaonoa 1817; Teehuteatuaonoa 1829; Kotzebue and Eschscholtz 1830) paint a surprisingly nuanced narrative of the women's participation in the *Bounty*'s onward journey.

She discusses how one woman jumped overboard to escape capture, while others who were "rather ancient" were seen as unappealing prospects by the British men and dumped on a nearby island. Discussions with Polynesian experts have helped illuminate the tension underpinning the women's blackbirding by Christian. There were no physical chains keeping the kidnapped women on board, only social fetters. Mauatua, Susannah, and Jenny (and Nancy, too) were the eager participants; the other women (lower-caste Tahitians) were bound to their mistresses by sisterly pressure.

Almost all of the events on Tubuai are extrapolated from Glynn Christian (1982) and from Heywood and Morrison's respective logs. It is footnoted in most accounts of the mutineers' time on Tubuai that there were two murders, one by Churchill and the other by Thompson. I have fleshed these out in greater detail. Often, sharpshooter Christian is depicted as the hero of the battle with the Tubuaians; this is not the case as he had a broken thumb from building the fort and was likely unable to fire a weapon.

Chapter 10: The Geometry of Solitude

After the exit of Bligh, Morrison, and Heywood from the narrative, there are no other witnesses who wrote about the *Bounty*'s journey firsthand. Only twenty years later, when Folger meets Adams, can we glean what happened after the vessel began its final haul into the unknown. There are numerous resources that have transcribed Adams's various conservations with passing captains (Becke 1898; Chamier 1838; Delano 1817; Fiske 1855; Hayes 1996; Pipon 1834; Raine 1821; Scott 1982; Shillibeer 1817; Staines 1815; "T. W." 1818). Later still, Jenny provides addition details via several interviews undertaken by journalists and explorers (Teehuteatuaonoa 1817; Teehuteatuaonoa 1829; Kotzebue and Eschscholtz 1830). Rosalind Young (1894), a direct descendant of Edward Young—born on Pitcairn—published a memoir of the island's early days; the first two chapters touch upon the island's settlement.

Interviews with Adams substantiate the trajectory of the *Bounty* after leaving many of the mutineers behind in Tahiti. Jenny's lines are borrowed from her interviews; we know Mauatua to be unwell during the journey as one of her alternate names—Maimiti—means seasickness.

Much of the other Englishmen's deliberations and intentions are carved out of classical and biblical references, which formed the backbone of their upbringing. We begin to see the first instances of cultural melding while the primary characters are crammed aboard the *Bounty*. European and Tahitian traditions start coming together, especially during Christmas festivities, which were held at sea, as the ship's arrival on Pitcairn (mutually agreed upon by historians) took place around late January, following several months without making documented landfall.

Numerous references to songs sung—especially by the Tahitian women—fill the annals of the island's history all the way up to the present day. Singing is a vital component of the Pitcairn condition—a way to express both joy and reverence. In several instances, songs are the essential components of plot points narrated in the local oral traditions. Never, however, is a song named explicitly. Careful research suggests that "Coventry Carol" was a very likely tune, as it came into prominence around this time, popularized by King Henry VIII, patron of the Royal Navy.

Chapter 12: *The Quiet*

Virtually all accounts of Christian on Pitcairn become noticeably threadbare when the action shifts from the *Bounty* to the mutineers' new island home. Only a small collection of secondary sources (Belcher 1870; G. Christian 1982; Delano 1817; Nicolson 1997; Shapiro 1936; Silverman 1967; Wahlroos 1989; Young 1894) diligently cull the extraneous primary sources—logs and interviews—into a legible timeline. The island's survey, the descending of their various belongings from the ship, and the killing of the dogs are documented in detail, as is the plotting out of land allocated to each Englishman. Christian's proclamations are quotes pulled from Adams's interviews.

Early attempts to redraw the scenes of the first two decades on Pitcairn prioritize the leadership of Christian and his fellow seamen. A dedicated effort has been made here to aggregate the oral stories of various descendants regarding the importance of the women's contributions in erecting the first homes and clothing for their cohabitants. Suffice it to say, had it not been for the women's knowledge of plant weaving, herbal medicines, and cooking, the little colony would not have survived beyond its first few months.

The islanders would for years unbury relics from the proto-Polynesians that first settled the island. Archaeological evidence has been documented by Glynn Christian (1982) as well as at the Norfolk Island Museum, and evidence of the obsidian mine exists even today.

The burning of the *Bounty* is vividly described by Nicolson (1997); elements are borrowed herein, including the way in which the residual tar helped ignite the sinking vessel. Both Jenny and Adams corroborate the notion that Quintal and McCoy were responsible for the ship's destruction. For details on Smith's dream, see Chapter 21.

Chapter 13: The Museum People

Beyond the scope of the professional maritime world, a handful of other documented visits to Pitcairn do exist (Ball 1973; Birkett 1997; Marks 2009; Marden 1957; Sala 2013), and all are worth exploring for other—different—perspectives on the island experience. Some of the information gleaned by these travelers has further amplified my research, particularly when delving into the backstories of certain modern-day characters. Marks notes that Steve Christian is a GBE.

Chapter 14: The Devil's Workshop

While on Norfolk Island, I had the privilege of rummaging through the archival notes at the Bounty Folk Museum; its owner had spent years studying the various Pitcairners, with a particular interest in Jenny and her "stirring" (as he refers to her machinations). Both trysts uncovered are germane to the eventual massacre of several Polynesian and British men. While other characters were more closely coupled up, Jenny had little regard for her partner, Martin. She was one of the few women who did not bear children.

The notion of a chore wheel, or an equitable sharing of duties, remains part of modern Pitcairn's framework, as does the rationing and sharing of newly procured items (fishing surplus, or gifts arriving aboard the freighter). Many of the social stipulations that helped govern the way the mutineers lived remain important elements of the present-day society.

Faahotu's death sets the island's chaos into motion, and while historians have largely agreed upon the timing of her demise, opinions are mixed on how she died: some say scrofula of the neck; others believe it was a goring of the stomach. Jenny suggests a swelling of the neck in her interviews (Teehuteatuaonoa 1817; Teehuteatuaonoa 1829; Kotzebue and Eschscholtz 1830). I am inclined to believe, however, that it was not scrofula, as she would have been contagious. No other islanders perished or were ill in a similar fashion. Faahotu's goring of the neck is an amalgamation of these two prevailing theories. The subsequent taking of Tararo's wife is well-documented in Jenny's interviews as well.

Multiple sources (including Nicolson 1997; G. Christian 1982; and oral traditions) note three separate occasions during which a passing ship almost discovered the mutineers' hideaway. This particular instance was likely the *Pandora* on its international manhunt supported by the British Crown.

Chapter 15: Pandora's Box

While the mutineers' timeline is recounted in an omniscient fashion, the fates of those left behind—like Bligh in his seabound tender and mutineers like Heywood and Churchill who remained on Tahiti—are forever unknown to Christian and his comrades as they were in real life. The fallout after the mutiny (the open-water expedition, Bligh's return to England, the *Pandora*'s search efforts, and the trials) is recounted in colorful detail by Bligh himself, Heywood, and Morrison (Tagart 1832; Morrison 1935; Bligh 1790 and 1937; Brunton 1989).

Chapter 16: Dreadfruit

Very little is known about the lives of the *Bounty*'s able seamen, as they were born into the lower echelons of society. The archives on Norfolk Island have done a reasonable job of cobbling together McCoy's (sometimes spelled McKoy) history and Scottish origins. Little is known about Quintal (sometimes spelled Quintrell, also known as Matt) beyond Bligh's physical descriptions of the seaman in his log. However, old muster records (collated by the Norfolk Island archives) show that he and McCoy served together on vessels in the Caribbean before signing up for the *Bounty* mission.

Minarii's encounter with Susannah is part of an implicit rite of sexual exploration—oftentimes non-penetrative—embedded in ancient Tahitian culture, during which young peers engage with one another before more conscious coupling and copulation occurs (Oliver 1974; Goldman 1970; plus interviews with Polynesian cultural specialists). Banks noted

in his logs that women possessed just as much influence over these escapades as men, and sexual play could be perceived as a pastime or sport.
The assumption can be made that Minarii and Susannah were sexually
intertwined, as her engagements with other men seemed to inspire jealousy in the young teen, which would soon lead to the murder of his
Polynesian comrade.

The changing of song lyrics to signify malicious intent on behalf of
the Polynesian men is an important moment in the Pitcairn tradition,
documented in virtually all accounts of the island's early settlement. The
intricacies of these machinations, however, have yet to be clearly parsed
out and defined. It is more likely that only a couple of women knew
of the Polynesian men's plans and used their singing to warn their sorority. Had Mauatua known of the scheming earlier, she would have
undoubtedly warned her husband, instead of being an active participant
in the chorus, as some versions of this vignette would suggest. Tararo's
subsequent murder is often depicted (Nicolson 1997) in an even sloppier
fashion—there was an attempt to poison him before his more violent
demise. Nancy's (also known as Toofaiti) participation can only be rationalized as a reluctant effort of loyalty toward the British men, just like
Tetahiti's (also known as Taaroamiva) killing of his cousin Oha (also
known as Ohu and Oher). Although never explicitly named as Christian's *taio*, it is impossible not to conclude that the Tubuaian was bound
to the lead mutineer by an oath of brotherhood.

Varying timelines detailing the early events on Pitcairn place the distillation of the ti root brandy either before or after the massacre in Chapter 18. It is most likely that the drunkenness began before, following a
period of indolence once the settlement's construction was completed—
with the women forcibly responsible for the menial chores, the men
searched for a drink. But more than establishing drunkenness as another
key factor in the society's near demise, this chapter presents the case for
nascent psychopathy (Patrick 2018, plus interviews with psychologists)
as a leading agent of decline, too—from the harming of small animals
performed by Minarii to the more tacit and extroverted exemplars in
McCoy and Quintal, respectively.

The births of Pitcairn's next generation (Daniel McCoy and Charles
Christian, and Thursday October and Matthew Quintal Jr. in Chapter
14) are documented on the island's official register.

Chapter 18: Hunting Pigs

Christian's Cave has become a point on the map of modern-day Pitcairn and is the location most closely associated with the mutineer's prolonged bouts of isolation and paranoia. His inner thoughts are extrapolated from universally agreed-upon elements of his biography, including romantic feelings for a cousin named Isabella and his familial connections to the Isle of Man. Christian's rumination about alternate futures at the start of the chapter is largely based on a popular theory held by some historians and many *Bounty* enthusiasts that the lead mutineer did not in fact perish with his peers but escaped back to England and lived out the remainder of his life in obscurity. More information on the subject can be found in the Epilogue's notes.

Massacre Day, as it's referred to by historians and amateur theorists, is perhaps the best documented event during the eighteen years of solitude on Pitcairn. Nicolson (1997), Glynn Christian (1982), and Wahlroos (1989) synthesized various accounts of the action and streamlined the timeline for easy perusal. Young (1894) also presents a brief account passed down from her grandmothers. In Jenny's interviews (Teehuteatuaonoa 1817; Teehuteatuaonoa 1829; Kotzebue and Eschscholtz 1830), she speaks candidly about how the Polynesian men "studied revenge." The killings were methodical, starting with Williams and Smith, who were largely perceived as the instigators of the great imbalances on the island, despite McCoy and Quintal being the outright aggressors. The unusual relationship between Brown and Martin has never been properly unpacked, but it remains curious why Brown—always a more agreeable character and thus granted safety from harm—would knowingly give up his life in a feeble attempt to save Martin, especially on an island where not only malice but selfishness is a hallmark of survival. A deeper relationship between the two men more properly explains these motives and why, in the early hours of the morning when all of the men were apt to be alone, the other mutineers were targeted and assassinated separately while Brown and Martin died side by side. This also better rationalizes Brown's willingness to partake in the Pitcairn adventure—as a gardener, he was merely an adjunct member of the *Bounty* and was never singled out as an instigator during the mutiny (Bligh 1790); perhaps he followed Martin. Martin's subsequent disinterest in Jenny, his consort, better explains her latent jealousy regarding the affection her Tahitian counterparts received (Teehuteatuaonoa 1817; Teehuteatuaonoa 1829; Kotzebue and Eschscholtz 1830).

Christian's murder occurs off the page to better cast a shadow of doubt over the circumstances of his death and further perpetuate the possibility that he was not in fact killed with the others. Those who subscribe to the notion that Christian was indeed shot during Massacre Day agree that his last words were "Oh dear" (Alexander 2003; G. Christian 1982), and that a second bullet was needed to put a more permanent end to his life, after which he did not speak.

Chapter 19: An Eye for an Eye

Like the specifics of Massacre Day, the details of the fallout—the revenge—have been compiled by numerous sources (including Nicolson 1997; G. Christian 1982). It is likely that Smith snuck up to Quintal and McCoy's hideout to encourage Minarii's murder; however, the evidence to support this notion is unavailable. As Susannah murdered Tetahiti with an axe, the history books place Young with Niau, teaching the Tahitian how to use a gun, only to fire the weapon at point-blank range into his face. The wearing of facial bones as jewelry is a newer tidbit of evidence that has emerged, perpetuated by oral tradition; some argue that Mauatua wore a skull fragment of her beloved Christian for many years after his death. Beechey (1831) refers to "five skulls" in Young's log, which has led historians to confirm Christian's murder, but it is possible that one, or several, of these unburied bones belonged to a Polynesian man instead.

Chapter 21: The Book of Fear

After Christian's death/disappearance from the narrative, it was Young who took over as leader of the island—a role he seemed to have held in a more unofficial capacity, leaving the men and women to their own devices while he dutifully detailed the banalities of their existence in an unused logbook rescued from the *Bounty* before its burning. Beechey (1831) candidly references the tome, citing various events that occurred on the island after Massacre Day and before the island's discovery by Folger in 1808. However, no evidence of this diary remains. Nicolson's

(1997) thorough record of births and deaths notes a child of Tevarua's surviving for only seven days.

Smith's dream and subsequent embrace of Christianity is a cornerstone of Pitcairn lore. It is one of the plot points most consistently told during Adams's repeated recollections of events on the island once passing ships began documenting his testimony ("T. W." 1818; Belcher 1870; Chamier 1838; Fiske 1855; Shillibeer 1817; Raine 1821). Adams's accounts of the Pitcairners' years of isolation waver in detail, but it's worth noting that the mentions of this nightmare—being pierced in the heart by an archangel—remain surprisingly consistent and should be examined in greater detail. Through conversations with a handful of psychologists (and resources like Mellman 2018), including clinicians in the metaphysical department at Canyon Ranch, the origins and details of Smith's dreams were likely trauma induced—a manifestation of some kind of Christian guilt—and stem from lived experiences occurring earlier in the narrative. The dream is a manifestation of his sudden and fervent desire to appreciate the Christian doctrine, his atonement for crimes committed or observed.

Like Christian, no first-person account of Young's actions remain, though via Adams we understand that his affinity for the Bible's teachings perpetuated much of his decision-making and thus his speech. The dialogue herein was pulled directly from the Bible's so-called wisdom literature (BibleProject 2014, 2015, 2016a, 2016b, 2016c, 2016d, 2016e; Breitowitz 2016). Seeds of Job's tears—still a popular decorative item on Pitcairn today—emphasize the importance of the book of Job in early island teachings. However, certain Western constructs like fear and dualities of good and bad were difficult for the Tahitian women to reconcile (Oliver 1974; Goldman 1970; plus interviews with Polynesian cultural specialists).

Quintal's abuse of Tevarua was continuous throughout their relationship but rarely dwelled upon by historians, as they were secondary characters relative to the Christian-Bligh narrative that has long captivated audiences. The most talked-about incident of abuse, first mentioned by Young (1894), was when Quintal bit off Tevarua's ear after being woefully disappointed with the size and quality of fish caught and cooked.

Shortly thereafter in the timeline, McCoy plummets to his death under suspicious circumstances. It is widely believed that he suffered delirium tremens after repeatedly ingesting over-proofed brandy from his improvised still. However, it is worth noting that Jenny (Teehuteatuaonoa 1817; Teehuteatuaonoa 1829; Kotzebue and Eschscholtz 1830) delivers an account of his demise with surprising detail—holding a giant boulder, or a large rock tied to his naked body—which suggests the possibility that she may have been somewhat responsible for his untimely end, or at least present and unwilling to stop it. Some of the archival notes at the Bounty Folklore Museum further detail Jenny's "stirrer" propensities; perhaps she was more of a puppet master than historians suggest.

Chapter 23: Time, Chance, and Death

The three vignettes in this chapter are the only documented events that occurred in this two-year time frame (Nicolson 1997). Generally they are glossed over as bullet points, but I've sought to flesh these occurrences out and lend them a more sculpted sense of cause and effect.

Historians have given little regard and dignity to the Tahitian women, especially the more tertiary characters like Obuarei (also referred to as Puarai, Opuole). We do not know the exact date of her death by falling, but—using Jenny's and Adams's interviews—know it occurred sometime from 1792 to 1799, before Tevarua's end. Some theorize that she, along with Faahotu, died quite early (and that Smith, like Williams, stole a new bride from the Polynesian men), but it is more likely that she dropped from the cliffs later on with witnesses—including Jenny and Tevarua— all around. A terrible event must have occurred during Jenny's planned escape to discourage her from trying again; it is likely that Obuarei was the casualty of this essay. Her death also lays the groundwork for Tevarua's purposeful demise; suicide was not customary in ancient Tahitian society but a learned behavior from the Christian Englishmen (Oliver 1974; plus interviews with Polynesian cultural specialists). Like fear, depression in Tahiti was viewed in a radically different manner; it was seen as a sickness, not a mood or facet of one's personality and being.

The sternness of Young's disposition when faced with the possible arrival of outsiders is underscored by his death threat, which, according to Adams's various accounts, was repeated on numerous occasions after the women tried to leave the island. There are passing references in the accounts of visiting captains that at one point the women sought to stage their own uprising, similar to the Polynesian men. The logic is sound; however, details are too murky to faithfully reconstruct a narrative beyond the raft of *Bounty* parts that fell apart at sea.

As detailed in Chapter 21, we know for certain that Tevarua was an active listener in the Christian missionizing because her death occurred in a distinctly Western fashion. Her suicide has long been a footnote, but upon consulting various psychological sources on the propensities of self-murder and the emotional damage caused by unwanted conversion (Weishaar and Beck 1992; Hui, Cheung, and Lam 2017; plus discussions with practicing therapists), I was able to better tease out other suicidal behaviors, like euphoria and the giving away of things. The treatment of Tevarua's character has largely focused on her physical abuse; the emotional abuse she sustained (as a low-caste Tahitian, she did not have any control over her departure from Tahiti) is equally important to acknowledge as well. Tevarua (also called Sarah or Big Sully) is perhaps the most tragic figure in the Pitcairn saga.

Chapter 24: Far from Help

My research on Pitcairn's modern history of sexual abuse occurred off island both before and after my visit. Marks (2009) is the primary resource on the intricacies of the rape trials, having spent time on Pitcairn herself during the court proceedings. Prochnau and Parker (2007) provide a worthy summary and additional details.

Chapter 25: Bury the Hatchet

The last well-documented event befalling Pitcairn's first generation is Quintal's most violent undoing. The multiple sources (including Nicolson 1997; Young 1894) that detail his murder are based upon an eyewitness account: Betsy Mills, daughter of mutineer John Mills, revisited her impressions of the killing several times during her ninety-three years of life. An eight-year-old at the time, Betsy—accompanying Thursday October and the other older children—saw the messy carnage in Young's cabin and construed that whatever plan Young and Smith had in mind, it was not cleanly executed. Although Smith/Adams places himself at the scene, he couches his actions as self-defense. The dreaming thread further serves Smith/Adams's intentions—Quintal's murder is the real-life echo of Smith/Adams's cosmic intervention.

Chapter 26: Children of Castaways

All versions of Pitcairn's register date Young's death to Christmas Day 1800, citing some kind of breathing issue as the primary cause. Evidence suggests that he had acquired the affliction many years prior—he was hampered by asthma and chest pains during Massacre Day—but the condition appears to have worsened following Quintal's butchering.

It is Jenny (Teehuteatuaonoa 1817; Teehuteatuaonoa 1829; Kotzebue and Eschscholtz 1830) who details the style of Smith/Adams's leadership as the final mutineer—his "sermonizing extempore." Nicolson (1997) logs the various goings-on after Young's passing before Folger's arrival: the falling death of Vahineatua (Mills's consort and Smith/Adams's eventual partner), the birth of Smith/Adams's children, and the marriage of Susannah and Thursday October.

Never has the arrival of the *Topaz* been documented from Smith/Adams's perspective, but we can rightly assume that the last mutineer purposefully let his fires burn, as great care was taken during any earlier instance of potential discovery. An island of children now, Pitcairn no longer needed to remain hidden; the second generation's reaction to Folger's arrival was captured in Folger's log (and Hayes 1996) and by Delano (1817).

Epilogue: Turn Off the Quiet

In many ways, my time on Norfolk Island afforded me a better opportunity to get acquainted with the mutineers' timeline, as more of the saga remains readily embedded in the islanders' psyche there. My extended visit to the Bounty Folklore Museum provided invaluable insight into the historical timeline elaborated in this book; the museum's founder had spent years cobbling together disparate factoids and accounts into a more streamlined summary of Pitcairn's first two decades and beyond. Hard-to-obtain photographs and log entries further aided my detailing of some of Pitcairn's finer points beyond the physical descriptors in early nineteenth-century journals and my own experiences on Pitcairn. Additionally, many citizens on Norfolk Island are in possession of artifacts and oral traditions—passed down from their ancestors in equal measure—that have not, until now, been a part of the *Bounty*'s story. It was on Norfolk Island that I fully appreciated the notion that Pitcairn's history was only half written. A fervent desire among the descendants exists to better represent the importance of the Tahitian women in the society's perpetuation—a task that can only be accomplished through the seamless blending in of some of the more intangible storytelling elements alongside the handwritten historical accounts of Bligh, Folger, and the other accidental explorers who have left their marks on the collective narrative.

As explained in this closing chapter, much of my research on Norfolk Island led me to unravel a series of alternate histories—fragments of storylines teased out across the generations that bore interesting subtheories about the leading mutineers in particular. Glynn Christian (1982) does a notable job of clearly enumerating the various ways in which Christian could have met his maker: death on Pitcairn in 1793, death in obscurity back in England at a later time, or, as some say, death as Adams, buried under the apocryphal gravestone mentioned in Chapter 22. The latter two notions are likely the result of wild imaginations, but it is tempting to wonder if Young and Smith/Adams were not as God-fearing as they purported to be. After Bligh's departure from the narrative, Jenny becomes the most trustworthy resource when deciphering this entire ordeal. Leaving Pitcairn in 1817, she gave three interviews (referenced many times herein) without fear of retaliation, which, interestingly, makes her the most important character in her timeline. Later, in 1831, the other Pitcairners (Mauatua and Susannah included) made their way to Tahiti as well and tried to reintegrate themselves into Polynesian society. The attempt was a disaster. After so much time away, the islanders hadn't built up an immunity to new viruses and bacteria that the European missionaries had brought with them to the island. Over a dozen Pitcairners quickly perished, including Thursday October, and after a few fatal months, the landing party soon returned home to their faraway enclave. Jenny, however, was unaccounted for. Several amateur historians, including myself, are still in pursuit of the answers regarding Jenny's ultimate fate. For now, she remains lost in the wilderness.

SELECT BIBLIOGRAPHY

Bible passages and unpublished materials—including oral traditions, interviews, and research—are referenced in the source notes organized by chapter. Museum research is listed at the end.

Alexander, Caroline. 2003. *The Bounty: The True Story of the Mutiny on the Bounty*. New York: Viking Penguin.

Ball, Ian M. 1973. *Pitcairn: Children of the Bounty*. London: Victor Gollancz.

Banks, Sir Joseph. [1773?]. *An Epistle from Mr. Banks, Voyager, Monster-Hunter, and Amoroso, to Oberea, Queen of Otaheite*. London: Jacobus Opano.

Barrow, Sir John. 1831. *The Eventful History of the Mutiny and Piratical Seizure of H.M.S. Bounty: Its Causes and Consequences*. London: J. Murray.

Beaglehole, J. C., ed. 1962. *The Endeavour Journal of Joseph Banks, 1768–1771*. 2 vols. Sydney: Trustees of the Public Library of New South Wales in association with Angus and Robertson.

———. 1974. *The Life of Captain James Cook*. Stanford, CA: Stanford University Press.

Becke, Louis, and Walter Jeffery. 1898. *The Mutineer: A Romance of Pitcairn Island*. London: T. Fisher Unwin.

Beechey, Frederick William. 1831. *Narrative of a Voyage to the Pacific and Beering's Strait, to Co-operate with the Polar Expeditions Performed in His Majesty's Ship Blossom.* 2 vols. London: Henry Colburn and Richard Bentley.

Belcher, Lady Diana Jolliffe. 1870. *The Mutineers of the Bounty and Their Descendants in Pitcairn and Norfolk Islands.* London: J. Murray.

BibleProject. 2014. "The Book of Genesis Part 2." Uploaded June 30, 2014. Video, 5:06. www.youtube.com/watch?v=VpbWbyx1008.

——. 2015. "Overview: Job." Uploaded October 22, 2015. Video, 11:00. www.youtube.com/watch?v=xQwnH8th_fs.

——. 2016a. "The Book of Ecclesiastes." Uploaded August 17, 2016. Video, 6:41. www.youtube.com/watch?v=VeUiuSK81-0&t=335s.

——. 2016b. "The Book of Job." Uploaded October 22, 2016. Video, 7:14. www.youtube.com/watch?v=GswSg2ohqmA&t=328s.

——. 2016c. "The Book of Proverbs." Uploaded May 4, 2016. Video, 5:30. www.youtube.com/watch?v=Gab04dPs_uA.

——. 2016d. "Overview: Ecclesiastes." Uploaded June 10, 2016. Video, 8:01. www.youtube.com/watch?v=lrsQ1tc-2wk.

——. 2016e. "Overview: Jonah." Uploaded April 12, 2016. Video, 9:00. www.youtube.com/watch?v=dLIabZc0O4c.

Birkett, Dea. 1997. *Serpent in Paradise.* New York: Anchor Books.

Bligh, William. 1790. *A Narrative of the Mutiny, on Board His Majesty's Ship Bounty; and the Subsequent Voyage of Part of the Crew, in the Ship's Boat, From Tofoa, one of the Friendly Islands, to Timor, a Dutch Settlement in East Indies.* London: G. Nicol.

——. 1937. *The Log of the Bounty: Being Lieutenant William Bligh's Log of the Proceedings of His Majesty's Armed Vessel Bounty in a Voyage to the South Seas, to Take the Breadfruit from the Society Islands to the West Indies.* Edited by Owen Rutter. 2 vols. London: Golden Cockerel Press.

Breitowitz, Yitzchak. 2016. "The Book of Job." Hidabroot, uploaded January 14, 2016. Video, 54:49. www.youtube.com/watch?v=e9LB47o4Q9M&t=2194s.

Briand, Paul L. 1966. *In Search of Paradise.* New York: Duell, Sloan, and Pearce.

Brunton, Paul, ed. 1989. *Awake Bold Bligh! William Bligh's Letters Describing the Mutiny on HMS Bounty.* Honolulu: University of Hawaii Press.

Burrows, M. 1853. *Pitcairn's Island: A Lecture Delivered at the Christchurch School-Room, St. Pancras.* London: J. Whitaker.

Carteret, Philip. 1965. *Carteret's Voyage Around the World 1766–1769.* Edited by Helen Wallis. Chicago: Northwestern University Press.

Chambers, Neil, ed. 2000. *The Letters of Sir Joseph Banks: A Selection, 1768–1820.* London: Imperial College Press.

Chamier, Frederick. 1838. *Jack Adams, the Mutineer.* London: H. Colburn.

Christensen, Alta. 1855. *Heirs of Exile.* Battle Creek, MI: Review and Herald Publishing.

Christian, Charles. 1818. *An Abridged Statement of Facts, Supported by Respectable and Undeniable Evidence: With Strictures on the Injurious Influence of Calumny, and a Display of the Excellence and Invincibility of Truth.* Douglas, Isle of Man.

Christian, Edward. 1795. *A Short Reply to Capt. William Bligh's Answer.* London: J. Deighton.

Christian, Fletcher [pseud.]. 1796. *Letters from Mr. Fletcher Christian, Containing a Narrative of the Transactions on Board His Majesty's Ship Bounty, Before and After the Mutiny, with His Subsequent Voyages and Travels in South America.* London: H. D. Symonds.

Christian, Glynn. 1982. *Fragile Paradise: The Discovery of Fletcher Christian, Bounty Mutineer.* Boston: Little, Brown.

Coleridge, Samuel Taylor. 1912. *The Complete Poetical Works of Samuel Taylor Coleridge.* Edited by Ernest Hartley Coleridge. 2 vols. Oxford: Clarendon Press.

Danielsson, Bengt. 1962. *What Happened on the Bounty?* Translated by Alan Tapsell. London: George Allen & Unwin.

David, Andrew C. F. 1981. "Bligh's Notes on Cook's Last Voyage." *Mariner's Mirror 67,* no. 1 (February): 102.

Delano, Amasa. 1817. *Narrative of Voyages and Travels, in the Northern and Southern Hemispheres, Comprising Three Voyages Round the World; Together with a Voyage of Survey and Discovery in the Pacific Ocean and Oriental Islands.* Boston: House.

Dening, Greg. 1992. *Mr. Bligh's Bad Language: Passion, Power, and Theatre on the Bounty.* Cambridge: Cambridge University Press.

Dick, William H. 1882. "The Mutiny of the Bounty and the Pitcairn Islanders." *Victorian Review 5.*

Ellis, William. 1829. *Polynesian Researches, During a Residence of Nearly Six Years in the South Sea Islands, Including Descriptions of the Natural History and Scenery of the Islands, with Remarks on the History,*

Mythology, Traditions, Government, Arts, Manners, and Customs of the Inhabitants. 2 vols. London: Fisher, Son & Jackson.

Fiske, Nathan Welby. 1855. *Aleck and the Mutineers of the Bounty: A Remarkable Illustration of the Influence of the Bible.* Boston: Massachusetts Sabbath School Society.

Folger, Mayhew. 1809. "Mutineers of the Bounty." *Naval Chronicle* (21): 454–455.

Frost, Alan. 2018. *Mutiny, Mayhem, Mythology: Bounty's Enigmatic Voyage.* Sydney: University of Sydney Press.

Goldman, Irving. 1970. *Ancient Polynesian Society.* Chicago: University of Chicago Press.

Hall, James Norman. 1934. *Tale of a Shipwreck.* Boston: Houghton Mifflin, 1934.

———. (1950) 2001. *The Far Lands.* Reprint, Honolulu: Mutual Publishing.

———. 1952. *My Island Home: An Autobiography.* New York: Little, Brown.

Hawkesworth, John. 1773. *An Account of the Voyages Undertaken by the Order of His Present Majesty for Making Discoveries in the Southern Hemisphere, and Successively Performed by Commodore Byron, Captain Wallis, Captain Carteret, and Captain Cook, in the Dolphin, the Swallow, and the Endeavour, Drawn Up from the Journals Which Were Kept by the Several Commanders, and from the Papers of Joseph Banks, Esq.* 3 vols. London: W. Strahan and T. Cadell.

Hayes, Walter. 1996. *The Captain from Nantucket and the Mutiny on the Bounty: A Recollection of Mayhew Folger, Mariner, Who Discovered the Last Mutineer and His Family on Pitcairn's Island, Together with Letters and Documents Never Previously Published.* Ann Arbor, MI: William L. Clements Library.

Henley, Jon. 2021. "France Has Underestimated Impact of Nuclear Tests in French Polynesia, Research Finds." *Guardian,* March 9, 2021. www.theguardian.com/world/2021/mar/09/france-has-underestimated-impact-of-nuclear-tests-in-french-polynesia-research-finds.

Hook, Milton. n.d. "Pitcairn Island." In *Encyclopedia of Seventh-Day Adventists.* Accessed January 2021. https://encyclopedia.adventist.org/article?id=782T.

Hough, Richard Alexander. 2000. *Captain Bligh and Mr. Christian: The Men and the Mutiny.* Annapolis, MD: Naval Institute Press.

Houston, Neal B. 1965–1966. "Fletcher Christian and 'The Rime of the Ancient Mariner.'" *Dalhousie Review* 45 (Winter): 431–446.

Hui, Harry C., Sing-Hang Cheung, and Jasmine Lam. 2017. "In Search of Psychological Antecedents and Consequences of Christian Conversion: A Three-Year Prospective Study." *Psychology of Religion and Spirituality* (9): 220–230.

Kennedy, Gavin. 1989. *Captain Bligh: The Man and His Mutinies*. London: Duckworth.

Kotzebue, Otto von, and Johann Friedrich Eschscholtz. 1830. *A New Voyage Round the World in the Years 1823, 24, 25, and 26*. 2 vols. London: H. Colburn and R. Bentley.

Lareau Web Parlor. n.d. "Crewmembers of the H. M. S. *Bounty*." Internet Archive. Accessed January 2021. https://web.archive.org/web/20080509070443/http://www.lareau.org/bounty2.html.

Lucas, Sir Charles Prestwood, ed. 1929. *The Pitcairn Island Register Book*. London: Society for Promoting Christian Knowledge.

Mackaness, George. (1931) 1957. *The Life of Vice-Admiral William Bligh*. Reprint, Sydney: Angus & Robinson.

Marden, Luis. 1957. "I Found the Bones of the *Bounty*." *National Geographic Magazine*, December 1957, 725–789.

Marks, Kathy. 2009. *Lost Paradise: From Mutiny on the Bounty to a Modern-Day Legacy of Sexual Mayhem, the Dark Secrets of Pitcairn Island Revealed*. New York: Simon & Schuster.

Marquand, Christophe. 1990. "23 Polynesians Convicted in Religious Witch-Hunt Murders." *Associated Press*, April 6, 1990. https://apnews.com/article/64cef6ef3791dfc0d5f2e13dcdc90398.

Masefield, John. (1905) 2010. *Sea Life in Nelson's Time*. Reprint, London: Nabu Press.

Maude, H. E. 1958. "In Search of a Home." *Journal of the Polynesian Society* 67, no. 2.

———. 1968. *Of Islands and Men: Studies in Pacific History*. Melbourne, Australia: Oxford University Press.

McKee, Alexander. 1961. *The Truth About the Mutiny on the Bounty*. London: Mayflower Books.

Mellman, Thomas A. 2018. "Sleep and PTSD." *Post-Traumatic Stress Disorder*, edited by Charles B. Nemeroff and Charles R. Marmar, 409–419. New York: Oxford University Press.

Metcalfe, Rowan. 2004. *Transit of Venus*. Wellington, New Zealand: Pandanus.

Morrison, James. 1935. *The Journal of James Morrison, Boatswain's Mate of the Bounty, Describing the Mutiny and Subsequent Misfortunes of the Mutineers, Together with an Account of the Island of Tahiti*. Edited by Owen Rutter. London: Golden Cockerel Press.

———. 2010. *After the Bounty*. Edited by Donald A. Maxton. Lincoln, NE: Potomac Books.

Mountain, Fiona. 2014. *Isabella*. London: Random House.

Murray, Reverend Thomas. 1857. *Pitcairn: The Island, the People and the Pastor*. London: Society for Promoting Christian Knowledge.

Nicolson, Robert. 1997. *The Pitcairners*. Auckland, New Zealand: Pasifika Press.

Nordhoff, Charles, and James Norman Hall. 1948. *The Bounty Trilogy*. Boston: Little, Brown.

O'Brian, Patrick. 1997. *Joseph Banks: A Life*. Chicago: University of Chicago Press.

Oliver, Douglas L. 1974. *Ancient Tahitian Society*. 3 vols. Honolulu: University Press of Hawaii.

Pacific Union College. n.d. "Pitcairn Islands Study Center." Accessed January 2021. https://library.puc.edu/pitcairn/index.shtml.

Patrick, Christopher J., ed. 2018. *Handbook of Psychopathy*. New York: Guilford Press.

Philbrick, Nathaniel. 2000. *In the Heart of the Sea: The Tragedy of the Whaleship Essex*. New York: Viking.

Pipon, Philip. 1834. "The Descendants of the Bounty's Crew." *United Service Journal* (part I): 191–199.

Pitcairn Islands Office. n.d. "Government of the Pitcairn Islands." Accessed January 2021. www.government.pn/index.php.

Pitcairn Islands Tourism. n.d. "Welcome to Pitcairn Islands Tourism." Accessed January 2018. www.visitpitcairn.pn/.

Preston, Diana. 2017. *Paradise in Chains: The Bounty Mutiny and the Founding of Australia*. New York: Bloomsbury Publishing.

Prochnau, William, and Laura Parker. 2007. "Trouble in Paradise." *Vanity Fair*, December 17, 2007. www.vanityfair.com/news/2008/01/pitcairn200801.

Raga, Suzanne. 2015. "The Super Luxe History of Pineapples— and Why They Used to Cost $8000." *Mental Floss*, June 25,

2015. www.mentalfloss.com/article/65506/super-luxe-history -pineapples-and-why-they-used-cost-8000.

Raine, T. 1821. "Captain Raine's Narrative of a Visit to Pitcairn's Island in the Ship Surry, 1821." *The Australian Magazine, or, Compendium of Religious, Literary and Miscellaneous Intelligence* (1): 109–114.

Reynolds, Pauline. 2008. *Pitcairn Tapa: 'Ahu no Hitiaurevareva*. Edited by Arthur Baysting. Papeete, French Polynesia: 'ana'ana Publishing.

Robertson, George. 1948. *The Discovery of Tahiti: A Journal of the Second Voyage of H.M.S. Dolphin Round the World Under the Command of Captain Wallis, R.N., in the Years 1766, 1767, and 1768*. Edited by Hugh Carrington. London: Hakluyt Society.

Rohrbaugh, Jackson. 2015. "What Is Madeira Wine?" *Wine Folly*, March 27, 2015. https://winefolly.com/deep-dive/what-is-madeira-wine/.

Rutter, Owen. 1936. *The True Story of the Mutiny in the "Bounty."* Boston: Newnes.

Sala, Enric. 2013. "Journey to the Pitcairn Islands." *National Geographic*, uploaded March 4, 2013. Video, 23:08. www.youtube.com /watch?v=yx8kjJgt_AE, 2013.

Scott, Brian W. 1982. "The True Identity of John Adams." *Mariner's Mirror* (68): 31–39.

Shapiro, Harry Lionel. 1929. *Descendants of the Mutineers of the Bounty*. Honolulu: Bishop Museum.

———. 1936. *The Heritage of the Bounty: The Story of Pitcairn Through Six Generations*. New York: Simon & Schuster.

Shillibeer, John. 1817. *A Narrative of the Briton's Voyage to Pitcairn's Island: Including an Interesting Sketch of the Present State of the Brazils and of Spanish South America*. Taunton, England: J. W. Marriott.

Silverman, David. 1967. *Pitcairn Island*. Cleveland, OH: World.

Staines, Sir Thomas. 1815. "Account of the Descendants of Christian and Other Mutineers of the Bounty." *Naval Chronicle* (33): 217–218.

Tagart, Edward. 1832. *A Memoir of the Late Captain Peter Heywood, R.N., with Extracts from His Diaries and Correspondence*. London: E. Wilson.

Teehuteatuaonoa [Jenny]. 1819. "Account of the Mutineers of the Ship *Bounty*, and Their Descendants at Pitcairn's Island." *Sydney Gazette*, July 17, 1819, 817.

Teehuteatuaonoa [Jenny]. 1829. "Pitcairn's Island—The Bounty's Crew." *United Service Journal* (part I): 589–593.

Topliff, Samuel. 1821. "Pitcairn's Island." *New-England Galaxy* (Boston), January 12, 1821.

"T. W." 1818. "John Adams of Pitcairn Island." *Gentleman's Magazine and Historical Chronicle* 88, part 2 (July): 38–39.

Wahlroos, Sven. 1989. *Mutiny and Romance in the South Seas: A Companion to the Bounty Adventure.* Topsfield, MA: Salem House.

Weishaar, Marjorie E., and Aaron T. Beck. 1992. "Clinical and Cognitive Predictors of Suicide." In *Assessment and Prediction of Suicide*, edited by Ronald W. Maris, Alan L. Berman, John T. Maltsberger, and Robert I. Yufit, 467–483. New York: Guilford Press.

Young, Rosalind Amelia. 1894. *Mutiny of the Bounty and Story of Pitcairn Island, 1790–1894.* 3rd ed. Oakland, CA: Pacific Press.

MUSEUM SOURCES

Archival text. Main Reading Room, Bounty Folk Museum, Burnt Pine, Norfolk Island, Australia.

Wall text. Bligh's Cabin, Bounty Folk Museum, Burnt Pine, Norfolk Island, Australia.

Wall text. Archival Wing, Norfolk Island Museum, Kingston, Norfolk Island, Australia.

Wall text. Main Building, Norfolk Island Museum, Kingston, Norfolk Island, Australia.

Wall text. Vestibule, La Maison James Norman Hall, Arue, Tahiti, French Polynesia.

INDEX

Aboriginal Australians, 45–46
Academy Award, 77–78
Adams, John
   description, 11, 150
   grave and headstone, 229–230
   identity, 17, 229, 253, 254, 257,
      275–276
   meeting Folger, 10–15, 229,
      257–258
   as mutineer, 12, 275
   and story of life on Pitcairn,
      274–275
Adams family descendants, 273
Adamstown, 150
Adventure Bay (Tasmania), 44
Aitutaki (island), 93, 94
alcohol making and drinking on
      Pitcairn, 156, 182–183, 186,
      195, 220–222, 250, 275
Ally (marketing executive), 33,
      34–35
animals from *Bounty*
   on Pitcairn, 126, 127, 129,
      130–131, 157–158
   on Tubuai, 93, 95, 97, 101

Arago (ship) visit to Pitcairn,
      259–262
arii (rulers) in Tahiti, 54–55,
      56, 57
arioi cult/sect, 60
Artocarpus incisa. See breadfruit
astronomy on Pitcairn, 246–247
azimuth compass of *Bounty*, 15, 16,
      63–65

Baby Sully, 108, 126, 158, 248
Banks, Joseph, 18–19, 20, 32
Batavia, and Bligh with crew after
      mutiny, 169–170
Bethia (ship), 20–21, 39
Bible
   cultural aspects, 68
   and fear of God, 217, 218
   justifications for behavior by
      Young, 248, 249–250
   as reference for mutineers,
      110–111, 122
   Young with Smith, 217, 220, 236,
      248–249, 253, 254
   Young with Susannah, 53, 66, 68

Bible (*continued*)
  Young with women, 110–111,
    217–219, 236–237
Big Fence (house), 142–143, 173
Bligh, William
  background and description, 21,
    25
  character and admiration seeking,
    18, 22, 37–38, 45, 64
  letter for command of vessel, 18,
    21–22
  reputation as commander, 41,
    47, 61
  in Tahiti with Cook, 21, 56
Bligh, William and *Bounty*
  behavior after Tahiti, 87
  cabin, 39
  as captain and other tasks, 21–22,
    28, 38–39
  control of crew, 62
  as Cook's son lie, 64
  crew description, 22–25
  and crew's goings-on, 39–41, 44
  departure for mission, 30–31
  departure from Tahiti, 71
  at *heiva*, 60–61
  lashes as punishment, 41–42,
    61–62, 65
  logbooks of Cook, 25–26
  logs, 40, 72, 168
  responsibilities of Fletcher
    Christian, 37, 39, 40, 44,
    45–46, 87
  runaways in Tahiti, 61–62
  sailing orders and route, 28
  in Tahiti, 54–55, 57, 65–66, 277
  theft of compass, 63–65
  Valentine's sickness and death,
    46–48

  watch shifts and orders for work,
    37, 39, 40
  wine on, 37, 49
  and women, 57, 65–66
Bligh, William and mutiny on
    Bounty
  fate afterwards, 104, 169–170,
    192
  in mutiny, 88–91, 93, 94
  return to England, 170, 277
  and story of mutiny, 9, 277
Bloody Bay (Tubuai), 94, 95, 96
blue eyes, 69
Bougainville, Louis Antoine de, 75
Bounty
  azimuth compass, 15, 16, 63–65
  breadfruit as mission, 20
  at Cape Horn, 42–43
  captain's cabin, 39
  crew and details, 22–25, 26–28,
    37
  crew goings-on, 39–42, 44
  departure for mission, 30–31
  departures from Tahiti, 70–71,
    93–94, 106–107
  equator crossing and ritual, 38
  fate and future on Pitcairn, 128,
    133
  food and provisions, 26
  landing on Pitcairn, 123–124
  logbooks of Cook, 25–26, 84
  logs of Bligh, 40, 72, 168
  map of voyage, xvi–xvii
  marine chronometer, 15, 16, 44
  mutiny (*see* mutiny on *Bounty*)
  Nomuka visit, 84–86, 87
  postponement of mission, 28–29
  preparation for mission, 20–21, 28
  proof given to Folger, 15, 16

refitting from *Bethia*, 20–21
returns to and resupply in Tahiti,
    92–94, 105
in Tahiti (*see* Tahiti)
Tenerife stop, 37–38
torching, 3, 133–134, 135
travel to Tahiti, 43–49
at Tubuai, 94–95, 96, 99, 101,
    103–104
turn to Cape of Good Hope,
    43–44
two-year journey for food, 33
use of parts by mutineers, 11, 13,
    128
at Van Diemen's Land
    (Tasmania), 44–46
watch shifts, 37, 40
water and wood restocking,
    45–46, 84, 87
wreck and remains, 263
See also Bligh, William and
    Bounty; mutineers
Bounty Folklore Museum, 276–278
Bounty today
    Bounty Day on Norfolk Island,
        272–276
    as business for Carol Warren,
        185, 188, 189–190, 213, 261
    museums, 185, 212, 276–278
    mutiny in movies and books, 3–4,
        34, 73–74, 80
    replica for movie, 74, 80
Bounty Trilogy (Nordhoff and Hall),
    208–209
Brando, Marlon, 34, 74, 78, 80
the Brando resort, 78
brandy from ti plant, 182, 195, 220,
    250, 275
breadfruit (*Artocarpus incisa*)

after mutiny, 91, 92, 93
agreement with Teina, 57–58
collection for *Bounty* in Tahiti,
    54, 55, 56, 57, 58–59, 61, 65
collection for Jamaica as mission,
    20–21, 22, 49, 54
departure of *Bounty*, 30–31
description and properties,
    19–20
second mission of Bligh, 277
Brenda (Steve's sister), 225–226
Britain
    convicts in Australia, 209–210
    and mutiny story, 16–17
    Operation Unique for sexual
        abuse of children on Pitcairn,
        240, 241–243, 244, 245
    Pitcairn Island as territory, 151,
        241–242, 243–244, 246
    in Pitcairn of mutineers, 153–154,
        160–161, 195
    and sexuality on Pitcairn,
        243–245, 246
British Overseas Territory, 151
Briton (ship), 17
Brown, William
    breadfruit cuttings, 54, 55
    description and as gardener, 54
    in massacre by Polynesians,
        196–197
    as mutineer with Fletcher
        Christian, 105
    surveying of Pitcairn, 123–126
    wife's indiscretions, 154–155
Burkitt, Thomas
    in attacks on Tubuai, 97, 98, 101
    description, 50
    in mutiny, 88, 89, 90, 172
    remaining on Tahiti, 105

Burkitt, Thomas (*continued*)
  seeking women on Tahiti, 50–52
  treason and hanging, 172
Byrne, Michael, 28, 31, 59

Campbell, Duncan, 20, 21
Cape Horn and *Bounty*, 42–43
Cape of Good Hope and *Bounty*,
  43–44, 73
Carteret (Captain), discovery and
  description of Pitcairn, 13,
  108–109, 123
Catholic mission and priests, 116
ceremonial gathering (*heiva*) in
  Tahiti, 59–61
children of mutineers on Pitcairn
  babies and births, 155, 160, 175,
  178, 199, 220
  inhabitants after 18 years, 256
  protection from mutineers,
  248–249
  and visit by *Topaz*, 256–258
  witnesses of murder, 253
children on Pitcairn today, sexual
  abuse and trial, 240–245
Christian, Charles (brother of
  Fletcher), 29–30, 106
Christian, Charles (son of Fletcher),
  178, 256–258
Christian, Fletcher before mutiny
  and brother Charles, 29–30,
  106
  as crew on *Bounty*, 24, 26, 27
  departure from Tahiti, 70–71
  description and background, 24
  desire to leave *Bounty*, 86–88
  and emotions, 58, 191–192
  in equator-crossing ritual, 38
  insults of Bligh, 87–88

as leader of landing party on
  Tahiti, 61, 64
and Mauatua, 60, 61, 67–70,
  93–94
and *Middlesex* mutiny story,
  29–30
on Nomuka, 84–86, 87
postponement of *Bounty* mission,
  28–29
responsibilities on *Bounty*
  before Tahiti, 37, 39, 40, 44,
  45–46, 87
skills with people and for work,
  24, 37–38
in Tahiti, 57–58, 64
women in Tahiti, 55, 60, 61
Christian, Fletcher in mutiny and
  after
  bed and sleep on Pitcairn,
  135–137
  and Bligh's fate, 104, 192
  Christmas celebration on Pitcairn,
  155–156
  concerns and angst on Pitcairn,
  128–129, 137, 191–193
  departure from Tubuai, 103–104
  departures from Tahiti, 93–94,
  105–106
  and emotions, 58, 191–192
  and John Adams, 275–276
  as leader on *Bounty*, 3, 91,
  103–109, 113, 121–123
  as leader on Pitcairn, 123, 126,
  128–129, 134, 159–160, 183
  legend of return to England, 274
  at lookout and fear of being
  found, 158, 168, 183, 191
  in massacre by Polynesians,
  197–198

and Mauatua, 198
in modern movies, 34, 74
mutiny decision and actions, 9,
   88, 89, 90–91, 94, 103, 104
and Polynesians' mutiny, 180–181
returns to Tahiti, 92–94, 103–104
search for island without natives,
   107–109
and second mutiny, 113
sight of Pitcairn, 122–123
and Smith's disappearance,
   100–101
surveying of Pitcairn, 123–126
on Tubuai, 94–96, 98–99,
   100–103
Christian, Isabel, 142–143, 145,
   261, 264
Christian, Nadine, 145, 265
Christian, Olive
   and *Arago* visit, 260
   description and as homestay
      parent, 140–141
   at house with author, 141–143
Christian, Olive and Steve
   author's time with, 140–147,
      151–152, 163–168, 172–174,
      187
   and closed-door bedroom,
      163–166, 174
   and descendants of Fletcher
      Christian, 140, 184
   general store and *Claymore*
      supplies, 145–146
   as homestay, 140, 144–145
   house (Big Fence), 142–143, 173
   stench in author's room, 163,
      172–174
   travels, 146–147
   visit to Lookout Point, 167–168

Christian, Randy, 145, 211,
   242–243, 265
Christian, Shawn
   and *Arago* visit, 261
   description, 174
   ham radio and logs, 165–166,
      174
   ignoring and meeting author, 174,
      211, 264
   as mayor, 151, 174
   old bedroom, 163–165
   rape and sexual abuse, 240,
      242–243
Christian, Steve
   description, 143–144, 147
   as Fletcher Christian's closest
      relative, 144, 147
   and outside world, 145
   sexual abuse, 241, 242–243
   weather updates, 164
   See also Christian, Olive and Steve
Christian, Thursday October
   birth, 155
   children with Susannah, 255
   and Quintal's murder, 253
   visit and encounter with Folger
      and *Topaz*, 9–10, 256–258
Christian, Trent, 272
Christian family at *Bounty* time, 30,
   277
Christian's Cave (Pitcairn), 191
Christmas in the South Pacific, 59,
   109–113, 155–156
Churchill, Charles
   in attack on Tubuai, 97–98
   on *Bounty* trip, 38, 40, 42
   in breadfruit deal, 58
   as crew on *Bounty*, 27
   death, 171

Churchill, Charles (*continued*)
　in mutiny, 88, 90, 91
　remaining on Tahiti, 105,
　　170–171
　as runaway on Tahiti, 61–62
Claymore (ship)
　author on, 116–120, 138–139,
　　264–265
　description and trip to Pitcairn,
　　115, 117–119, 145, 148–149
　return for departure, 263–264
　supplies for Pitcairn, 145–146
closed-door rooms in homestays,
　　163–166, 174, 188
coffee plants and berries, 228
communications on Pitcairn, 142,
　　165–166
Cook (Captain, James)
　in Adventure Bay, 44
　Bligh with, 21, 56
　changes in third visit, 69
　death in Hawaii, 21, 23, 25, 69
　logbooks, 25–26, 84
　on *Resolution*, 21
　reverence for in Tahiti, 54, 69
"Coventry Carol" (song), 111–112,
　　156, 178, 235
cow of Cook, 93, 97, 98

dead bodies, on ships, 47–48
democracy on Pitcairn, 151, 158,
　　159–160, 195
discovery and naming of Pitcairn, 3,
　　13, 108
dogs
　care and love from Jenny, 100,
　　109, 127
　as danger, 129
　slaughter, 129, 130–132, 135

Down Rope (Pitcairn) and falling
　　visitor, 224–227
ducats legend of Pitcairn, 274

Eden, as notion, 74–75
Edwards, Edward, 170, 171–172
Elizabeth (author's friend), 268–270
Endeavour (ship), 18–19
etchings on Pitcairn, 225, 226–227
explorers, and paradise, 75
eye color, 69

Faahotu, 63, 127–128, 156–158, 160
fear (*mehameha*) and fear of God,
　　217, 218
Folger, Mayhew
　and *Bounty* story, 9, 11–12, 16–17
　capture by Spanish, 16
　encounter with islanders and
　　invite to island, 7–10, 256–258
　finding Pitcairn, 6–7
　mapping of Pitcairn, 16
　meeting John Adams, 10–15, 229,
　　257–258
　and proofs of *Bounty*, 15, 16
　supplies search, 5–6
fort (Fort George) on Tubuai, 95,
　　96–97, 98, 101, 103
Friendly Islands, 84, 86
Fryer, John, 41, 89, 90

Galapagos tortoise on Pitcairn, 146,
　　230
Gambier archipelago, 115–116
general store on Pitcairn today,
　　145–146
Gibson, Mel, 34
goats on Pitcairn, 157–158, 167, 168
goods, in *Bounty*'s days, 32–33

Hall, Conrad L., 78
Hall, James Norman
  attempt to reach Pitcairn, 80
  copy of Bligh's *Bounty* logbook,
    72, 168
  life and background, 72–73
  and *Men Against the Sea*, 168–169
  museum to, 81
  and *Mutiny on the Bounty*, 73
  and *Pitcairn's Island*, 172
Hall, Kate, 76–78, 79, 80
Hall family, 76, 77, 80, 81
Hall Rutgers, Nancy, 81–83, 244
Hallett, John
  in and after mutiny, 90, 170
  on *Bounty* trip, 38
  as crew on *Bounty*, 23, 26, 27
  treason of Heywood, 172
ham radio of Shawn Christian,
  165–166, 174
Hawkesworth's Voyages, 108
Hayward, Thomas
  in and after mutiny, 90, 170
  on *Bounty* trip, 38
  as crew on *Bounty*, 23, 26, 27
  treason of Heywood, 172
heiva (ceremonial gathering) in
  Tahiti, 59–61
Heywood, Peter
  on Aboriginal Australians, 46
  on *Bounty* trip, 38, 62
  connection with Fletcher
    Christian, 24, 26, 30, 55,
    106, 192
  as crew on *Bounty*, 24, 25, 26
  and legend of Fletcher Christian
    in England, 274
  and *Middlesex* mutiny story, 30
  in mutiny, 91

  remaining on Tahiti, 106, 171
  and Smith's disappearance,
    100–101
  treason verdict and pardon, 172,
    274
  on Tubuai, 95, 96, 100–101
  women in Tahiti, 55–56
Highest Point (Pitcairn), 143
Hill of Difficulty (Pitcairn), 127,
  140
HMAV *Bounty. See Bounty*
homestay on Pitcairn today,
  140–142, 184
Huggan, Thomas (Doc), 22, 42,
  46–47, 58

Itia, and Bligh, 57, 65–66

Jenny
  on *Bounty*, 109, 113
  death of remaining Polynesians,
    204
  discontent and desire to leave
    Pitcairn, 153–154, 160–161,
    162, 178–179, 204, 231
  dogs care and love, 100, 109, 127
  and dogs slaughter, 130–131,
    134, 135
  and Faahotu's death, 160
  in massacre's aftermath, 204, 206
  as name, 66–67
  nighttime outings, 153, 154–155,
    161–162
  plan and warning of mutiny by
    Polynesians, 178–179
  preparation and attempt to leave
    Pitcairn, 231–233, 234
  recollections of Pitcairn, 275, 278
  return to Tahiti, 278

Jenny (*continued*)
  and second mutiny warning, 113
  social changes from British, 63,
    278
  and Tararo's death, 180
  as Teehuteatuaonoa at *heiva*, 59
  on Tubuai, 99–100
  and visit by ship, 234
Job (of Bible), 218–219
Job's tears, 219, 228, 236, 260,
  273
Jonah and the whale, 125, 202

La Maison James Norman Hall
  museum, 81
Landing Place (Pitcairn), 126, 139,
  232
Larcum Kendall marine
  chronometer of *Bounty*, 15,
  16, 44
latitude, in charting, 107
Ledward, Thomas, 46, 58, 62,
  89–90
longitude, and charting as problem,
  107
Lookout Point (Pitcairn), 158,
  167–168, 182–183
Los Angeles, and return to modern
  world, 268–270

Mai (islander), 59
Maimiti. *See* Mauatua
mana, description, 68
manahune, 56, 57
Mangareva, 115–116
marae, description, 60
Martin, Isaac, 105, 155, 196–197
Mary (Shawn's mother-in-law),
  264–268

Massacre Day, 194, 195–199,
  249–250
Mataohu. *See* Susannah
Matavai Bay (Tahiti), 53–58,
  92–94, 105
Matthew Junior, 160
Mauatua
  bed and sleep on Pitcairn,
    135–136, 137
  children, 155, 160, 178, 191, 199
  concerns on Pitcairn, 128–129
  and cultural differences, 68–69,
    156
  death of remaining Polynesians,
    204
  dizziness and health, 127, 128,
    129, 137
  and dogs, 129, 131, 135
  early days on Pitcairn, 127–128
  and Fletcher Christian, 60, 61,
    67–70, 93–94, 198
  at funeral of Huggan, 58
  gift to Fletcher Christian, 70
  at *heiva*, 60
  as leader of the women, 134–135
  and massacre of whites, 197–198
  Minarii's banishment, 201
  and mutiny against whites, 178,
    179, 180
  return of *Bounty*, 92–94
  in search for Pitcairn, 108, 109
  seasickness, 109, 123, 137
  and second mutiny on *Bounty*, 113
  Susannah's pregnancy, 63
  on Tubuai, 95, 96, 101, 103
  and violence on women, 63
  and visit by ship, 233, 234
  and women's departure from
    Pitcairn, 232

Maui (god), 70, 94

Mavis (Jay and Meralda's mother), 227

McCoy, Daniel, 175, 256–258

McCoy, William
alcohol making and drinking, 156, 182, 220, 221–222, 275
in attack by Polynesians, 195–196, 199–200
background and views, 175–176
Christmas on *Bounty*, 110–111, 112–113
control of Pitcairn, 183, 194–195, 202–203
as crew on *Bounty*, 28, 176
death, 222
eavesdrop by Bligh, 39–40, 41
in Minarii's death, 203
morning rounds on Pitcairn, 175
as mutineer with Fletcher Christian, 105
in mutiny, 89
plot to retake control of Pitcairn, 202–203
and Quintal, 39–40, 176–177, 182–183
surveying of Pitcairn, 123–126
torching of *Bounty*, 133
tracked and joined by Minarii, 200–202
on Tubuai, 100–101

medical clinic on Pitcairn, 239–240

Mehetia (island), 48

Mele (Nancy's daughter-in-law), 82

Melva (at tourist office), 148, 149, 150

Men Against the Sea (Hall and Nordhoff), 168–169

merchandise, in *Bounty*'s days, 32–33

Michelle (on Norfolk Island), 273, 276

Middlesex (ship), 29–30

Mills, John
in massacre by Polynesians, 195
as mutineer with Fletcher Christian, 104, 105
in mutiny, 88, 89, 90

Millward, John
in attack on Tubuai, 97, 98
description, 50
in mutiny, 90
remaining on Tahiti, 105
as runaway on Tahiti, 61–62
seeking women on Tahiti, 50–52
treason verdict and hanging, 172

Minarii
death, 202–204
description, 177
Fletcher Christian and Mauatua in massacre, 197–198
as fugitive, 200–202
joining mutineers, 107, 198
in massacre of whites, 195, 196–198
with Quintal and W. McCoy, 195, 200–204
in ratio of women and men, 159
as servant to whites, 195
surveying of Pitcairn, 123–126
with Susannah, 177
violence on Polynesians, 179–180, 201

Miz T (Galapagos tortoise), 146, 230

Moira (on Norfolk Island), 276–277

Morayshire (ship), 210, 272–273

Motu Mapeti (Tahiti), 76–78, 79
movies, on *Bounty* mutiny, 34,
　　74, 80
Mururoa atoll, 114–115
museums about *Bounty*, 185, 212,
　　276–278
mutineers
　　and Christmas, 59, 109–113,
　　　155–156
　　departures from Tahiti, 93–94,
　　　105–106
　　description, 3
　　events in mutiny, 88–91
　　fate and future of *Bounty*, 128,
　　　133
　　Fletcher Christian as leader on
　　　Bounty, 3, 91, 103–109, 113,
　　　121–123
　　grievances and second mutiny,
　　　113, 121
　　hunt by *Pandora*, 170–172
　　islanders joining *Bounty*, 93, 104,
　　　106–107
　　pairings with women, 106, 108
　　on Pitcairn (*see* Pitcairn Island
　　　and *Bounty* mutineers)
　　remaining in Tahiti after mutiny,
　　　105, 106, 170–171
　　remaining with Fletcher Christian
　　　after Tubuai, 103–104, 105
　　returns to Tahiti, 92–94,
　　　103–104
　　search for island without natives,
　　　107–109
　　search for Pitcairn, 3, 13,
　　　108–109, 113, 121
　　torching of *Bounty*, 3, 133–134,
　　　135
　　trial in England, 172

　　on Tubuai (*see* Tubuai)
　　See also individual mutineers
mutiny on *Bounty*
　　curse on people involved, 80
　　description and result, 3
　　events on ship, 88–91
　　Fletcher Christian's decision and
　　　actions, 9, 88, 89, 90–91, 94,
　　　103, 104
　　in Folger's encounter with
　　　islanders, 9, 11–12, 16–17
　　in movies and books, 3–4, 34,
　　　73–74, 80
　　rebranding as coup, 96
　　reimagined by Hall and Nordhoff,
　　　73–74
　　second mutiny, 113
　　story as legend, 33–34, 73, 74, 75
　　and tourism in Tahiti, 74
　　See also Bligh, William and
　　　mutiny on *Bounty*
Mutiny on the Bounty (books by Hall
　　and Nordhoff), 73–74
Mutiny on the Bounty (movie), 34,
　　74, 80

names and landmarks on Pitcairn,
　　149–150
Nancy, 159, 161, 178, 179, 180
Niau
　　control after massacre, 204
　　death, 204–206
　　joining mutineers, 107
　　in massacre of whites, 194,
　　　195–197
　　as servant to whites, 195
　　surveying of Pitcairn, 123–126
9/11 terrorist attacks, 79
Nomuka (island), 84–86, 87

Nordhoff, Charles, 72, 73, 168–169

Norfolk Island
  Bounty Day event, 272–276
  Bounty museum searches, 276–278
  and descendants from Pitcairn, 208–209, 210, 273
  description and travel to, 209, 271–272
  as penal settlement, 209–210
  return of some Pitcairners, 210
  theories about Pitcairn stories, 275–276
  visit by author, 271–276

nose flute, 234–235

nuclear testing, 115

obsidian, 128

Obuarei, 133, 216–218, 231–232, 233

Oha, 104, 159, 177, 179, 181–182

Operation Unique, 240, 241–243, 244, 245

Orion, 110, 112, 193, 219, 247

Pandora (ship), 170–172

"Pandora's Box," 171

paradise, as notion, 74–75

Pare (Tahiti), 59

petroglyphs on Pitcairn, 225, 226–227

philately and Pitcairn, 34

pineapples, in *Bounty*'s days, 32

pirates, 114

Pitcairn Island and *Bounty* mutineers
  alcohol brewing and drinking, 156, 182–183, 195, 220–222
  animals from *Bounty*, 126, 127, 129, 130–131, 157–158
  babies, births and children, 155, 160, 175, 178, 199, 220
  Bounty at, 123, 126, 128, 133–134
  control by Quintal and W. McCoy, 183, 194–195, 201
  daily duties of women, 178–179
  descendants to Norfolk Island, 208–209, 210, 273
  description as paradise, 126
  development as colony, 153, 155, 158
  digging of weapons, 233–234
  discovery and naming, 3, 13, 108
  division into parcels, 134
  ducats legend, 274
  earlier inhabitants and structures, 124–125, 126, 127, 129, 180–181
  Fletcher Christian as leader, 123, 126, 128–129, 134, 159–160
  fruit and food, 124, 228
  gardens, 124, 127, 129, 156–157
  inhabitants after 18 years, 256
  landing of mutineers, 126
  mapping by Folger, 16
  meetings and votes, 128, 129
  in mid-nineteenth century, 209
  obsidian, 128
  and passage of time, 235–236, 237
  Pitkernese dialect, 207
  Polynesians (*see* Polynesians on *Bounty* and Pitcairn)
  protection of children, 248–249
  return from Norfolk Island, 210

Pitcairn Island and *Bounty*
mutineers (*continued*)
search by mutineers, 3, 13,
108–109, 113, 121
ship in sight, 161–162, 172
sighting and surveying by
mutineers, 122–126
as slice of England, 153–154,
160–161, 195
use of *Bounty* as materials, 11, 13,
128
village and housing place and
setup, 126–127, 129–130, 155
visit by British ships in 1814, 17
visit by Folger on *Topaz*, 7–15,
256–258
visit by ships, 233–234, 255–257,
274–275
watch for ships and lookout, 155,
158, 168, 182–183, 191
whalebone comb, 127
wives and women, 158–159,
178–179, 206
See also individual mutineers and
women
Pitcairn Island today
alcohol, 186
arrival of author, 138–142
attitude toward sexuality,
243–244, 245
bar and trivia challenge, 223–224
Bounty museum, 185, 212
as British territory, 151, 241–242,
243–244, 246
church and religion, 185–186,
211–212
clinic and doctor, 239–240
communications with world, 142,
165–166

description and life on, 34,
150–151, 152
fruit and food, 143, 146, 270
general store, 145–146
as halfway point for vessels, 240
homestay, 140–142, 184
in imagination and as paradise,
3–4, 34
immigration to, 148
inhabitants and families, 151,
184, 185, 260–261
injuries and medical help, 144,
226, 228, 230, 239
and legend of *Bounty*, 33–34,
147
map, xviii–xix, 149
merchandise for tourists, 188
names and landmarks, 149–150
non-community residents, 240,
242, 244–245
outsiders and hospitality, 139,
152, 174, 210–211, 212,
213–214, 240, 262
petroglyphs on stone, 225,
226–227
power shut off at night, 1–2,
142, 187
prison, 147–148, 211, 242–243
rats, 172–173
school, 142
sex crimes research by author,
245–246, 247
sexual abuse of children and trial,
240–245
spiders, 212–213
tourism, 34, 35, 189–190,
210–211
tourist office, 147–150
town on (Adamstown), 150

transportation to, 2, 34–35,
148–149
travel insurance, 226
trip of author to, 4, 33–35
visit by *Arago* and sailors,
259–262
See also individual inhabitants
Pitcairn (ship), 186
Pitcairn's Island (Hall and
Nordhoff), 172
Pitkernese dialect, 207
poepoe grass/reeds, 217–218, 228
Polynesians on *Bounty* and Pitcairn
control after massacre, 201, 204
death of last men, 204–206
domination by and inferiority to
whites, 160–161, 177, 195
internal violence, 179–180, 201
joining mutineers on *Bounty*, 93,
104, 106–107
massacre of whites, 194, 195–197,
198, 199, 201, 249–250
in men/women ratio on Pitcairn,
159
mutiny against whites, 178–179,
180–182, 201
parcel of land on Pitcairn, 134
as servants to Quintal and
W. McCoy, 195
women (*see* women with
mutineers and on Pitcairn)
power shut off at night on Pitcairn,
1–2, 142, 187
Presser, Brandon
and *Arago* visit, 260
arrival on Pitcairn, 138–142
back in modern world, 268–270
in bar and trivia challenge,
223–224

in *Bounty* museum, 276–278
with Carol and Jay Warren, 184,
186–190, 207–209, 211–214
on *Claymore* to Pitcairn, 116–120,
138–139
and *Claymore* to Mangareva,
263–265
and closed-door rooms, 163–166,
174, 188
departure from Pitcairn, 264
Down Rope visit, 224–227
ignored by residents, 139, 140,
174, 211
injury and clinic, 230, 239
at John Adams grave, 229–230
knowledge of Pitcairn, 3–4,
33–34
Lookout Point visit, 167–168
Mangareva visit, 115–116
with Mary after Pitcairn,
264–268
Motu Mapeti visit with Kate
Hall, 76–78, 80
nights on Pitcairn, 1–2
on Norfolk Island, 271–278
with Olive and Steve Christian,
140–147, 151–152, 163–168,
172–174, 187
outing with Meralda Warren,
227–228
sex crimes research, 245–246, 247
and Shawn Christian, 174, 211,
264
stench in own bedroom, 163,
172–174
in Tahiti, 75–76, 81–83, 115,
265–268
travel insurance, 226–227
trip to Pitcairn, 4, 34–35

prison on Pitcairn today, 147–148,
   211, 242–243
professor from New Zealand, 117,
   118, 223–224, 225, 226,
   246–247

QSL cards, 165, 166
Quintal, Matthew
   alcohol brew and drinking, 156,
      182, 220–221, 250
   on *Bounty* trip, 39–42
   character, 40–41
   Christmas on *Bounty*, 110–111,
      112
   control of Pitcairn, 183, 194–195,
      201, 202–203
   as crew on *Bounty*, 28, 176
   death as solution, 248–249,
      250–253
   descendants, 273
   dogs slaughter, 130–131, 135
   grievances and second mutiny, 121
   joined by Minarii, 200–202
   killing of Minarii, 202–204
   in massacre by Polynesians, 196,
      199–200
   and W. McCoy, 39–40, 176–177,
      182–183
   mellowing out, 236
   murder of, 251–252
   as mutineer with Fletcher
      Christian, 105
   in mutiny, 89
   on Nomuka, 84, 85
   plot to retake control, 202–203
   shooting in Tonga, 108
   sight of Pitcairn, 122
   and Smith's disappearance,
      100–101

as source of trouble, 248–249
   and Susannah's pregnancy, 236
   torching of *Bounty*, 133, 135
   on Tubuai, 99, 100–101
   violence and lashes on *Bounty*,
      41–42
   violence on Tevarua, 63, 131,
      178, 215, 221, 235
   and Young's survival, 200–201

raatira, 56, 57
Raiamanu's house, 75, 76, 81
rats on Pitcairn, 172–173
religion on Pitcairn of mutineers.
   See Bible
religion on Pitcairn today, 185–186,
   211–212
Resolution (ship), 21
Rutgers, Nancy Hall, 81–83, 244
Rutgers, Nicholas/Nick, 81, 82

Saint Michael's Cathedral, 116
Saint Paul's Pool (Pitcairn), 177, 186
school on Pitcairn today, 142
scurvy, 26, 47, 50
seasickness, 118–119
9/11 terrorist attacks, 79
Seventh-day Adventists on Pitcairn,
   185–186, 211–212
sexual abuse of children on Pitcairn
   today, 240–245
slave trade, 20
Smith, Alexander
   in attack on Tubuai islanders, 97,
      98, 132–133
   and death of Quintal, 248, 249,
      250–253
   disappearance on Tubuai,
      100–101

doubts about Young, 249–250

dreams (nightmares), 132–133, 193–194, 216–217, 251

fencing of garden, 154, 157, 253

interest in religion, 217, 220, 236–237, 254–255

and Jenny's name, 66–67

as leader on Pitcairn, 254–255

in massacre by Polynesians, 194, 195, 199

as mutineer with Fletcher Christian, 104, 105

in mutiny, 89, 275

past identity, 253, 257

and visit by ship, 256, 257–258

wives and children on Pitcairn, 255

women in Tahiti, 55, 67, 100

South Pacific, description and modern history, 114–115

spiders on Pitcairn, 212–213

Spithead naval yard, 28–29

stamps of Pitcairn, 34

stargazing on Pitcairn, 246–247

stars in southern skies, 70, 110, 135–136

Sully (Baby Sully), 108, 126, 158, 248

Sultan (ship), 278

superstores, 32, 35

Survivor (series), 79

Susannah

bathing, 53, 206

children with Thursday October, 255

Christmas on *Bounty*, 110–111, 112

in daily gathering of women, 178

departure from Pitcairn, 231–232, 233

dogs slaughter, 131–132

encounter with Young, 51–53, 66

at *heiva*, 59

killing of Tetahiti, 205–206

and Minarii, 177

pregnancy, 62–63, 236

premature birth of Tevarua's baby, 215

red feathers, 96

return of *Bounty*, 92

sight of Pitcairn, 122

song for Tevarua and toll of time on Pitcairn, 234–236

and Teimua, 201

thatching work on Pitcairn, 130, 131–132

Young and the Bible, 53, 66, 68

Swallow (ship), 13, 108

"Sweet By and By" (song), 261–262

Taaroa, 96, 97

Tagus (ship), 17

Tahiti

arrival of *Bounty*, 48–49, 53–54

author's time on, 75–76, 81–83, 115, 265–268

breadfruit collection for *Bounty*, 54, 55, 56, 57, 58–59, 61, 65

breadfruit in, 19–20

cultural differences with crew, 66, 68–69, 110

departures of *Bounty*, 70–71, 93–94, 106–107

emotions in people, 58

Endeavour in, 19

and fear (*mehameha*), 218

funeral of Huggan, 58

Tahiti (*continued*)
  Hall and Nordhoff in, 72–73
  heiva (ceremonial gathering),
    59–61
  incident with young woman,
    50–53
  mutineers remaining after mutiny,
    105, 106, 170–171
  Pandora in, 170–171
  as paradise, 74–75
  rain, 76
  returns and resupply of *Bounty*,
    92–94, 105
  rulers (*arii*), 54–55, 56, 57
  runaways from *Bounty*, 61–62
  secrets from *Bounty*, 54
  social changes, 63, 278
  social structure, 54–55, 56–57,
    60, 68
  tattoos, 57, 60
  theft of compass, 63–65
  tourism from mutiny on *Bounty*,
    74
  travel of *Bounty* to, 43–49
  visits by British, 19, 21, 56
  women's sexuality, 52–53, 55–57,
    243
taio
  and crew of *Bounty*, 61, 64
  definition, 61
  Tetahiti's pledge to Fletcher
    Christian, 179, 181–182, 204
Tamatoa, 95–96, 97, 101
tapa cloth, 8, 51, 127, 129, 161,
  193, 227, 235
Tararo
  attack and killing by Minarii,
    179–180
  joining mutineers, 107

  loss of wife, 159, 178
  in mutiny against whites, 178–179
  nighttime visits by wife, 161,
    178, 179
Tasmania (Van Diemen's Land),
  visit by *Bounty*, 44–46
tattoos, 57, 60, 274
Teatuahitea, 154, 204–205
Tedside (Pitcairn), 175, 189
Teehuteatuaonoa. *See* Jenny
Teimua
  death, 201
  joining mutineers, 107
  in massacre of whites, 194,
    195–197, 201
  as servant to whites, 195
  surveying of Pitcairn, 123–126
Teina (ruler)
  Bounty in domain of, 58–59
  Bounty's departure from Tahiti,
    70–71
  and *heiva*, 59–60
  and missing compass of *Bounty*,
    64–65
  return and resupply of *Bounty*,
    93
  visit for breadfruit, 56, 57–58
Teio, 175, 255
Tenerife stop of *Bounty*, 37–38
Teraura. *See* Susannah
Terii (caretaker), 77, 79
Teriipaia, Tarita, 74
Tetahiti
  affair with Teatuahitea, 154,
    204–205
  control after massacre, 204
  joining mutineers, 104
  and killing of animals on Tubuai,
    97, 101

in massacre of whites, 195,
196–197
mutiny against whites, 179
plot for death of, 204–206
and Polynesians' mutiny, 181–182
as servant to whites, 195
taio pledge to Fletcher Christian,
179, 181–182, 204
Tetiaroa (atolls/island), 61–62, 78
Tevarua
Christmas on *Bounty*, 110–111,
112
departure from Pitcairn, 231–232,
233
dogs slaughtered, 130–132
interest in religion, 217–218, 219,
237
and passage of time, 235–236, 237
premature birth and death of
baby, 215–216
song from Susannah and toll of
time on Pitcairn, 234–236
thatching work on Pitcairn, 130,
131–132
violence from Quintal, 63, 131,
178, 215, 221, 235
walk and suicide, 236–238
Thompson, Matthew
in attacks on Tubuai, 101, 102
on *Bounty* trip, 38, 40
in breadfruit deal, 58
as crew on *Bounty*, 26–27
death, 171
killing of Tinarau's brother, 102
in mutiny, 90
remaining on Tahiti, 105, 171
ti plant and brandy, 182, 195, 220,
250, 275
Timor, and Bligh after mutiny, 169

Tinarau
as leader on Tubuai, 96
raids on and battle with
mutineers, 97, 98, 100, 101–102
and Smith's disappearance,
100–101
Tofua, 86, 169
Tongatapu, 108
Topaz (ship)
finding land, 6–7
leaving Pitcairn and capture by
Spanish, 16
seal hunt and supplies search,
5–6
visit to Pitcairn, 6–7, 257–258
tourism on Pitcairn
as initiative, 34, 35, 189–190,
210–211
tourist office, 147–150
transport to Pitcairn, 2, 34–35,
148–149
travel insurance for Pitcairn, 226
Tubuai
animals of mutineers, 93, 95,
97, 101
attacks on mutineers, 97–98,
100–102, 132–133
colony breakdown, 98–99
departure of mutineers, 103–104
description, 94, 95
as destination of mutineers, 94
fort of mutineers (Fort George),
95, 96–97, 98, 101, 103
people and politics, 94–95,
96–97
plans of mutineers, 95–96
and Smith's disappearance,
100–101
women on, 99–100

Up Tommy's (house), 184, 186–187,
     188

Vahineatua, 255
Valentine, James, 27–28, 46–48
Van Diemen's Land (Tasmania),
     visit by *Bounty*, 44–46
venereal disease, 62
VHF radio, 142
vinho da roda, 36–37, 156, 274

Warren, Carol
  and *Arago* visit, 260, 261
  as a Christian descendant, 188
  description, 186, 187–188, 190
  outing with author, 188–190
  role on Pitcairn and *Bounty*
     business, 185, 188, 189–190,
     213, 261
  younger days, 265
Warren, Carol and Jay
  author's time with, 184, 186–190,
     207–209, 211–214
  description of family, 184,
     187–188, 265
  food and meals, 207–208, 214
  house (Up Tommy's), 184,
     186–187, 188
  room with closed door, 188
Warren, Charlene, 184, 259
Warren, Darralyn, 184, 208
Warren, Jay, 185
  See also Warren, Carol and Jay
Warren, Meralda, 227–228, 260,
     261–262
Warren, Pawl and Sue, 223–225
whalebone comb, 127
Whale's Tooth Inn, 223

Williams, John
  Christmas on *Bounty*, 110–111,
     112
  killing by Polynesians, 195
  as mutineer with Fletcher
     Christian, 105
  new wife, 158–159
  surveying of Pitcairn, 123–126
Winchester, Sarah, 72
wine, 36–37, 49, 156, 274
women with mutineers and on
     Pitcairn (as a group)
  and "Coventry Carol," 111–112,
     178, 235
  daily chores, 178–179
  departure attempt, 231–233
  first encounter in Tahiti, 50–53
  in Massacre Day, 197–198, 199
  Mauatua as leader, 134–135
  pairings and ratio on *Bounty*, 106,
     108
  and return of *Bounty*, 92–93
  and sexuality, 52–53, 55–57, 243
  on Tubuai, 99–100
  as wives, 158–159, 178–179, 206
  and Young with the Bible,
     110–111, 217–219, 236–237
  See also individual women

Young, Edward
  alcohol brewing, 275
  beheading of last Polynesians,
     206
  Bible justifications for
     un-Christian behavior, 248,
     249–250
  and Bible with Susannah, 53,
     66, 68

and Bible with women, 110–111,
217–219, 236–237
on *Bounty* trip, 42
capacity for violence, 234
Christmas on *Bounty*, 110–111
as crew on *Bounty*, 25
death and funeral, 254
death of Quintal, 248–249,
250–253
encounter with Susannah, 51–53,
66
at *heiva*, 59
journal writing, 237

in massacre by Polynesians,
200–201, 249–250
as mutineer with Fletcher
Christian, 103, 105
plot against Tetahiti, 205
religious guidance to others,
217–219, 236–237
sight of Pitcairn, 122
and visit by ship, 233–234,
249
and women's preparation to
leave, 231
Young/Yung, Simon, 139, 140

Brandon Presser was born in Ottawa, Canada, and has lived in Paris, Tokyo, and New York City. Called a "rough-and-tough adventurer" by *Entertainment Weekly*, he has visited over 130 countries, and his travel writing has been featured in numerous publications including *Bloomberg*, *Harper's Bazaar*, *Condé Nast Traveler*, and Lonely Planet. He holds a bachelor's degree from Harvard University.

PublicAffairs is a publishing house founded in 1997. It is a tribute to the standards, values, and flair of three persons who have served as mentors to countless reporters, writers, editors, and book people of all kinds, including me.

I. F. STONE, proprietor of *I. F. Stone's Weekly*, combined a commitment to the First Amendment with entrepreneurial zeal and reporting skill and became one of the great independent journalists in American history. At the age of eighty, Izzy published *The Trial of Socrates*, which was a national bestseller. He wrote the book after he taught himself ancient Greek.

BENJAMIN C. BRADLEE was for nearly thirty years the charismatic editorial leader of *The Washington Post*. It was Ben who gave the *Post* the range and courage to pursue such historic issues as Watergate. He supported his reporters with a tenacity that made them fearless and it is no accident that so many became authors of influential, best-selling books.

ROBERT L. BERNSTEIN, the chief executive of Random House for more than a quarter century, guided one of the nation's premier publishing houses. Bob was personally responsible for many books of political dissent and argument that challenged tyranny around the globe. He is also the founder and longtime chair of Human Rights Watch, one of the most respected human rights organizations in the world.

.   .   .

For fifty years, the banner of Public Affairs Press was carried by its owner Morris B. Schnapper, who published Gandhi, Nasser, Toynbee, Truman, and about 1,500 other authors. In 1983, Schnapper was described by *The Washington Post* as "a redoubtable gadfly." His legacy will endure in the books to come.

Peter Osnos, *Founder*